DATE DUE

OCT 1 9 03		
12-19-03		
JAN 14 '04		
JUN 3 '04		
JUL 14 '04		
9-17-04		
JAN 1 4 2005		
MAR 0 1 2005		
8-12-05		
MAR 2 3 2006		
JUL 0 2 2006		
DEC 0 4 2006		
JUN 0 7 2007		
APR 2 1 2008		
SEP 1 7 2014		

GUT FEELINGS

Other Hay House Titles of Related Interest

❀ ❀ ❀

BOOKS

BodyChange™, by Montel Williams and Wini Linguvic

Eating in the Light: Making Your Way to Vegetarianism on Your Spiritual Path, by Doreen Virtue, Ph.D., and Becky Prelitz, M.F.T., R.D.

Dr. Citron's Evolutionary Diet, by Ronald S. Citron, M.D., and Kathye J. Citron

Heal Your Body A–Z, by Louise L. Hay

Losing Your Pounds of Pain: Breaking the Link Between Abuse, Stress, and Overeating, by Doreen Virtue, Ph.D.

Vegetarian Meals for People On-the-Go: 101 Quick & Easy Recipes, by Vimala Rodgers (May 2002)

The Yo-Yo Diet Syndrome, by Doreen Virtue, Ph.D.

AUDIO PROGRAMS

Body Talk: No-Nonsense, Common-Sense, Sixth-Sense Solutions to Create Health and Healing, by Mona Lisa Schulz, M.D., Ph.D., and Christiane Northrup, M.D.

Eating Wisdom, by Andrew Weil, M.D., with Michael Toms

❀ ❀ ❀

All of the above are available at your local bookstore, or may be ordered through Hay House, Inc.:

(800) 654-5126 or (760) 431-7695
(800) 650-5115 (fax) or (760) 431-6948 (fax)
www.hayhouse.com

GUT FEELINGS

From Fear and Despair
to Health and Hope

CARNIE WILSON

with
Mick Kleber

Hay House, Inc.
Carlsbad, California • Sydney, Australia

Published and distributed in the United States by: Hay House, Inc., P.O. Box 5100, Carlsbad, CA 92018-5100 • (800) 654-5126 • (800) 650-5115 (fax) • www.hayhouse.com

Writer: Mick Kleber • *Contributor:* Doug De Vito
Editorial supervision: Jill Kramer • *Design:* Summer McStravick • *Indexer:* Joan Shapiro

Library of Congress Cataloging-in-Publication Data

Wilson, Carnie, 1968–
    Gut feelings : from fear and despair to health and hope / Carnie Wilson.
      p. cm.
    Includes index.
    ISBN 1-56170-907-7 (hardcover)
      1. Wilson, Carnie, 1968 ---Health. 2. Overweight women--United States--Biography.
  3. Gastrectomy--Patients--United States--Biography. 4. Women singers--United States--
Biography. I. Title: Gut feelings. II. Title.

RC628 .W525 2001
362.1'96398'0092—dc21
  [B]

                                        2001024950

ISBN 1-56170-907-7

04 03 02 01   4 3 2 1
1st printing, September 2001

Printed in the United States of America

To Mom and Dad and Wendy—
we've all helped each other to grow.

CONTENTS

Acknowledgments..xi
Introduction: Listening to My Gut..............................xiii

Chapter 1: Born to Be Fat 1
Chapter 2: Chubby Childhood 17
Chapter 3: Songs, Sex, and Smoke 47
Chapter 4: Making It Big 59
Chapter 5: Heavy Duty 75
Chapter 6: Larger Than Life 87
Chapter 7: Sizing Things Up 103
Chapter 8: You're in Love 119
Chapter 9: Decision of a Lifetime 131
Chapter 10: Going Public 163
Chapter 11: Getting Down 179
Chapter 12: Be My Baby 203
Chapter 13: The Weight Is Over 217

Appendix: Asking the Experts

Interviews with:
- Alan Wittgrove, M.D., Bariatric Surgeon.............237
- Sharron Dalton, Ph.D., R.D., Nutritionist..........252
- Steven Heymsfield, M.D., Endocrinologist 263
- Myles S. Faith, Ph.D., Psychology Professor 276

Index..291
About the Author 301

ACKNOWLEDGMENTS

THIS BOOK COULD NOT BE THE CELEBRATION OF EMOTION THAT it is without my husband, Rob. Thank you, my angel, for our bond, our friendship, and our loyalty. I love you forever.

My thanks to Mick Kleber—your dedication and sensitivity have helped me express what's in my heart.

My gratitude to Mickey Shapiro, Dr. Jonathan Sackier, and the team at Spotlight Health for the vision that saved my life and inspires so many others; to Hay House for the opportunity to connect with kindred spirits everywhere; to Dr. Alan Wittgrove, Leslie Jester, and everyone at Alvarado for your care, concern, and complete professionalism; to Dr. Marc Schoen, Lisa Roth, and Jeff Panzer for your faith, devotion, and constancy; to my family and friends, who have enriched my life with deep affection and unconditional acceptance—to Jonah for beating "the curse" on your own, and to Pam Miller for turning my life around and teaching me discipline and appreciation.

The people in your life are what make each moment precious—and I want you all to know you mean the world to me.

Listening to My Gut

I T'S ONLY 100 MILES FROM THE BIG HOUSE IN BEL AIR WHERE I grew up to Operating Room 4 at the Alvarado Hospital Medical Center in San Diego.

But it took me 31 years to get there, and along the way it was a wild ride.

From a childhood of rock 'n' roll fantasy and family tragedy to adulthood in the public eye, it's been a lifelong battle to control an overpowering obsession with food that packed 300 pounds on my body and threatened to destroy my health.

As a child, I developed an appetite for attention and a craving for calories that became deep-rooted aspects of my personality, feeding a vicious cycle of bingeing, dieting, losing, and gaining even more that swamped me for decades with embarrassment, anger, panic, and frustration.

At the same time, my life has been filled with wonders— a famous father who gave me the gift of music, a mother whose love gave me the strength to overcome my pain, a sister who's always been there to share the heartache and help me cope, and a husband whose devotion and compassion gave me courage as I've gone through changes that have shaken my sense of who I am.

I've been to the top of the charts, in front of the cameras, and in the spotlight of center stage. I've felt thrilling highs and crushing lows, fame and fortune, rejection and despair—and I've pushed myself from the lap of luxury to the brink of self-destruction.

I put the food in my mouth time after time after time. I kept eating and eating and eating when I knew I should stop. I did it to myself, and I had to risk it all for a chance at transformation and happiness.

These are the landmarks on my journey to that day in August of 1999 when I shared my desperation with the world, put my life in the hands of cutting-edge medical technology, and left behind the body that I'd loved and hated for as long as I could remember.

As I write this almost two years later, I've lost more than 150 pounds. But this isn't a book about how to lose weight. There are hundreds of books out there that claim to know the answers to weight-loss success. I've read a lot of them, and none of them worked for me.

This is also not a life story, because in many ways the life I've always dreamed of is just beginning. But this *is* about the feelings that have shaped my life—about food, family, fame, flesh, and fear—and how these factors have influenced the choices I've made in the life I've lived until now.

Through it all, the advice my mother gave me as a little girl has been with me: "Always listen to your gut," she would say. And I know that sounds ironic, because my gut became a burden that almost killed me, and I literally had to change my guts to save my life. But in one way or another, everything I've ever done has been based on my gut feelings.

That's why I wrote this book.

In my gut, I know that telling my story is what I have to do now—just as I came to know that my only hope for survival was gastric bypass surgery, and that putting my problem on display was the best thing I could do for myself and millions like me.

And although I'm not looking for praise or sympathy, it's taken some guts to do this. It's not easy to open up your body and your life to be scrutinized and judged by others. But it's always been my style to put it out there.

I've grown up surrounded by the buzz of celebrity, and I've always known that my destiny was to give myself to others and to make people love me for who and what I am. Maybe some of these feelings come from missing my dad's love for so many years, from not understanding how much he really loved me. Maybe I'm just emotionally needy and always will be.

But from an early age, I can remember feeling deep inside that something wasn't right, that somehow *I* wasn't right. Even when I became successful myself as a performer with Wilson Phillips and the host of my own television show, that sense of being inadequate or deficient became more consuming than ever.

I buried these feelings with rushes of pleasure from food—and later from drugs—and I learned to enjoy my role as "the fat chick" with the sassy shtick and in-your-face attitude. I fed on "fat power" and stood up for size acceptance. But on the inside, I was suffering in a private hell of guilt and shame as my eating raged out of control, my body ballooned, and I eventually became so obese that every day was a physical ordeal and an exercise in deadly denial.

Bottom line, no matter how much others cared for me—whether it was loved ones or friends or millions of fans—I couldn't find a way to care for myself until finally I took control and made a decision that changed my life.

Now I have a stomach the size of a lemon, and the meals I eat are tiny. But the fat that almost smothered me to death is gone for good, and the fear of tomorrow is a fading memory. Now I can focus on the future of my dreams and believe that there's a real chance I can get there.

If *you* are obese, your dreams are probably the same—to feel normal and attractive, to love and be loved, and to live a long, healthy life. It makes no difference whether you're rich or poor, young or old, black or white, male or female. It doesn't matter what you do or where you're from. When you're headed down a road of misery, only *you* can change the course so that your dreams have that chance of coming true.

You have to listen to the feelings deep in your gut, get your head straight about what you need in order to be healthy and happy, and go for it. That's how it's been for me, and I know it's hard. I also know that it takes more than a medical procedure to turn your life around. Just because you lose a lot of weight doesn't mean that all the other baggage disappears.

I'm a work in progress with many issues to resolve. But where once I felt cursed, now I feel blessed. I've got a handle on my health, I've found the love of my life, and I'm excited about what lies ahead.

There's still a lot I need to do to feel comfortable with who I am and what I'm meant to be. This book is part of that process, and if my experience can inspire those who live each day with a heavy load of heartache, hopelessness, and humiliation to move in a healing direction, then my blessings will mean even more because I've shared them.

Some of you may pat me on the back and say, "Wow, you've been through a lot, but you turned your problems into something positive. You could've been six feet under."

Others will say, "You're a spoiled kid of a rock star who took the easy way out."

But it doesn't matter what gets said about me. I've made my choice, and I'm on my way. I've listened to my inner voice, and I'm here to tell my story for all of you who need to know that there's hope out there. Obesity doesn't have to be a lifetime sentence. You *can* beat the odds.

But whatever path you choose, remember this. *No matter*

how much you weigh, no matter what you look like, you deserve respect and love, most of all from yourself.

I just couldn't love myself or let others love me when I knew my body was a ticking time bomb.

For me, the answer was an operation that helped me commit to a new lifestyle of healthy habits. It's not for everyone, and perhaps it's not for you. But if you know you've got to do something to rescue your health from a downward spiral that's sucking your spirit down with it, you've got a friend who's been there and wants to help.

I feel that in my gut—now more than ever.

CHAPTER ONE

Born to Be Fat

I've been overweight as long as I can remember. I was probably on my way to being fat from the moment I was born. It's hard to tell from looking at my baby pictures because almost every baby looks chubby. But there's a picture of my sister, Wendy; my oldest friend, Chynna Phillips; and me when we're somewhere between five and six years old. It's the first group shot ever of Wilson Phillips, and the only topless one—so far.

We're standing there in a line, our arms around each other's shoulders, wearing nothing but big smiles. When you look at Wendy and Chynna, you can see their ribs peeking through the skin that's tight on their tiny torsos. Their arms are skinny, and their faces are slender. And there I am on the left side, and I've already got this plump little body, a baby belly, a roundish face, and pudgy little arms. There isn't a bone in sight.

I look cute and happy, but there's no question who's going to grow up to be the fat one.

Experts will tell you that weight problems are a complex combination of genetic and environmental factors. Some people are born with a predisposition for putting on weight.

Others develop bad eating habits. They eat too much of the wrong foods too often. In my case, it was both—big time.

My dad was tall and slim as a young teenager, but by the time the Beach Boys exploded, he was steadily gaining weight. In the '70s, he beefed up to 310 pounds on a diet of ice cream and birthday cake for breakfast, lunch, and dinner. My mom was never really fat, but she's been on every diet you can think of—many with me—and she's lost and gained the same 30 pounds over and over in her life.

Both of my parents came from homes where weight control was not a family tradition. My dad's father, Murry, was a heavy guy in more ways than one, who knocked back a steady diet of high-cholesterol foods until he died of a heart attack when he was only 56. Both my grandmothers suffered from illnesses complicated by weight. Mom's mother, Grandma Mae, had diabetes early on, and it was very bad as she got older. Dad's mom, Grandma Audree, also became a diabetic, and she died of heart and kidney failure.

So fate probably handed me a bunch of fat genes from the start, and the eating habits I learned at home did the rest. I grew up in a family where everyone loved to eat. We practically worshiped food—and not the healthy kind.

Mom was always into junk food. She loved bread and doughnuts and chips—anything sweet or crunchy—and there were always lots of goodies around our house—until I got ahold of them. We almost never had vegetables because Mom didn't like them. As kids, she and her sisters wouldn't eat them unless my Grandma Mae covered them with chocolate pudding—not exactly a nutritional solution to picky eating. So you wouldn't find too many veggies on the plates at our home, unless you counted the french-fried onion rings with our steaks and mashed potatoes.

We ate a lot of heavy meals, and we rarely skipped dessert. We all loved food, and we also loved to talk about it—what we *had* eaten, what we *were* eating, and what we *were going* to eat. Food was fun, and it filled the void that Mom and Wendy and I would sometimes feel, because there was something missing in our lives—a sense of complete family.

Dad wasn't around much, almost never for dinner. He was always off doing his own thing, playing the piano, or hanging out somewhere in the house in his own space. Once in a while he'd show up in the kitchen, bolt down some food, and then he'd be gone again.

By the time I was born, he was already an icon of pop music. He had written and produced some of the all-time great songs of his generation and had turned the world on to surf, sun, custom cars, and California girls. One journalist said that my father invented California, but he was just a high school kid from Hawthorne and a dysfunctional family when the '60s swept him up and seduced him. Drugs and alcohol put him into a headspace where there was little room for anything or anyone but music—and eventually even that suffered with him.

Wendy and I ate our dinners alone, sitting at the kitchen counter watching television—just the two of us. I'm not sure when my mother would eat. I just know we never had dinner together—except for one night when Mom was determined that we'd eat a civilized meal like a normal family. We all sat down at the dining room table, and Mom brought in the steaks. She put Dad's plate down in front of him, but she'd forgotten to bring him a knife and fork.

By the time she got back from the kitchen, Dad was gone and so was his steak. He'd picked it up with his hands and wolfed it down so fast I couldn't believe it. It was like he inhaled it, and before Mom sat down, he had disappeared into another part of the house.

The house in Bel Air was so enormous that disappearing was easy. I have this vision of my father roaming among the

22 rooms. You could never be sure where he was or who else might be there. I used to wonder what he was doing, what he was thinking, and why he seldom had time for me. It hurt me that he was so remote, so strange. I'd cry and ask my mother why he was that way, because I thought he didn't love me.

I know now that Dad was struggling with mental illness, and his own dad had never shown his sons what it's like to be a loving father. Dad didn't know what to do with a little girl who wanted to play with him or just be close to him. Nowadays, we know how to treat depression, and he has been so much happier, thankfully, and lives a normal, healthy life.

"Your dad has problems," Mom told me, hugging me and kissing me and wiping away my tears. "He's a musical genius, though, and you can be proud of that forever. He does love you. He just doesn't know how to show it." These comforting moments usually ended with a Twinkie or a Hostess cupcake to help the sad feelings go away.

Mom worked overtime to give me the attention and affection I sorely needed. She held me and kissed me and rubbed my back until I fell asleep. She laughed at my jokes and told me how beautiful and special I was. She taught me to find the patch of blue sky among the clouds, and she protected me from the volatile lifestyle that surrounded me.

But she had her hands full with two young daughters and a husband who was caught up in self-destructive tendencies—and I didn't make it any easier for her. I was a headstrong, spoiled kid who could be very hard to deal with. I drove my mother nuts until I got whatever I wanted. Maybe it was toys or clothes or something I really didn't need. Often it was food.

She spoiled me because she loved me, and she knew I really needed love. She cared for me and helped me feel safe and strong. My mom gave me the emotional tools to survive when things didn't go my way. She helped me believe I could do anything, no matter what others did to hurt me or what I did to hurt myself.

When I was young, I didn't understand how precious her love was. I didn't understand that my father was trapped in a dark place and couldn't help himself out. All I knew was that something was missing inside of me that was supposed to be there. There was a hole in my life that needed to be filled up. So I turned to the world for attention, and I filled the hole with food.

I can trace these feelings back to when I was four years old. In 1972, the Beach Boys decided to get away from Los Angeles and make an album in Holland. So the family picked up and moved to a big house in a little town called Laren, just outside of Amsterdam. My mom was excited because she and her sister, Dee Dee—who'd had a girl group in the '60s called The Honeys—planned to make a new record there produced by my dad.

But Dad hadn't been on the road in seven years. Those six months in Holland were tough for him, and they were hard for me as well. Dad was uncomfortable, and the pressure was on Mom to make things work for us. We were all stressed, and I was afraid to be in a strange place where everyone was talking in a different language.

I missed my friends at preschool back in Los Angeles, and I didn't know anyone at the school in Laren. Wendy was too young for school, so she stayed at home with Mom—and my cousin Jonah was in other classes, not with me. Even though all the kids spoke English, I felt odd and lonely and out of touch.

While we were away, my mother made cassette tapes of us to send back to our grandparents. When I listen to them now, I hear this hysterical little girl, laughing and singing and trying to shock people with naughty words. I was this crazy, outrageous, nutty little ham, cracking up at my own jokes, but underneath it all I can feel the desperation I was feeling then.

There's a moment on one of the tapes that gets to me more than anything else. Right in the middle of everything, Mom says, "Don't worry about what *she's* eating, Carnie. Here's yours."

There it is at four years old. There's my personality. My own food wasn't enough. I wanted some of Wendy's. The habit was there before I was old enough to even know what I was doing.

I don't remember anything about eating in Holland, but by the time we were back in California, I was simply mad for food. The sight and smell of it just thrilled me. I was overwhelmed by the flavors of different foods, and I couldn't wait to eat. Food just took over my whole being.

More than anything, I wanted sugar. It was all I craved. I was on a mission for sugar at all times. I remember being frantic about it and begging anyone I was with, "Can we go get some food? Can we go to the store? Can I get some Twinkies? Can I get a Hostess pie?" I was obsessed with the sweetness and the rush of sugar, and I was sneaking food whenever I could, shoving it in my mouth before anyone would see me.

I remember sitting on the kitchen floor, straddling a box of cake mix, eating the raw powder and just loving it. I stole packets of powdered goat's milk from my baby-sitter's purse because it was sweet, and I had to have it. Once I ate a whole can of frosting and got really ill. All that sugar gave me awful stomachaches and diarrhea. I didn't like being sick, but I wanted the sugar so badly I didn't think about what would come later.

My mother was concerned, because even though she wouldn't catch me eating, she could see that I was gaining weight. When I was six, she took me to the doctor to have my thyroid checked.

"Her thyroid is a tiny bit low," the doctor said, "but not enough for medication."

"But why is she gaining weight?" my mother asked. "I don't see her really eating more than Wendy."

The doctor told me I was overeating and eating the wrong foods and that I needed to get it under control, because as I got older it would be harder and harder to lose weight. I just felt awkward, like "What the hell is wrong with me?" But I had no idea what to do about it or how to control myself.

We tried not to snack and to eat balanced meals. But one way or another, I was going to get that food. I didn't care. I would sneak it from everyone, anytime I could. It was always, "Can I have a bite?"

At home, I'd eat off my sister's plate and finish anything she left behind. I'd eat off her plate before she even started. At school, I'd ask people for stuff from their lunches, and on the way home, I made our carpool driver stop at 7-11 so I could get a Slurpee, some Twinkies, and a bag of chips. When we had a baby-sitter, I would beg mercilessly, "Please, can we get some ice cream? Can we get some frozen yogurt?"

It was like this basic instinct gone berserk—like the whales having to go up to Alaska or the bees having to get that pollen for their honey. I *had* to get it. And I remember always feeling like I wasn't going to get enough. I'd panic until I got that food, and then for a while there was comfort.

On the weekends, we'd go to Grandma Mae's and Grandpa Irv's little house off Melrose Avenue in West Hollywood where my mom grew up. Grandma and Grandpa were the cutest, most loving couple ever. They loved to invite people into their home, and everybody adored them, including my dad. They adored him in return, and trusted him to marry their 16-year-old daughter.

Grandpa was a dead ringer for Albert Einstein, with this thick German accent—the sweetest, most tender man. He had the biggest, softest hands, and was just so gentle. If there's any-one who's influenced me in terms of a male role model, it would be Grandpa Irv.

Grandma Mae had a great sense of humor and had the fun-niest laugh you've ever heard. She was the prototypical little Jewish grandmother. The first thing she'd say is, "Are you hun-gry? What do you want to eat?"

I'd walk in, give her a big hug, and head straight to the kitchen to see what she was cooking that day. Then I'd go to the freezer in her second refrigerator where she kept the sweets she used for baking—bags or Tupperware bowls filled with chocolate, butterscotch, and peanut butter chips. I'd shovel handfuls of these chips into my mouth as fast as I could. Next, I'd go in her cabinet for some potato chips, mat-zos, cookies, or peanut butter and stuff my face until someone would come and say, "Hey, what are you doing? What are you eating?"

"Nothing," I'd say. Then I'd go play the piano until dinner.

When we finally sat down, the spread was always huge. We'd have brisket, chicken, fish, blintzes, latkes, and kugel—all in one meal. Dinner there was so much different than it was at home. We'd all be at the table, raving about how delicious everything was. Grandma Mae had no teeth, and she looked like an adorable little frog when she ate. Grandpa Irv would be smacking his lips and slurping away.

By the time dinner was over, I was ready to pop, and everyone would moan and complain about how full they were. But five minutes later, we were all set for dessert. Grandma Mae was crazy for sweets, and she'd have fresh fruit, home-baked cookies, fudge, cakes, pastries, mandel bread, and ice cream. It was unbelievable.

When she'd come to our house to baby-sit, I remember her getting out of the car with bags and bags of food. She'd always bring a big bottle of matzo ball soup with these amazing matzo balls that were so hard they'd sink to the bottom of the bowl.

I'd watch her in the kitchen over the sink or the stove, whipping up an incredible cheese soufflé that would melt in your mouth. Later she'd lie down on the floor in our bedroom, her head on her arm with a little Kleenex in her hand, waiting for us to fall asleep. Often she'd be snoring before we were.

With my Grandma Audree, it was different. We always went out to dinner.

Grandma Audree had a wicked sense of humor, and we spent many years together hysterically laughing until we would cry. We loved to fart together. I would call her and fart for her over the phone, and all I could hear was this woman hysterically laughing on the other end. She was the coolest, hippest grandmother you've ever seen.

She wasn't really a cook, but she was very dramatic about food, and she loved to eat. Sometimes it was hamburger platters with deep-fried zucchini circles, and the incredible French onion soup smothered with cheese at the Hamburger Hamlet on the Sunset Strip. More often than not it was Caesar salad, steak, and mashed potatoes—our family favorite—with all the fattening trimmings that made the meal seem extra special.

I didn't really worry too much about the fact that I was fat until the teasing started. I was used to being the heaviest kid in my class, and everyone accepted me because I was outgoing and fun. I was just as active as all the other kids, taking gymnastics and ice skating lessons, and my weight didn't stop me from making friends and being popular.

The first teasing I remember was about my name.

I was born in 1968, and "flower power" was in full bloom. When it came time to choose my name, something floral seemed natural.

"How about 'Carnation'?" proposed my dad.

"I like it," said my mom. "But it seems too long."

"Okay," said Dad. "How about 'Carnie'?"

They both loved the name, and today I love it, too. But as a kid, I thought it was a curse. *Carne* means "meat" in Spanish, and this was hysterically funny to some of the meaner kids in kindergarten and first grade.

"Carnie, *carne!* Wow, have *you* got a lot of *meat* on you!"

I wasn't laughing, and I couldn't believe that my parents had saddled me with this sick joke.

"How could you give me a name like Carnie?!" I'd demand of my mom. "How could you do this to me? It's the worst name ever!"

"No, it's a great name," she'd say. "It's different. Be proud of it. You might be teased right now, but one day the boys are going to say, 'Oh, Carnie, Carnie'—and then they'll kiss you. One day you're going to be very happy with your name."

She was right, but at the time I couldn't imagine that that day would ever come. I was also annoyed because they'd never given me a middle name like everybody else. It was just another thing that made me feel like I was odd.

In the second grade, my parents enrolled me in a private school called Oakwood that specializes in the arts. That meant a bus ride from Bel Air over the hills into North Hollywood and back every day. It was a long ride, and there were two brothers on the bus who made it a miserable trip for me and my cousin Jonah.

"Hey, fatso," they'd say, "you've got the biggest stomach I've ever seen. How come you're so fat?" I remember crying, but they'd just laugh and tease us even more. I pleaded with the bus driver to make them stop, but nothing worked. It was devastating day after day, and I began to feel ashamed of my body.

"Why are those boys so mean?" I'd ask my mom, crying and feeling so unhappy about my weight.

She'd wrap her arms around me and tell me not to listen to them. "It isn't important how you look on the outside; it's who you are on the inside that counts," she'd say. "You're a beautiful person, but they just can't see it because they don't know you."

"I hate them," I'd say.

"Don't hate them," she'd reply. "That's bad karma. The feelings you send out into the world come back to you. One day those boys will be sorry they were mean to you, because their karma will come back to them, and they'll pay the price for what they did."

These words of wisdom were soothing, but the teasing was still painful, and I ate everything in sight to comfort myself and take my mind off the distress I knew would come the next morning and then again in the afternoon.

By the time I was nine, I weighed 110 pounds, and I was tired of being teased. I was also getting more and more self-conscious about my size. At summer camp the year before, one of the counselors had cuddled me and called me her "cute little butterball," and although I was happy that she liked me, it hurt my feelings a little.

I began to develop an interest in fashion, and I wanted to look better. It was the late '70s, and disco style was everywhere. I wanted to go rollerskating in satin shorts, to shake my little booty in tight designer jeans, and to look really hot. But when I looked in the mirror, it was more like Dumbo than disco, and I wasn't happy about it.

My mom understood and would try to help me, but there was always a good excuse to break this or that diet for some special occasion—or even if it wasn't that special. As my dad became more and more remote, my mom made sure our lives were filled with fun—and where there was fun, there was always food.

My Uncle Carl, who'd been the chubby baby brother in the Beach Boys, knew how heartbreaking it was to be fat as a kid, and his son, my cousin Jonah, had a problem similar to mine.

Carl and my mom got together and decided to do something serious to help Jonah and me lose weight.

So that summer we went to Weight Watchers camp—and we went every summer for the next seven years.

I remember riding in the car with my parents up the coast to San Luis Obispo where the camp was located that year. Wendy and Chynna came along for moral support. We'd all gone to summer camp together in Malibu for a couple of years, and it was fun. But this was a camp for fat kids, and we were all kind of sad that this had to happen to me.

I didn't know what to expect, and I was upset, but my dad came up with a way to keep me smiling.

We stopped at a drive-in for cheeseburgers, shakes, and fries—my last "bad meal" before camp. Dad ordered a hamburger, and instead of wolfing it down in his normal style, he shoved the whole thing in his mouth and left it there bulging in his cheek.

"What are you doing?!" we all shrieked hysterically, because he looked about as goofy as you can get. "I'm savoring my food," he said with this mock serious look on his face that was *too* funny. He kept that burger stuffed in his cheek for the next hour, and we laughed all the way to camp until the time came to drop me off—and then the tears began.

I said good-bye, and I cried as I watched them drive away, but I didn't cry for long.

It was summertime, and I was determined to have fun no matter what. So was everyone else. Over the next seven weeks, I made lots of friends and had a great time. We'd put on plays, go swimming, do activities—and we exercised and learned about food. But the best part was that we were all in it together, and we didn't feel like outcasts.

After a few years of this drill, we'd learn to spend our energies in other ways—like figuring out how to cheat.

A big part of the fun of fat camp was cheating. It didn't take long to find out which counselors could be bribed to smuggle in a loaf of bread and a jar of Jif. Or which pizza house would make a delivery through the window.

The lengths kids would go to to cheat were often inspiring, especially on Sundays. We'd be struggling through our calisthenics, and one of the counselors would ask, "Who's going to church today?"

Everybody would raise their hand, no matter what religion they were.

Even though the services were Catholic—and I'm technically Jewish—I'd say, "I want to go, I want to go." After all, it was either church or exercise, and for me there was the added bonus of communion. I'd kneel there praying, just waiting for that wafer to drop on my tongue and melt in my mouth. It was gone in a second, but the sensation was just so decadent, it might as well have been devil's food cake.

All the kids were obsessed with finding new ways to score that next delicious morsel of forbidden food. Each Monday came the moment of truth when you got weighed, and everyone would know who was breaking the rules. But no matter how guilty you felt for that moment, the urge to sneak a snack was overwhelming.

One summer it got serious when I tried to sneak out for a Snickers bar with two other girls. We were all huge, trying to squeeze through this narrow gap in the locked gate to get to the store before anyone would know we were gone. In the frenzy, I got pushed out of the way, lost my balance, stepped into a ditch, and broke my ankle.

One of the gardeners heard me moaning and came over to pick me up, but he couldn't get me off the ground. It took two of the staff members to lift me up, and I walked around for the rest of the summer with a cast on my leg.

In spite of it all, I still managed to lose weight every summer, and the sense of accomplishment would be great for a while.

When I was 12, it was time to take the big step from grammar school to junior high, and I wanted to look really good. There was a big party to kick off the new school year, and I was fresh from fat camp, 25 pounds lighter and ready to show off my new body.

The thrill of going shopping for new clothes was almost overpowering, and my heart was racing as my mom told me, "You're going to have the best time. Everyone's going to say 'Wow, you look so great.'"

And she was right. The looks of amazement and appreciation on people's faces were worth the weeks of dieting, nutrition classes, and boring exercise. I felt this special energy, and the attention was like a drug.

But as the weeks passed from fall into winter, the buzz faded away. The old habits and feelings reappeared, and the weight came back. Before I knew it, the school year was ending, and I was heavier than I'd been the year before.

My mom would ask me, "Do you want to go again?" and I'd say yes because I wanted to be with people who didn't care if I was fat. I wanted to lose some weight even though I knew I'd gain it back again. I wanted to come back feeling slimmer and sexier, even though I knew it wouldn't last.

Every year I'd tell myself, "This time I'm not going to cheat." But it never worked out that way. It was too hard, and too tempting—and there were temptations other than food.

When I was 13, I smoked my first cigarette at fat camp. Pretty soon I was doing it every day, sneaking around puffing on menthols, feeling cool and sexy. Two years later, at 15, I smoked my first joint there—and I loved it. That was my last summer in the program.

Was the $20,000 worth it for all those years of losing the same pounds over and over? It's hard to figure. Those summers were positive experiences for me, and they exposed me to some of the best information about healthy eating and dietary discipline you can find anywhere. Weight Watchers helps a lot of people, and some of the kids at camp got a handle on their problem for good.

But for me, seven years of fat camp couldn't change the complex dynamics of haywire genetics, psychological issues, and environmental factors that kept me from controlling my unhealthy relationship with food. I was out of control, ready to party, and headed down a heavy road.

CHAPTER TWO

Chubby Childhood

Before I started fat camp—even though I was teased at school from kindergarten on—I wasn't really aware that I was fat. I knew I was eating all the time. I knew I was hungry. I knew what the doctor had told me about my eating, and I felt odd now and then. But for some reason, it never sunk in that I had a weight problem.

When it came to the teasing, I was more confused than anything else. It was like, "What did I ever do to *them?*"

My family and friends all accepted my weight as a part of who I was, and although my dad was sort of an absentee father, in every picture you see of me as a child, I have a big smile on my face. I was a happy, active, very social kid, and I was surrounded by love.

My mom was at the center of this incredible support system. Mom is someone whom I model my life after. I want to be like her. I love it when people tell me that I remind them of her because it's such a compliment. I know that my life wouldn't be the same without her.

She's just such a great person, mother, friend, and partner, and she's so much fun to be around. She makes the most of her life, and that's been a big inspiration to me. It's like her middle name should be "carpe diem." She's just like boom, boom, boom. Let's go and explore and do and be and see—and eat. She loves to eat, and my dad does, too—tremendously. I know that's where I got it from.

But my mom has such a peculiar and particular passion for the actual act of eating—the whole experience. My dad eats really fast and loves his food. But he's quiet about it. When you eat with Mom, she moans and groans with pleasure.

I grew up thinking about food as a celebration—and it *is* to most people, families, religions, and cultures. In our house, the best *time* in the world was mealtime. And the best *thing* in the world was a tasty fuckin' tortilla chip with great salsa. Oh, man. So Mom was always making sure we had food.

My mom has been young all my life. She was 14 when she met my dad, 16 when she got married, and only 20 years old when she had me. I feel she sacrificed her childhood to raise Wendy and me. It's so incredible to know that someone has done that for you. At the same time, I feel sorry that she spent so many years on us, making sure we were okay and ready to go off in the world on our own.

That's what happened. I moved out when I was 18, and then Wilson Phillips started. By 21, I was doing my own thing, supporting myself.

Mom was always proud, always supportive of whatever I've done in my life. She's been very giving and has always put us first. That's what she *did,* and that's what she *does.* I love it that she's free enough now to do the things that she wants to do.

She's so happy since she met Daniel, her new husband. He's such a doll and so sweet to her. She's always laughed, but with Daniel she laughs more than ever. She has such a magical, contagious, warm, spiritual, funny laugh—and he makes that come to life every day. It's a pleasure to see her laugh and feel free, and it's wonderful to see her happy.

Mom was always very concerned about me and my weight. She'd say, "Carnie, I'm getting scared for you. I wouldn't want anything to happen to you." It would make me feel terrible because I always wanted to make Mom proud—which I did. I still love to make her laugh, and she has always been my biggest fan.

But when it came to my weight, I just couldn't do it for her, and I couldn't do it for me or anyone else. When I finally did do something, I think she kind of went into shock.

MOM'S VERY CLOSE TO HER TWO SISTERS. My Aunt Barbara got into training animals for movies. She used to bring baby tigers and other wild animals to our house like they were normal pets. When I was 12, she moved away, so we didn't see her as often. But Aunt Diane—the family calls her Dee Dee—was like a second mom to us. "I've never had children of my own," she'd say. "You'll be the closest thing I'll ever have."

Dee Dee has such a great sense of humor, and no one has a bigger heart. She's a very talented woman in her own right. She's co-written songs with Dad, and I'm very proud of her. Everyone loved Dee Dee because she just talked, talked, talked. I think I inherited my motormouth from her. It just seemed like wherever we were, Dee Dee was there, too.

Another lady who was always there—even on the day I was born—was Cherie Champion. Cherie's been my mom's best friend for 33 years. If Mom went away for the weekend, we'd go to Cherie's apartment and she'd take great care of us. Auntie Cherie was just a fireball and always funny. There was so much laughter. I remember Mom, Dee Dee, Barbara, and Cherie—everybody laughing so hard they were peeing in their pants.

We went on skiing trips together. We went to the beach together. We had parties at the house on the holidays. Everyone was there enjoying themselves. There was this dark side of dysfunction, but there was also family love, and everybody having fun. When I look back through all the family photos, there's Mom, Dee Dee, Cherie, Francis, and cousin Ginger—always, always close—and everyone still is.

There were my childhood girlfriends—Chynna, Shawn Kay, Tiffany Miller, Julie Siegel, and Jenny Brill.

And of course, there was Wendy.

When Wendy was born and Mom brought her home, my first words to her were, "I love you, Wendy," and I kissed her. You hear stories about children who are threatened when their siblings are born. I never was. I was always the big sister. I looked out for her and protected her—and I made her laugh. I still do.

Wendy's like a twin. We couldn't look any more different, but I've always had such a close connection with her. We don't even have to speak to know what we're thinking. I love her more than anything in the world, and I feel so fortunate that she's my sister. We've always felt that way about each other.

Mom always said to us, "You two are so lucky to have each other, so blessed. Always be good to each other. Always be fair to each other and respect each other. Always love each other—because there's nothing in the world like having a sister."

Mom feels that way about her sisters, and it was so special for her to be one of five girls who were growing up together, experiencing things together. There was this feeling of major strength and girl power. It's the same thing for Wendy and me.

There was never any competition with her. We each had our strong points, and we learned to appreciate them in each other. That doesn't mean that I couldn't understand why she never had to struggle with weight. But she couldn't have been more supportive.

"I know how hard it is for you," she would say. "I feel so sorry. It's not fair. How can I help you? What can I do?" But there was nothing she could do. She couldn't stop me from eating—my food and hers. As soon as the plates were put down on our counter, I'd want a bite of hers.

I didn't hate her because she was thin. I was just confused and troubled about it.

All of a sudden, she started growing really tall, and I was short. She started becoming this really pretty girl, and I was this big clown. I was purposely loud so that I'd get attention, and I was funny so that people would notice my personality rather than my body. Wendy didn't always have to say something—and a part of me was envious and jealous.

I went through a lot of issues and insecurities about Wendy. But how could I blame her for my esteem problems? She wasn't out to hurt me. She'd never hurt a fly. I learned through therapy that just because she's taller or slimmer doesn't mean that I'm *less* of something. It took me a long time to realize this, and I still struggle with it.

But there's been a love like no other—a bond so deep—that's very strong between us. And it always will be. Wendy is so sweet, so fair and caring. She's so different from me in so many ways. She's introverted, shy, and soft-spoken—but really smart, and funny as hell. Sometimes I admire the way she doesn't have to state her opinion. She doesn't have to prove a point like I've always had to do. I respect her for that.

I always thought that she was more feminine than I was. I was the abrasive and aggressive broad; Wendy was the kind and gentle girl. I think we admire our strengths and our weaknesses, and we honor them.

When we were younger, Wendy used to tattletale on me, antagonize me, and piss me off—and I used to beat up on her a little bit. I'd scratch her and bite her and hit her. When I got older, I felt really bad about it. I was in that stage of therapy where I was thinking about my family and what everyone meant to me. I had to apologize to Wendy.

"I'm so sorry if I ever put you in an uncomfortable position," I said. "I just want you to know how much I love you and how grateful I am that we have each other."

There's been more pain in these last ten years for both of us because we've realized how things have affected us, and what we did and didn't have as children. But growing up together, we always had each other. We sang together, we partied together, and we laughed and cried together. I just can't imagine not being with her or talking with her. I respect her so much as a person and as an artist. Our relationship is so special. There's nothing like it in the world.

The love I felt from Mom and Wendy and our family and friends helped me through the really painful years on the way to adolescence. These were the years when I was teased the most. I was starting to get really heavy for my age, and I was in that awkward stage of being fearful of any type of discipline with my weight.

Everyone began to show their concern, and that's when I got nervous about it. I started to realize that I had a problem. It dawned on me when I went to fat camp that first year. *Hey, I thought, I'm not going to a normal camp. I'm going to the camp where the fat kids go.*

Growing up, I was never ashamed of the importance of food. I was never really self-conscious about eating in front of someone. My friends and family all loved food, so it wasn't really an embarrassment to eat. It was more of a frustrating thing, like, "There's Carnie overeating again." It was sort of expected of me, part of my personality, part of the package.

My mom and my psychologist used to say to me, "Yes, you are indulgent and sort of a glutton when it comes to food, but you also have that in other areas of your life—the hunger for success, the desire to be outgoing."

I was very active as a youngster, even though I was overeating the wrong foods. I used to ice skate. I did gymnastics. I swam.

I played volleyball. I loved to roller skate.

I always remember wanting to put on a show, to make people laugh and get a reaction. I just wanted to shock people. My mom was the best audience. She was the one from the beginning saying, "Oh, you're so funny," or "You're so talented," or "Boy, you can really sing!"

I wasn't a shy, withdrawn fat kid. I was a social butterfly, in the school plays, very popular with my schoolmates—the class clown. I made everyone laugh.

I worked at being funny because I felt so out of place. My identity was shaped by the fact that I was fat. I was the fat one—but the one with the personality, the one who was entertaining, the one always joking.

Because I was overweight, I think I was expected to be funny. So I was.

Deep down I was hiding the pain of feeling different, but I also *wanted* to be different. I liked the attention. I enjoyed being the one people remembered. I was big, but everyone liked me, and I became sort of comfortable with that.

It was a major contradiction because I wanted to be like the other girls in terms of size, but I liked who I was. I was content to be original. I got so used to being the chubby one that I somehow felt good in that role.

I'd think about it and ask myself, "Why? Why am I this way?" But I didn't know the answer. Maybe there was so much instability and pain and abnormal family life that I just wanted to be strong, and I equated being heavy with being strong.

Sometimes people want to beef themselves up with food because they think the world says, "When you're big, you're powerful." When you're feeling very powerless as a child because people do things to you, and you're being moved around, and you don't have a voice, one of the ways you can feel like a powerful person is to get physically big. You bulk up. I think that's one of the things that could have been happening in my life.

I didn't feel pretty like the other girls, so I decided to get tough. In the sixth grade playing softball, when I'd step up to bat, everybody backed up. I remember thinking, *Yeah, that's right, you motherfuckers. You better back up because I'm going to show you my strength. I'm the biggest, strongest girl here, and I'm going to hit this ball harder than any other girl on this team.*

I wanted to prove that I could do it, and I had the power to hit the ball, but then I couldn't run the bases very well. I usually made it to first base, sometimes second. I don't know if I ever hit a home run. I just wanted to seem strong.

When your weight becomes part of your identity and you equate it with your power, it becomes harder and harder to let it go. If somebody's been thin all their life and they start to put on a little weight, they think, *I'll just take it off.* But if you've been fat all your life, it becomes your Achilles' heel. You start thinking of yourself as not just the fat one, but the one who'll gain it back again if you lose it.

Then you start feeling that people *expect* you to gain it back. It becomes a self-fulfilling prophecy—or more like a curse.

My cousin Jonah and I always felt cursed. We'd spend hours crying and talking about how cursed we were. We felt we were blessed in many ways, but in the food department, we were born under a bad sign. We still say it now, even though Jonah has lost 115 pounds and kept it off for ten years. We'll always have a little curse on us, and that's the way it is. We've got to deal with the struggle—and it will always be a struggle.

At home, Mom tried to get a handle on my problem. We did everything but put me in a cage. She even put locks on the refrigerator door. The worst thing about it was that the doors were glass. You could see the food inside.

But it didn't last for long because I'd just get food from somewhere else.

My dad was gaining weight during this period as well. He was working with some trainers and getting help from one of his cousins who was a Los Angeles Laker. He'd come over to shoot hoops with Dad. Everyone knew that I was gaining weight, too, and they wanted me to lose weight along with my father. "If Brian's doing it, we've got to get Carnie to do it, too," they said, "because we don't want her to be heavy as an adult."

So at the same time that I started gaining weight, I started running on the treadmill and playing basketball. I have a terrible memory of something that happened to me when I was seven. One day when I was running on the treadmill, Dad's cousin wouldn't let me get off. He kept making me run and run and run.

"You're fat," he said, "and because you're fat, you've got to lose this weight. You can't be fat. You've got to get healthy."

I was crying hysterically, out of breath, exhausted, and this was very traumatic for me. When I told Jonah, we decided to get revenge. We took a rock and carved "Fuck You Asshole" on the door of his silver 450SEL Mercedes. Then we peed in his apple juice bottle and left it in the back seat.

The next day we were at Brother Records Studio where the Beach Boys were recording the *Beach Boys Love You* album, one of my favorite records. Mom had come to Wendy and asked, "Who did this?" because she knew Wen would tell. Sure enough, Wendy tattled on us, and we got in big trouble. We had to make an official apology, and my mom had to pay for the Mercedes to be repainted. This was supposed to be a big lesson, but we felt great about it.

I remember another bad experience that happened while my dad was working for the first time with a psychologist, Dr. Eugene Landy, in 1977. I was nine years old, in the third grade, and going through a period where I was angry, talking back, and out of control with my eating. My mom was desperate because Dad was clearly having his problems, she was trying to raise Wendy and me by herself, and I was rebelling.

I was up to 110 pounds, and Mom was terrified for me. She didn't know what to do, so she thought that while Dad was getting training, maybe I could get straightened out as well.

Dr. Landy, who eventually had his license revoked, convinced my mom to put me on a "token" program. I had to earn red, white, or blue tokens by making my bed and doing other chores around the house. Then I could cash in the tokens to earn my breakfast or my lunch for school, or even to come out of my room. The idea was to teach me discipline. "You're lazy," he said. "You're not helping out. You've got to learn to do these things."

So I went on this program, and I remember sharing with my friends how embarrassed I was that I didn't have a lunch one day. I felt like this worthless person because I didn't have enough red tokens.

One day I was outside playing, and one of Dr. Landy's team that watched over my dad was watching over me. His name was Joey.

"Okay, it's time to come in," he said.

"No," I said back. "I want to play some more."

"Get your ass in the house," he said, and he grabbed me.

I remember fighting him off, and he called Dr. Landy and said, "I don't know what to do with her."

"Throw her in the sauna," said Landy.

So Joey dragged me upstairs and locked me in the sauna.

It wasn't turned on, but I was terrified. I was in there probably 15 minutes, screaming and crying, until my mom arrived.

"What the hell is going on here?" she screamed at Joey. "Where's my daughter? What have you done with her? Get out of my house, and don't ever come back here again."

She unlocked the door, and I remember running into her arms. I was frightened and ashamed because it was all linked to my behavior and my eating. But no kid should have to go through that.

Around this time, I had a moment with my dad that I'll remember forever. One night he woke me up about 11 o'clock and asked me if I wanted to have some cereal. We went down to the kitchen, and Dad poured us two bowls of raisin bran. Then he poured half-and-half over the flakes.

"Raisin bran tastes so much better with half-and-half," he said.

I can almost taste the creamy flavors now—the crunchy flakes and the sweet raisins. It was so good—it was like food ecstasy—sitting with my dad, grooving on the fats and sugars and carbohydrates. Nutrition was the last thing on my mind. We were together, the rush was delicious, and that was all that mattered.

WHEN MY PARENTS WERE DIVORCED A COUPLE YEARS LATER, I was sad because I knew they weren't going to be together and I wasn't going to be seeing my dad every day. I think my mother just wanted to get us out of what had become a very unstable environment.

We moved to a big house in Encino with a huge pool. It was a wonderful place, and we had so many great times there with our friends and our dogs—Louie, Banana, and Hana. People would come over all the time. Compared to the house in Bel Air, it was so sunny and bright, and I was glad to get out of that dark old house. We had so many great times in our new home, and I treasure my memories of those days. I cherish the music and the friendships and the many people who showed me so much love. Most of all, I cherish the laughter we shared with each other.

Not long after that, I began to diet continually—on and off from age 12 all the way through high school. In the eighth grade, I started to binge and purge. I'd eat and then make myself throw up. I'd been doing it for about a month when I went to the doctor for my yearly checkup. He looked down my throat and asked, "Are you throwing up?"

I admitted that I was.

"Well, you better stop," he said. "I can see that it's beginning to damage your esophagus. That's really dangerous, and you can kill yourself by doing that. So you have to stop."

I stopped right away because he scared me—and I didn't want my mom to find out. Looking back, I just can't believe I did that. It's so frightening—all the things that I've tried, and all the failures. Mentally, it was so hard to just keep failing.

Weight was always an issue with me, no matter where I went. If I went to a girlfriend's house, her mother would ask, "Can you have this?" One day I was at the house of a very close friend of mine who also had a weight problem. We were 13. Her stepdad saw us snacking and said, "You shouldn't be eating. You're just pigs."

Everyone knew that I had a weight problem, and I was always the one who was going to eat more. I don't think anyone knew how to handle it.

MY MOM, HER SISTERS, AND MY GRANDMA always used to talk about their "thunder thighs."

"It's part of our genetics," they'd say. "We just have that look. And Wendy is so lucky because she's thin."

It was never, "Carnie is so unlucky because she's fat." It was just that Wendy didn't get that and I did. It was a part of who I was—Carnie's struggle.

From such a young age, it was, "What are we going to do? What's the latest thing?"

"Let's go on the Beverly Hills Diet."

"Let's go to the Lindora Clinic and get the shots."

"Let's do the starvation diet."

"Let's do Jenny Craig or Pritikin or Weight Watchers."

We were always on some kind of program, and we did them together. So I never felt alone in the battle because Mom, Dee Dee, and Jonah were right there with me. Dad was sort of in and out. Wendy never had a problem.

We were measuring our food, eating low fat, and then we'd all go out and binge on junk food. We went to the movies a lot, and that was always the perfect excuse to blow the diet. We'd devour candy, sodas, hot dogs, nachos, and huge buckets of popcorn.

We did a lot of social things together, too. There were tons of parties all the time, especially on holidays, and everything revolved around food. You never knew who would be stopping by. One day I opened the door and Shaun Cassidy was standing there, wanting to see my dad. I just about jumped out of my skin—he was so cute.

Another time, Paul and Linda McCartney came by with their kids, and we all stood around the piano singing "My Bonnie Lies Over the Ocean." Of course, anytime there were guests, the food would be rolled out for everyone. It was just a huge thing, and we'd hardly ever exercise. Mom played tennis, but most of the time the calories going in were greater than the calories being burned.

So we'd be back on the latest fad diet. On the Beverly Hills Diet, we'd have a huge plate of pineapple for breakfast, then carrots and broccoli for lunch. And we were all starving. It was the most unsatisfying, unhealthy thing. Then we'd have a dinner of nothing but steak. The next day we'd start with grapes. It was crazy.

It went on like this for a week—because who can eat fruit for a week like that? We all had canker sores in our mouths after the pineapple day. We'd drop ten pounds in seven days, then we'd gain it all back in two weeks.

We used to take Ex-Lax together to get the food out of our bodies. Once we went to Chicago for Passover, and we all knew we were going to eat like pigs. So we thought we'd take Ex-Lax and just shit it out. We indulged ourselves, overate, and we all took more Ex-Lax than we should have. It was a horrible experience. We were shitting in our pants for a couple of days.

Mom, Dee Dee, and I went together to the Lindora Clinic for a series of shots made from the urine of pregnant women. The shots were supposed to make your body burn fat. I was hoping, "Please, God, let this be the cure. Let this be the one that does it." I needed to lose 40 or 50 pounds, and I really got into the program. I'd check my urine with a ketosis stick to see if I was burning fat, and I lost probably 30 pounds or so.

But as usual, when the program was over, the weight came back and then some.

I went on Dexatrim when I was in junior high, but it totally wigged me out, and I got so hyper, I just ate more and more. I did both Jenny Craig and NutriSystem. We'd buy the food and stick with it as long as we could. Then we'd go right back to our bad habits.

Diet after diet led to failure after failure, and as I rolled into my high school years, my weight kept climbing. Some days I wanted desperately to be thinner. Other days it was okay to be heavy. And although I dreamed more and more of my future in show business—a future I couldn't count on—the unhealthy pattern for the future of my health was set.

I was on my way into the danger zone.

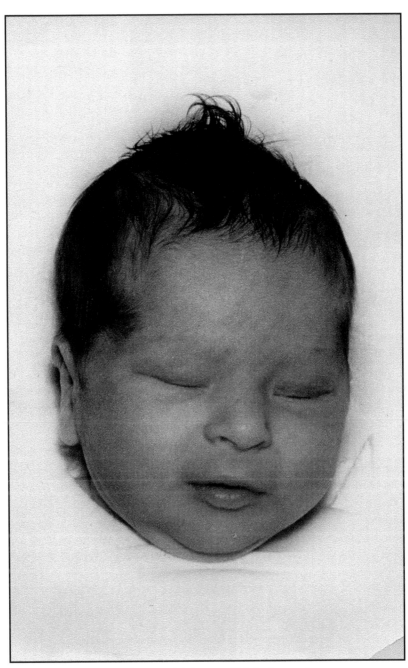

Congratulations! It's a girl! My first picture.

Always a Daddy's girl.

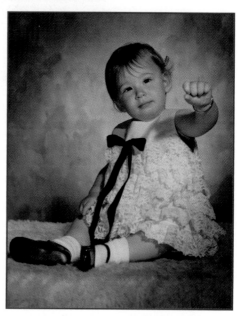

Mommy says to wave hello!

Wendy (right)
and me:
Always pals.

Wendy (left) and
me with Mom.

Playing around with Dad.

Wendy and me onstage performing at a Beach Boys concert.

Two of my favorites—eating and making Mom laugh.

A grand performance for the family.

Clowning around with Wendy . . . as usual!

Wendy and me weighing in
at elementary school.

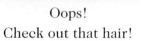

Oops!
Check out that hair!

"I'd like a piece this big, please!" (age 7).

Daddy and I are twins—minus the beard!

Halloween costumes made by Mom.

Home from Fat
Camp, hoping my
schoolmates will
"flip" over my
new figure.

My yearbook
photo (age 15).

Feeling big
and depressed.
Please pass
the joint!

Me at 19
years old in my
first apartment,
weighing 225 lbs.,
and not happy.

I lost 80 lbs. with Lisa
Roth's help. (From left:
Auntie Dee Dee, me,
Mom, and Wendy.)

Grandma Mae (left)
and family friend
Gwen (right)—two of
the sweetest women.

Grandpa Irv at my high
school graduation. He's
an Einstein clone!

Grandma Audree
with her famous
rose-tinted glasses.

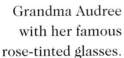

A Wilson family Christmas at Mom's house—Wendy; cousins
Jonah, Justyn, and Michael; me; and Carl.

My cousin
Jonah and
me looking
like brother
and sister.

Wendy, Chynna, and me at a post-Grammy party in 1989,
one year before Wilson Phillips.

Tour manager Steve Hoffman (far left), me,
Chynna, and Wendy on a private tour jet—lucky us!

First radio station concert in Phoenix (it's 114 degrees!).

Lisa Roth and me on the tour bus.

Shooting "The Dream Is Alive" video. Notice the
shadowing under my chin to hide excessive weight?

(Photo: Henry Diltz)

My buddy Jeff Panzer,
an SBK executive.

From the
"Flesh and
Blood" video.
I'm hiding
behind the
piano.

Wilson Phillips at
the MTV Awards.

Robert Palmer
and me at the
Royal Albert
Hall before
our perform-
ance together.

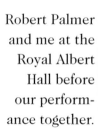

CHAPTER THREE

Songs, Sex, and Smoke

My first love is music. It always has been. It's such a huge part of my being, and I've always known it. I remember feeling it when I was as young as four, certainly by the time I was six.

I knew I wanted to be a singer when I heard voices like Barbra Streisand and Karen Carpenter. My parents loved the Carpenters, and we played their records all the time at home. It didn't matter whether you liked that style of music or not. It was the magic in Karen's voice that was so soothing, and the lushness of the layered harmonies that were like soft clouds of sound.

My dad particularly loved the song "Be My Baby," by the Ronettes. He played it every single day—sometimes over and over—for as long as we lived together. Dad was blown away by Phil Spector's "wall of sound" production, and Ronnie Spector's voice had a yearning quality that knocked him out again and again. He couldn't get enough of "Be My Baby." To him, it's the greatest record ever made.

All kinds of music were always playing in the house, so Wendy and I were just constantly exposed to it. We had a big family room with an incredible stereo system, and Mom and

Dad had this huge wrought-iron shelving unit filled with albums. We used to go through the collection and just blast the music and dance and sing. It was something that gave us so much pleasure.

There was always someone visiting, and whoever came through that front door would have to watch Wendy and me perform. They didn't have a choice. We'd bug them until they sat down, and then we'd sing our hearts out into hairbrushes or broomsticks with the big fireplace behind us.

Sure, we did other things that little girls do—sports, putting on makeup, playing dress-up. But that was more when we were alone or with Mom. We'd be in her bathroom and put on her nail polish and makeup, and she would teach us about beauty.

But we spent most of our time singing to our favorite music.

We had no idea we'd ever do it in front of thousands of people, but at the age of five, I made my stage debut with Wendy. It was the first of many times we sang backup for the Beach Boys in concert.

All the Beach Boys took their kids on the road. We'd go to the gigs, sing onstage, hang out backstage, eat constantly, and have so much fun. Grandma Audree was often there with us, laughing and having a great time. There was nothing she liked better than to see her sons perform. It was a wonderful musical experience, and everyone supported each other in those days. It felt more like a family than it did at home.

But Dad didn't like going on the road. He didn't like to perform. He was in and out. But most of the time he stayed home.

I remember a huge thrill one night at the Forum in Los Angeles. It was the first time Mom ever let me wear high heels. They were actually wedges, but they were high, and I was feeling really cute.

Daddy was back on the road with the band, and there was

a huge banner saying **"Brian's back! Welcome back, Brian!"** I was really proud of him, and it was a great feeling, because usually he wasn't on the stage. But that night he was there, and it was awesome.

I went out to the center of the stage all by myself, stepped up to the microphone, and said, "Ladies and gentlemen, please welcome the Beach Boys!"

Memories like this are so special because Dad didn't share himself with us that often. Most of the time he didn't really think about us. He was always busy at the piano, and once in a while we'd make him play something, and we'd sing it. But these moments were very scarce.

I've been making music of my own since I was 18 months old. We had a fantastic Hammond B-3 organ that my dad played now and then. Sometimes he'd put me on the bench next to him, and my little hands would go for it. I loved to watch him and be like him.

I started on the piano when I was in kindergarten, and Wendy and I took lessons for about ten years. We loved to perform for Mom and Dad, especially because it was the best way to get our father's attention. He'd sit back, close his eyes, and smile as he listened.

It was a rare chance for us to make a connection with him, and these were moments we cherished. There are only a few others, and even though they're little moments, they're all I have, so they mean so much.

When I was ten, Dad taught me how to play "Rhapsody in Blue." He'd learned it by listening to a recording over and over until he got every note. He didn't read the music. He just played it on the piano every day. When he showed me how to do it, I felt like I tapped into something very close to him, and that was the coolest. Another time he taught me "California Girls" and "Sloop John B," and I was so happy to share this bond with him.

When I was 12—this was a year after my parents were divorced—he came over one day to our new home in Encino. He sat down and said, "Play something for me. I love to hear you play."

So I played, and he sat back like he always does and closed his eyes. I could see how much it meant to him, and I felt so proud that somebody who knows music and just *is* music was so deeply affected by my playing. I think he enjoyed the way I played, but what he loved was that it was his daughter playing.

It was like, "Hey, this is my daughter, and I'm her dad. This is her talent, and some of it came from me. I may not have been the perfect father, but I gave her something beautiful that will last forever."

Music was our connection—our easiest connection—and it still is. We have painful connections, too. But music is our most natural. We can't explain it. It's just there.

HARMONIZING CAME NATURALLY TO WENDY AND ME. Mom has the gift of harmony, too. I remember riding down Sunset Boulevard in her little brown Mercedes convertible, listening to Bob Seger or the Beach Boys and singing along. She'd teach me how to go below the melody for the low harmony, and Wendy would go for the high part. There's something magical about singing harmonies together, and when we'd make our voices blend just right, I'd get off on it so much. I dreamed of making music and having an acting career.

At Oakwood I started working in the drama department in the seventh grade. After years of subjects that didn't hold my interest, it was like coming home.

I'd done two national commercials when I was younger, and the feeling had been so positive. *Okay, I may be heavier than the other kids,* I thought, *but I can do this—and I'm good.*

Drama was the perfect outlet for my outgoing side. I could win people over with my acting. A wonderful teacher named

Sabel Bender constantly encouraged me to work hard at bringing my characters to life. On the opening nights of our productions, I'd tell her how nervous I was. "Good," she'd say. "Now direct that energy into your performance. You'll be great!" She'd always compliment me on my strong stage presence, and her inspiration helped me build confidence that has influenced me for the rest of my life.

By this time, I was already into boys, and my attitude toward my weight began to change. I had a few close girlfriends, and we were chunky together, but boys weren't part of our social life until around the fifth grade. I remember at that time I had a crush on a couple of boys, but they wouldn't give me the time of day. They wanted the thin blonde girl with the big blue eyes. Everybody wanted her, including the guy I just adored.

I was so in love with him, and we became close friends, but he never really wanted me. I'd go over to his house or call him on the phone, and we'd talk about the girls he liked. I'd give him advice, but inside I was dying for him. I was dying for that moment when he'd finally realize that I was the one for him.

"I really appreciate your friendship," he'd say. And I wondered if he didn't want me because I was heavier than his ideal girl.

Later we wound up having sex together once, and I was his first. But he never wanted me for a girlfriend, and my heart still aches a little when I think of him. I ran into him several years ago. He's now the dean of an exclusive private school in Los Angeles, has children of his own, and is still as handsome as a god.

But I had other boys who liked me. I always had a boyfriend. So it wasn't like I was this loner fat girl who never had a date. I was very popular, but I know the feeling of being rejected by the men you want, how it is to feel like you're not worth anything because you don't look a certain way, and the loneliness when they're not paying attention to you. It's sad, and it can be self-depleting.

There were times when I was attracted to guys and they'd just tell me that they couldn't get around my weight. It was so crushing that I can't dig up the actual memories. But it's one of those things that needs to be verbalized. When you feel rejected, you need to talk about it with people who care, and hopefully they'll comfort you.

They'll say things like, "He doesn't know what he's missing. You're a great person. One day you're going to find someone who really loves you for who you are." That's what I got from my mom and all my friends. They helped me believe that having a good personality is so much better than having looks—and that the boyfriend of my dreams would be there for me when the time was right

I actually had my first boyfriend when I was five years old. He had the cutest freckles, and I had a major crush on him.

"Do you think he likes me?" I asked my mom.

"Sure he does," she said.

I remember going to his house to play. But we were five. What were we going to do?

At six I was taught how to French-kiss by a gorgeous boy named Jeffrey Knott, whose parents were friends of the family. I remember how unbelievably warm and fabulous his mouth was.

In the fifth grade, I had my first feelings of wanting to kiss the boys like the other girls did. During lunch period or recess, there would be games of Truth or Dare or Spin the Bottle. I always watched, but I never had the courage or confidence to play. I was afraid to be embarrassed. There were so many boys I wanted, but God forbid if they were grossed out and said no—it would have been too devastating.

A year later, I had two boyfriends on the string, and kissing was no problem. I was actually starting to think about sex. Looking back, I remember feeling sexual at a young age. I always knew there were ways to feel good and that the hormones would kick in. Growing up, I felt very open, and my mom was very cool about sex and feeling good. She caught me playing with myself early on, and she said it was normal, but there was a time and a place. She told me it was natural to discover your body, and that as I got older, these feelings would come more into play. I was mature for my age, just like my mom was, and I had my first period when I was ten. Once it all started, I knew I was a sexy little thing even though I was 25 or 30 pounds overweight. I lost my virginity when I was 13, but I didn't realize I was more advanced than most of my group. I thought I was the oddball and the outcast, when I was actually the one having sex before everyone else was.

Now I wish that I'd waited. I'd never encourage anyone to have sex at 13 years old. But I wasn't promiscuous. I'd been with my boyfriend for two years when we first made love. I remember going to spend the night at his house.

"Now don't do anything I wouldn't do," my mom said.

"Don't worry," I said. "I will."

"Carnie," she said, "please be careful."

My boyfriend had put the stereo together and had changed his room around just for me. His parents were home, and we tried to be very quiet. He had a little condom, and it was a very sweet thing. We thought we were being responsible, that we were ready, and that we were in love. Even so, I was nervous that I'd gotten pregnant, but my period arrived on my 14th birthday.

A year later, I had my first experience with marijuana, and I found my drug of choice—next to food, which has been the most powerful drug in my life, and probably always will be. But I loved the feeling of being stoned, and the smell and taste of pot—I still do. I'll smoke it occasionally now, but I don't buy it anymore or keep it in the house—and that helps me—because if there's dope around, I'll smoke it. I can't control myself.

The marijuana smoking started out as social. In the beginning, I wasn't using it to cover up my feelings. I experimented a couple times at camp, and gradually I started smoking more often.

I never smoked it at school—on campus. I'd get in the car during free periods and go for a drive with my friends and our little pipe—and we'd get high. On the weekends, it was definitely the thing to do. We'd get the giggles and the munchies, and it was a blast.

When it came to smoke, my mom was liberal. She was hip about it, but she didn't condone it. She'd talk openly to me about drugs because she'd seen how devastating they could be.

"You've got to be really careful," she'd say. "You could react the way your dad reacted to drugs. Everyone's body is different, and we all have different chemical make-ups, but you never know how your body is going to react. So, please don't do drugs. It's dangerous, and I want you to promise me."

She was scared about me and pot, but I was basically a good kid. I wasn't a troublemaker, and she had a tremendous amount of faith in me. She believed that I had a good head on my shoulders, and she trusted me to take care of myself—and I did. I never went so overboard that I put myself or others in jeopardy.

But Mom knew I was partying. We'd sneak out or say we were going to the mall, get in the car, park somewhere on the street, and light up joints. Most of the kids were doing it, and many of their parents had no fucking clue. Today it's even worse.

It wasn't until later—during the Wilson Phillips years, when she saw I was getting stoned all the time—that Mom got really worried. She was seriously concerned.

"You've got to get a handle on this," she said. "Do you need to go into rehab?"

I'd say no and I'd stop for a while.

Other times I lied to her, and she knows that now. I'd say I wasn't smoking, but I was. She always offered her help, anything that she could do for me.

"I just want you to be honest with me," she'd say—and I usually was. But there were times when I wasn't.

Pot wreaked havoc with my weight. Once I started smoking regularly, I put on 50 pounds. I'd smoke, get the munchies, and I'd eat. Then the buzz would go away, I'd smoke again, and I'd eat even more.

Dope stimulates your senses, so everything tastes extra good, and you just can't get enough. When I was high, it seemed like I didn't realize how much I was eating. You just don't. You smoke and you're ravenous.

I remember getting high and going to Dupar's Restaurant. I'd eat a patty melt—a fried hamburger on grilled sourdough bread with grilled onions and tomato and lots of melted cheese. Then I'd eat a huge order of fries, and a big piece of hot pecan pie with a scoop of vanilla ice cream. That's probably 150 grams of fat right there.

I'd consume huge amounts, and then an hour later at home, I'd make myself a sausage sandwich with cheese or sour cream and ketchup. I was obsessed with cheese. I'd melt cheese in a cup and eat it like soup. I still eat cheese every day. I just love it. But now it's a good thing. I feel liberated because I can eat just a little, and I can stop.

I used to have get-togethers almost every weekend my junior and senior year with a group of five guys who were my closest friends—Maury, Jonathan, Josh, Chris, and Tucker. We had the greatest times together.

This is the way I've socialized for most of my life. I've hardly ever gone on dates. I went on a date with my first boyfriend, Gary, to see the movie *Urban Cowboy*, and he gave me a kiss on the cheek—my first kiss. But most of the time guys would come over and hang out.

These five boys used to come to my house every weekend, and they'd keep me in stitches for hours doing these routines like a slapstick comedy team. They were all so bright and talented in their individual ways, and I was the only girl—getting all the attention—so I was in heaven.

I was absolutely mad for Maury, but I had those feelings that he didn't always want to be with me because of my weight. We'd have passionate sex and great fun together, but he'd say, "We're really good friends, and it would just kill me if something happened to our friendship. So I just don't think we should become committed to each other."

These boys were my dear friends, and they made me feel sexy and appealing to men. When I look back, I think they really helped me to be open and comfortable around people. I felt I'd be accepted by men because I had these male friendships, and I'm grateful for these wonderful guys who took me in and didn't judge me. This was so important to me, because as high school came to a close, I was judging myself and not making the grade.

The pressure really started to hit me because I knew I didn't want to go to college. At Oakwood, it seemed like everyone was very bright, and everybody was going to college—except me.

I was a shitty student, and my grades were terrible. I was always distracted, and I had no attention span. All I wanted to be was social, so I didn't care about my studies. I'd get an A in drama and maybe a B in Spanish if I was lucky. The rest were C's and D's. My teachers all liked me, and sometimes they'd even let me slide by with F's. No one seemed really concerned because everyone took it for granted that I was going to be an entertainer.

In the plays at school, I was always cast in leading roles, but never the beautiful female lead. I was sort of proud to be the ditzy mom or the wacky housekeeper. It was natural for me, but there was still a little part of me that was hurt. It was like I didn't qualify, I didn't have what it took—and that made me feel bad.

But the part of me that perseveres, the part of me that's the true optimist, would say, "Okay, I didn't get the part of the stunning heroine, but I'm going to play the funniest house-keeper ever. I'm going to be the strongest mom you've ever seen." And my contributions were always appreciated.

In the ninth grade, I played the magician's assistant in *Carnival*, one of my favorite roles ever. It was very special to me because this was one of the few times my dad came to see me perform. My character was voluptuous and charismatic, and I got to prance around in these great costumes and sing my heart out. Everyone was knocked out by my work—but there was only one opinion that really mattered.

After the curtain came down, my dad came up to me. He had tears streaming down his face. "Your voice, Carnie" was all he said.

Those words meant the world to me.

But I was worried that there wasn't a real career in those kinds of parts. A talent scout saw me in some of the plays and hooked me up with an agency. I started going on auditions, but I didn't get any roles. As graduation got closer and closer, everyone seemed to have their future all planned, but mine was a big question mark. Each day the anxiety grew stronger and stronger.

I toyed with the idea of auditioning to go to Juilliard. But I really didn't want it, and I never pursued it. I never even took the SAT's. All I knew is that I wanted to get out of high school. That's when the smoke got heavy—and so did I.

CHAPTER FOUR

Making It Big

B y October of 1986, my classmates had gone to college, and I was smoking the equivalent of about five joints a day. As soon as high school was over, I'd moved out and gone on my own. I had my own apartment, and I was in that party-hearty summertime mode. I'd have a lot of friends over, and we'd have a blast just being crazy teenagers and enjoying our freedom.

My plans to be an actress weren't really working out, and I was doing bongload after bongload of strong pot, day and night.

Then one day Chynna called up.

"Hey, my friend Owen has this idea," she said.

I didn't really know Owen then. She went to Oakwood like I did, but she was a grade ahead. Chynna knew her because Owen is Cass Elliot's daughter—Mama Cass from the Mamas and the Papas. Chynna's father is the late John Phillips, the founder of that group, and her mother is Michelle Phillips, the beautiful blonde in the Mamas and the Papas who went on to become a successful actress and a wonderful friend.

We decided to meet at Mom's house. For some reason, Owen couldn't make it that day, but Chynna did. Owen's idea was to form a group of kids whose parents were '60s musicians and do some charity concerts. She was thinking of Donovan's kids, Frank Zappa's kids, and kids from the Grateful Dead's families. We all sort of knew each other.

But the only kids who ended up wanting to do it were Chynna, Wendy, Owen, and me.

"We've got to do this," we said. "Let's just start singing."

Of course, we'd all grown up hearing our parents' music, which has some of the greatest harmony arrangements ever. In high school, I started getting into Crosby, Stills, and Nash; the Eagles; and Fleetwood Mac—major harmony groups. I'd get kids together from my class, and during recess we'd sit on the benches outside and sing. We'd do songs like the Eagles' "Seven Bridges Road." I'd say, "Okay, you do this part." Then I'd sing the part until one of the other girls would get it. Then I'd say to another, "And you sing this part."

It would go like that until we'd have these three- or four-part harmonies that I could hear in my head all in sync. Technically they wouldn't be perfect, because I'd never taken music theory or composition. But I just knew what was natural to me, and it sounded great to everyone else.

I felt like it was what I was meant to do. I've always been kind of bossy—even as a little kid I wanted to pick the music and tell everyone else what to do. This was so right for me, and everyone knew it. I felt important and so at home, and it was obvious to me that music—and particularly harmony—was my thing.

By 1986, when Wendy and Chynna and I started singing together, we were listening to albums by Stevie Nicks, Genesis, and Heart. Every week we'd buy new CDs with our allowances, and they were precious to us. We'd sit around in a circle on the green carpet in Wendy's room and play these songs over and over. Then we'd sing along and start harmonizing together.

Owen was part of it for a while, but when we'd sing together,

her voice stood out so much that it didn't fit into the blend. She's a great singer, but it seemed like Wendy, Chynna, and I were meant to be a trio. We'd spent our lives growing up together, performing and having fun, singing and acting and dancing. It was so natural for us to form a group because that's what we've always done. We'd been singing together our entire lives.

We thought long and hard about it, and we felt terrible. But we had to tell Owen that she wouldn't be part of our group, and it was really devastating for her. The good news is that we became best friends, and I've always encouraged her. She's a great singer. And years later—when the opportunity presented itself—Owen, Wendy, and I performed in some shows with Al Jardine. So we all ended up singing together anyway.

Wendy, Chynna, and I started meeting regularly to rehearse. When Mom eventually heard us harmonizing, she was really flipped out. She always enjoyed hearing Wendy and me sing, and we were always doing it. We were never embarrassed to sing in front of anyone. But when she heard the three-part harmonies with Chynna, she knew we were on to something.

So did Michelle Phillips. She put us in touch with Richard Perry, a famous record producer who's worked with everyone from Barbra Streisand, Tina Turner, and Harry Nilsson to Ringo Starr and Tiny Tim. Richard liked our sound, and he took us under his wing. He brought us into his studio to make some demos.

We were working with songs by other writers, but at one point Richard said, "You've got to start writing your own songs. You're creative people. You've got it in you—and that's how you can really make some money."

He hooked us up with Glen Ballard, who was already known as a strong writer in those days. He'd been a staff writer for Quincy Jones and had co-written "Man in the Mirror" with Michael Jackson. Today he's famous as the producer for Alanis Morrisette, No Doubt, and the Dave Matthews Band—and Wilson Phillips—to name a few. In 1986, he'd just become an independent producer. We were so lucky to make this connection, and we shared many precious moments together, along with our engineer, Francis Buckley. None of us had any inkling of the wild ride that was in store for us.

Glen is an awesome talent, both as a composer and behind the glass. He worked with us for the next two years, crafting our sound and honing our material. I'd write and rehearse during the day, then go home at night and get high—and of course I'd eat.

Chynna had decided to get sober and had started therapy. I could see she was getting her life together, while I was feeling more and more out of control with my dope smoking and the constant munchies. In the nine months since the end of high school, I had put on 60 pounds and had ballooned up to 225.

Chynna could see what was happening with me. "Therapy is really great, Carnie," she said. "You should do this."

I knew I had an addiction to pot, and I wanted to get off it. Memories had been coming up from my past, and I was disturbed that I wasn't seeing my dad. I wasn't around him, and I missed him so much. I needed to figure some things out. At the same time, I was so thrilled to be in the group—a real musical group—that I wanted to direct my energy into healing places.

So I took Chynna's advice, and I started therapy with a wonderful psychologist, Dr. Marc Schoen. I'm very thankful I did, because it has really helped me. It's been everything.

With Marc, I discovered that I hadn't felt safe as a child. I'd turned to food for safety—and then eventually marijuana to numb the pain from all that. We started working on tools to help me feel safer and better about myself, using hypnosis to help me relax into a natural high instead of smoking marijuana.

I'd come in to some sessions loaded, and Marc would say,

"We can't make any progress if you're stoned." He made me realize that I had a substance abuse problem, and we battled it together, but it was hard to break the habit.

Meanwhile, Michelle had also put us together with her publicist, Warren Seabury, who started to get serious about our image as a group. "It's time to get some publicity so the major record companies will be interested," he said. And I started to get nervous.

Jesus, I thought. *I better get in shape.*

I started feeling this pressure about my physical presence, and as my 20th birthday approached and my weight climbed toward 235, I knew we were going to be professionals. We were working toward being famous and being in the limelight. In my therapy, I was going through these steps of discovery and healing, going in and out of sobriety, and just being wild.

I saw turning 20 as a milestone for me. I wanted to start a new decade for myself in a much more positive way. I knew that I had only one year left to get my act together. My mom had promised me, "I'll support you until you turn 21—but that's it." I was stressed about that deadline, and I wanted to start a real career and make money.

I wanted to become viable on my own, I wanted Wilson Phillips to succeed—and I wanted to lose 100 pounds.

Warren could see I needed help. "I'm going to hook you up with someone," he said. "She's a fitness expert, and I think you'll really get a lot out of meeting her."

I MET LISA ROTH JUST BEFORE I TURNED 20 IN APRIL OF 1988.

Lisa is a very special person who became one of the most important positive influences in my life. I'm really grateful for all the ways she enabled me to grow stronger. She changed my life because she helped me become aware of my feelings in a different way than my mother and my therapist did. She was my nutritionist, my trainer, and my friend.

Although Lisa's not in favor of weight-loss surgery, I don't think I would have ever have developed the confidence and courage to take that step without the wisdom and support she gave me. In spite of her reservations, she's been there for me in every way.

I got together with Lisa because I was really worried about coming out to the world being obese, and for the first time, I was sick of being fat—or so I thought.

Lisa has a philosophical as well as a practical approach to nutrition and health in general. She teaches you that we're emotional as well as physical beings, and if you really want to get to the bottom of an issue or a problem, you have to cover all the bases.

Marc was more in the head. But Lisa always combined the head *and* the heart, which is what is so wonderful about her.

In the beginning, we talked about nutrition—what's a carbohydrate, what's a protein, what's fat. We talked about the food groups, and what happens in your body when you eat the different ones. She encouraged me to keep a food journal, which I did on and off for a while, but it was hard for me to stick with it.

We spent time making sure I understood how different foods affected my body. She told me that it's not as much about the food itself as it is about how you *think* about yourself. She focused on the importance of insight and self-inquiry and how they affected your issues—whatever they were—whether it was a food, weight, or health issue.

Of course, many people with weight problems have genetics working against them. If your parents are heavy, or fate handed you a bunch of fat genes, it's going to be harder for you to keep weight off. But your attitude and the way you approach your weight will also affect it. We're nothing but a lot of neurotransmitters and hormones, and it's all interconnected. Your head's attached to your body, so if you want to control one, you've got to learn to control the other.

Lisa taught me that there are always good reasons for what we do, even if what we do is bad for us. We have to understand the reasons behind our behaviors before we can change them. She also taught me that when something negative happens in your life—someone lets you down or you make a mistake—it can lead to a positive outcome. These general life lessons helped me grow and mature so that I could focus on the specifics of my weight.

Some people with weight issues use food like a drug to protect themselves from emotional pain. If you're not feeling good about something or you're uncomfortable or there's anxiety, it's human nature to reach for something that will make the discomfort go away.

Putting on weight and keeping it on can be a form of denial. It's a way to *not feel*. Pot does the same thing. So what Lisa helped me do was look at the issues I was avoiding at all costs, and learn ways to use my pain as a teacher. I had to realize that I wasn't always going to feel good every day about myself or my life, and that's okay.

The fundamental issue for me was that I didn't feel worthy of being loved—and I still struggle with that feeling today after more than a decade of therapy and lifestyle coaching. It would be easy to blame these feelings on my father's absence in my childhood. It would be just as easy to say I felt inferior because I've been fat my whole life.

Understanding why you overeat is a complex mystery that usually can't be solved with simple explanations, and it can be very painful and frightening when you get down to the issues that cause you to abuse your body by overeating. It's very scary and uncomfortable—and desperate dieting can make it worse instead of better.

Crash dieting gets your body so confused that eventually

it goes into second gear to ensure its own survival. Your metabolism slows down, and everything you put into your body just stays there. It's a built-in natural mechanism. By the time I got to Lisa, I'd been up and down so many times that my body didn't know which way it was going.

But your body is extremely resilient, and there are many things you can do to rev your metabolism up again. One of them is to eat, which is unheard of in the diet world. But you have to put gas in your car before you can drive it. So it only makes sense that you have to eat so that you can exercise enough to burn off the excess pounds.

Lisa and I concentrated on making the right food choices and exercising regularly. This was a mantra I'd heard since I was six. It had been drilled into me summer after summer at fat camp. Maybe it worked for other people, but I never bought into it totally because something would always happen that would make me feel the irresistible urge to eat. The drive to get that food fix was so powerful that nothing could stop me.

The problem wasn't understanding nutrition. You have to take what you know and successfully apply it to your daily life. So Lisa and I examined everyday experiences, everyday obstacles—whether it had to do with family or work or life in general—that would trigger unwanted emotions, and we worked on figuring out how these emotions fit into the scheme of things. Lisa coached me through those moments, helping me develop a process of self-observation and the strength to confront my weaknesses.

This process is the foundation for fixing anything you want to change about yourself—whether it's health and well-being, relationships, finances, or any other aspect of your life. You just have to make it work—and we did.

I think we succeeded because the environment was very controlled. The Wilson Phillips record deal hadn't happened yet, so I had plenty of time to work on myself. I wasn't performing in public, but I could feel it coming, and we focused on all the issues that being in the public eye accentuates.

I could always count on Lisa coming over three days a week, sometimes four, showing up at my door in the morning with that beautiful long hair and lovely smile. We'd take long walks together, bouncing things off each other. I could ask her anything, and she would give me advice. It could range from "How does this shirt look on me?" to "Why do I feel this way?"

We found that we had a spiritual connection, and we related in so many ways—especially when it came to our mutual love of peanut butter! She helped me reach a level of personal success I'd never achieved before, and she became one of my closest friends.

In nine months, I lost almost 90 pounds. In the meantime, we finished a four-song demo tape that Glen took to Charles Koppelman, the president of SBK Records. When we signed our deal with SBK in January of 1989, I weighed 148 pounds, and I had never felt better in my life.

But once we got the record deal and things started jumping, it became hard to manage it all. We started recording immediately, and my controlled situation began to unravel. Now there was real pressure to make a record that would sell. I started to eat, and the scale began to move back in the wrong direction.

We'd been in the studio for a few weeks, and I'd gained about eight pounds, when some executives from the record company came over. We played some tracks for them, and one of the guys said, "Everything sounds great, but there's one thing."

Then he looked at me and said, "Carnie, what are we going to do about this weight problem?"

In front of everybody.

"We're going to have to get a hold of that," he said.

Later, when he got to know me, he learned to look at my character and my talent—and my weight was never an issue. He believed in me and became a really good friend. We had some great times together on the road and in Japan.

But I'll never forget what he said that day and how he said it.

When they left, I burst into tears. I felt like a piece of shit, like I was going to sabotage the group before we even got started.

Suddenly I was back on the bus, a fat little girl going over the hill to Oakwood. I remembered my mother's words—"It's not how you look on the outside, but who you are on the inside that counts."

Nobody had told this guy.

Chynna and Wendy were great. So were Glen and Francis, our engineer. "Don't even think about that," they said. "That's bullshit. What the fuck does he know? We love you the way you are—and so will everyone else."

But that moment was really, really hard for me. *Jesus,* I thought. *I just lost more weight than I've ever lost in my life, and here's someone saying I'm a fat pig.*

I started to panic, feeling very exposed, unprotected, and unsafe. I just wasn't comfortable in my own skin at that weight. It scared the shit out of me. I wasn't ready to be thinner. That's the bottom line.

But making the album was a fantastic experience—like an incredible creative experiment. We wrote six of the ten songs, and it was such great teamwork. We all worked on the songs together, except on "Hold On."

That was a different situation. "Hold On" was written when Chynna was struggling with her sobriety. It was the song that she wrote to get herself through it.

Glen wrote the music that became "Hold On" and gave the tape to Chynna. She went home and basically wrote 95 percent of the song. We didn't even really get a chance to contribute. But it was so great when she first sang it to us that we just went, "Oh my God, it's wonderful."

I did some of the harmonic arrangements for "Hold On," and many of the harmonic arrangements for both albums. I don't feel that I ever really got acknowledged for that. When we were singing in that studio, the three of us were always there for each other. We listened to each other sing every note, and we spent months and months recording. Glen was behind the board, and we were, too—especially me.

Glen did most of the arrangements, both the music and the vocals. But I made a major contribution on the vocals, too. Everyone relied on my ear, even Glen. "How was that take?" they'd ask me. "Was it sharp or was it flat?"

When people would come to the studio, they'd say, "Jesus Christ, you're a producer."

Our sound originally came from me saying, "You sing this high part, and you sing here, and I'll sing here." That's where it came from, and it should be known—because let's fucking face it, I sure wasn't known as the beauty of the group.

When we did the photo sessions for the album cover, they put me in a big coat. Then we did two videos back to back. I was about 185 pounds, and I was starting to get fat again. The stylist that we worked with tried to be sensitive—but *I* was the one who was sensitive. Custom clothes had to be made for me, and I felt bad about it. I was the one who needed a special wardrobe because I was too fucking fat.

I still looked good. I wore that beautiful Richard Tyler suit in the "Hold On" video as we marched down the boardwalk in Venice. It was a great shot, and we all loved it. I felt like the big one, but I told myself I was glamorous in a different way.

But it was a weird feeling, because here I was about to be a professional singer with two gorgeous girls, and I began to get excited about the fact that I looked different.

It was something that was my power. It was my ability to stand out. I wanted to confront people with "Does it really matter what I look like? Or are you going to hear me sing?"

I wanted to say, "Watch this, motherfucker."

I was just used to being fat. After years of being that way, I had changed, and I just wasn't ready. I wasn't comfortable letting that go. So I embraced my role as the heavy one.

I used my personality just like I always had. "Maybe I'm not going to strut my stuff," I told myself, "but I'm definitely going to make you laugh." I knew that I'd make a powerful impact.

The record was released, the label went into high gear, and we were off on a whirlwind promotion tour. We'd do our interviews at radio stations, and I was the one doing all the schmoozing, always cracking jokes with all the jocks. Wendy and Chynna weren't really into that. It wasn't as easy for them, so they relied on me. I was the motormouth who spoke for the group—and sometimes I said the wrong things.

We'd fly to three, four, or five cities in one day in 10- to 20-day spurts. It was the most draining thing any of us had ever been through, and we were just physically exhausted. But it was so exciting because we were climbing the charts. We were selling 100,000 albums a week. We were traveling around the world, performing to huge crowds, and it was an amazing time. We couldn't believe it.

I'll never forget the phone call I got in my hotel room in Tokyo at 4 A.M. with the news we'd gone to number one—the top of the Billboard singles chart! This was a dream come true, a fantasy from my childhood, and a definite goal from the first moment we decided to be a group. I was so ecstatic, I screamed at the top of my lungs. In the next room, Wendy thought I was going psychotic—and I was.

The schedule was so erratic, we were eating and sleeping at insane hours. For me, that meant a lot of bingeing and smoking. SBK hired Lisa to join me on the road because they were concerned I was losing the battle with my weight.

"Anything you want, if it's going to make you feel better," they said. "If it's going to help you lose weight and feel good about yourself, then go for it." Lisa came on the six-week tour that we had with Richard Marx. We walked together, and she helped me with my food and my choices. I didn't find out until later that they were charging it against my royalty income. In the end, I paid for it myself.

It was really great to work with Wendy. We've always felt so lucky that we got to work with each other and share the experience of our music. We'd always done that as little girls, so being on the road together and performing together was the most natural thing in the world. It was really funny, too, because when we'd record songs in the studio and when we were onstage, it was impossible not to laugh. We'd look at each other, and we'd start cracking up in the middle of a song. We did a lot of laughing.

But the pace was unbelievable, and the schedule was relentless. We even had Jonah and Jeff Panzer—SBK's video executive—travel with us so we'd feel more secure. In a sense, we were babies, and it was all new to us. But I don't care if you've been in the business for 50 years, that schedule was impossible.

We all got very ill. Chynna and Wendy were both hospitalized for dehydration and exhaustion. I just ate myself sick.

I started to have those feelings of being the outcast during the "You're in Love" video. That was the first time that I really saw myself as huge. I was probably around 210.

We were onstage in Atlanta in front of 10,000 people making this video. Wendy and Chynna were in these tight little dresses, and I was in this huge, long black skirt with a big black-and-white striped blazer over it. They were dancing around, and I was barely moving. I looked like a blimp, and I felt enormous.

"Okay, you're huge," I told myself. "Just don't think about it. Just sing your heart out, and people will still love you."

There was this guy in the front row who was hysterically crying the whole time, screaming my name. He was holding out this dollar bill, begging me to sign it. So I did, and he almost passed out.

I knew I had a special connection with my fans. It was the same thing with Wendy and Chynna. We all had our own separate followings, and there was something for everyone in the group.

I always tried to pat myself on the back. That's what got me through it, because as soon as I'd get home and close the door I'd say to myself, "Oh my God, you're such a fat piece of shit."

Everything triggered eating with me. Everywhere I turned, there was another reason to eat—the pressure of being in the group, making the music, and working with the record company. We were like guinea pigs, and they didn't care about our health. We were all very unhealthy in our own ways. I just ate to make myself feel better, but before I knew it, I looked at the scale and I'd gone from 185 to 240. But I just kept going.

People would say, "How do you do it? How do you stay so confident?" I didn't even know. I was on autopilot. I was running on gut instinct—just get out there and make the most of it no matter what you look like or how you feel. I didn't get a chance to feel anything.

If I was doing an interview or if I was onstage, I didn't really worry about my weight. I just gave it my all. I was the big one, the funny one—but I was never the pretty one. Standing next to Chynna and Wendy, what do you want? I was so crazy and busy with the huge success that we had in such a short period of time, I was blocking it out.

You're thrown out in the public eye, and if you have any insecurities, they just get magnified. You go for that comfort. You go for that food.

Having a camera on you, being photographed all the time, there's the constant pressure of being looked at more often by a lot more people. You see yourself on camera or in pictures, and you go, "Fuck. Look at my chin—make that my *chins.*"

I was in a group with two very beautiful, very thin young women, and I kept getting fatter and fatter, so it was hard. People who knew me realized that I had a personality, and there was much more to me than my stomach or my chins. I tried to never let it bother me, but I would see articles in the tabloids where they would say stuff about my weight—and I got upset about it.

How did I deal with it? I just said, "Screw them. Who cares what they think? They don't know me. That bullshit is just what they do." But it still hurt.

Lisa taught me that in the short term, you have to put these painful feelings on the backburner so they don't prevent you from moving on. But you're not going to resolve the real issues unless you gain some understanding about where your feelings are coming from. You have to work through them to figure out what they are, what validity they have, and what really matters.

You have to constantly remind yourself that you need to do this work—and it's not something you really want to do. That's why interacting with other people can help you tremendously. I learned a lot working with Wendy and Chynna. We were strong because of the values we shared, but it took a breakup for us to appreciate our differences.

Lisa and I continued to try a lot of cognitive techniques, looking at how I was thinking about different things, figuring out what was important and what wasn't. And Lisa was always very encouraging about my therapy. "Are you seeing Marc this week?" she'd ask. So Marc and Lisa were two people in my life who continued to give me that support—as well as my mother and Wendy, who were always there for me—even though I was failing miserably with the weight issue.

Wilson Phillips sold 11 million albums worldwide, and in some ways it was like a dream come true—money, travel, fame. In other ways, it was an absolute nightmare.

CHAPTER FIVE

Heavy Duty

W e went right into the second album after two-and-a-half years of nonstop work. We had incredible success, and now we had the crushing burden of doing it again—but this time we wanted to write the entire album.

"We love writing," we said. "Let's go. Let's do it. Let's have a good time. Let's write about what we're feeling."

What we were all feeling had to do with our issues in therapy—and that's what that whole second album is. It's one big sink with three faucets all turned on full blast. We called it *Shadows and Light*.

Glen helped us through it, and we just poured our hearts and souls and guts into that album. It all led me to just eat more, to stuff my feelings down, and to wallow in those bad habits.

I was sober for 18 months during the project—very clear-headed—and it was scary for me, because I wasn't smoking. I was feeling every feeling—all the anxiety of the new release and everything left over from the first album. The label didn't want us to just match the success of *Wilson Phillips*, they wanted us to beat it. There was a lot of hype and a lot of "sophomore jinx" flop sweat.

Was this one going to be as good as the first one?

So far as the critics were concerned, it couldn't be any worse. The critics always hated us, and our reviews were always terrible. I don't think we ever got a good review. We were too pop, too sappy, too clean for the critics—and we looked like spoiled Hollywood kids who didn't work at our success.

But people loved us. We were youthful and fresh, and we had melodies and harmonies. Our songs were about love and relationships.

Children who were 7 and adults who were 55 loved our stuff. People would exercise to our songs, eat to our songs, make love to our songs, and have children to our songs.

But the second album wasn't as successful as the first one, probably because it wasn't as pop, and it wasn't as commercial. This time around, the subject matter was heavy-duty, and I think we were all so tired of mixing that album that sonically it wasn't as good as *Wilson Phillips*. But I thought there were some of the prettiest vocals I've ever heard on that album. Every time I listen to it, I cry. So do Wendy and Chynna. We're very proud of it.

All I have to do when I see Glen is say, "How pretty is *Shadows and Light*?"

He just looks back at me and says, "It's one of my all-time faves."

The record sold three million copies around the world, but to our label and our management, this was a failure. "Do the math," they said. "*Wilson Phillips* sold 11 million units. This one did only three. It's a stiff."

We were furious. I was ready to vomit on that outlook, no matter how much money went into it.

One big mistake we made was changing management for the new project. And if dealing with my image for *Wilson Phillips* was hell, it was way worse the second time around.

For *Shadows and Light,* my weight went through the roof,

but I wasn't paying attention to it. Our new management company was a very successful team, but they had a history of breaking up groups. Journey, Heart, Fleetwood Mac, The Eagles—the list goes on and on. Their method was to take somebody out of the group and make them so egoed out that the other members were just nonexistent. Their mantra was "Sex sells, and that's the bottom line."

We decided to have Herb Ritts shoot our album cover. Herb has to be one of the best. He's directed all of the Calvin Klein *Obsession* ads, and has photographed just about every sexy superstar on earth. We'd seen Janet Jackson's video, "Love Will Never Do Without You," which Herb directed—and she looked so gorgeous in that sexy little top and those perfectly weathered jeans.

Janet was on fire, and we wanted to sell records like that. But we were really nervous about our image, because we were coming from this wholesome place. That's the way people thought of us. Maybe they could make Chynna and Wendy look as hot as Janet Jackson—but I was more the size of *Mahalia* Jackson. I was around 240, and how were they going to make 240 look like 140?

Herb took some awesome photographs of us, and they airbrushed and retouched my face and waist so much that it didn't even look like me.

When it came to making the videos, it was a huge ordeal for the record company—and also for us. I literally had heartburn, indigestion, and diarrhea because I was so nervous. Our physical image was so fucking important that nothing else mattered. Sometimes you just have to shut up and show up. That's how I felt.

We hired Michael Bay to direct our first video, "You Won't See Me Cry." He went on to make big feature films such as *The Rock*, *Armageddon*, and *Pearl Harbor*. He was a hot director, and all the women in his videos looked fabulous.

We hired a stylist who was very popular, and she had us wearing lingerie that made us look like we were high-class hookers. We went from the girls next door to the whores next door—and it wasn't good. I knew in my heart that it was fucked up from the start, and I was jealous and upset that I looked huge and ridiculous trying to be sexy next to Chynna and Wendy in their undies.

We were all wearing wigs and extensions, and the whole thing was very strange, like a bizarre Victoria's Secret commercial. It was absolute torture for me. They had ten corsets custom-made for me from Frederick's of Hollywood. They were designed to really hold me in, like something from the 19th century. I remember feeling like I was suffocating, and the wires and stays in the corsets were cutting and bruising my skin.

My chest and waist were squeezed so tight that my tits were touching my chin. I could barely even talk, and there was no way I could sit down. I kept saying to myself, "Don't worry. They'll figure out a way to make this look good. You've got a pretty face, and even though you're fat, you're still pretty." Somehow I could always talk myself into feeling better, but the minute I was alone, the feelings of shame and anger and frustration became almost unbearable.

One night after the shoot, I remember being in my kitchen trying to get this fucking thing off my waist. But I couldn't get it off—and I was freaking out, running around and screaming as this corset cut into my stomach. I was so fucking mad at our management and the label and the video directors and society—and myself. How did I get to this point?

It just hurts so much to remember all this. Why couldn't I just be me and let it all hang out—literally hang out? But at the same time, I wanted to look good, dammit. I wanted to look as good as Wendy and Chynna.

I wore a corset in all three videos for *Shadows and Light*. All the shots of me were carefully designed to hide my weight and make me look as thin as possible. I wasn't allowed to move, or the illusion would be spoiled and you'd be able to see my double chin—and then we'd have to do it all over again.

Yet part of me was thrilled because I appeared thinner. Some of the tricks were working. Another part of me was embarrassed and confused. Why am I being judged like this? What's wrong with the person I am? So what if I'm heavy? Is that a fucking crime?

And then I'd look at Wendy and Chynna looking so amazing, and I just wanted to do whatever it took to look good, too.

The strange thing is, I really like how I looked in all the videos. They did a great job. We worked with incredibly talented people—with amazing artists like Paul Star for makeup and Peter Savick for hair. By the time they got through with their magic, I always thought that I looked really pretty.

But as time went on, for each video I got heavier and heavier, and it became more and more of a struggle to get that look. So they started to just cut me out. We'd watch the rough cuts, and out of 80 shots, there'd be only 7 of me.

I was thinking, *What the hell is going on here?* But I knew exactly what was going on. The record company would get phone calls and letters saying, "Why are you hiding Carnie? Don't cover her up. It's not fair." There were people who were sticking up for me, and that was really important to me because it sort of validated what I was feeling—or what I was lacking.

Jeff Panzer was responsible for making all the Wilson Phillips videos, and he was trying to satisfy the record company. In spite of all the things they made me do, I still love him. He always said to me, "The bottom line is that I want to make you look great. I want you to watch these videos and say, 'Godammit, I look great.'" And I did.

But in my heart, I knew that we were still trying to cover me up—and I played along with the game. I felt so ashamed that I was almost brainwashed into thinking, *I'm not worthy of showing my body or my chins or whatever.* So I went along with it. But Jeff and I both knew it was bullshit, and he believed in my talent in spite of my weight. "I don't care if you weigh 500 pounds," he'd say. "You can do anything." I adore him for that, and I always will.

I thought we made great music videos together, and I was proud of our work, self-conscious or not. I owe those good feelings to Jeff.

People would come up to me and say, "Your videos are so great." And they'd whisper in my ear, "I think you're the prettiest." I would take that, and it would make me feel really good. But it also made me mad, because what they were really saying was, "Despite of what the majority of the public thinks, I can see through physical beauty. I know what true beauty is, and it lies within."

Now that *is* a beautiful statement, but I didn't want to feel that. I was tired of being "the other one" with the different kind of beauty.

When I was working, I'd just bite the bullet, but when I was alone, I'd get pissed. "What am I doing? I'm fat, and I can't hide it. If one day I feel self-conscious, then I *will be.* The next day I might feel totally confident, and fuck you all. Yeah, I'm fat, but it doesn't mean I can't sing. It doesn't mean I can't entertain you. My beauty doesn't necessarily have to be so physical. It's coming through my voice. It's coming through my songs. It's coming through my personality and my special energy."

I started making excuses so that I wouldn't have to make some appearances, but at this point I wasn't feeling so physically handicapped. I was big, but I was able to pretty much do what I wanted to do. I was just feeling emotionally abused. How did I deal with the stigma and physical ordeal of being obese? I dealt with it by being outgoing and funny, and I started smoking huge amounts of marijuana again, getting stoned out of my mind so I didn't have to think about anything.

As the *Shadows and Light* project was coming to a close, everyone was emotionally exhausted from the experience. Then in October of 1992, Chynna told Wendy and me that she needed a break. She was feeling really overwhelmed and wanted to do a solo project. She wanted to work on her own stuff.

"I'm just leaving temporarily," she said. "We're not breaking up. We're just taking a long break. We'll make another record one day."

I think we all needed a break.

Wendy and I were very frustrated—and we were both really mad and upset and scared. We didn't know what to do. I think I was angry because there was nothing I could do about it. Things were spinning out of control again, and I was helpless. I couldn't say, "Chynna, you can't leave." I couldn't hold it together, and neither could Wendy.

So I felt the pressure of having to go back to the label and say, "Guess what? We're not staying together forever. We're not going to make ten albums in a row. We're not going to have a string of hits anymore." I was completely terrified, and I was embarrassed. I felt like the company had put $80 million into our future, and now we *had* no future. The pressure was so intense that I was fearful. What was I going to do now?

On the other side, I was devastated that Chynna had chosen to do this. Chynna and I had been friends forever. She was my first friend—I knew her before I even knew Wendy. Our dads played basketball together, and our mothers would take us to the park in baby carriages when Chynna was about three months old and I was a newborn. Michelle likes to joke about how bald I was as a baby, and that my mom tried to put this little pink bow barrette in the five strands of hair on my head.

Chynna's like a sister—we feel that close. We have a very intense relationship because we've always had very strong personalities. So sometimes we bump heads. But I've always admired things about her, and I think she's always admired things about me. Of all my friends from childhood, Chynna is probably the closest in my heart. I have such a deep, deep love for her. It's so powerful, and it always has been, and we'll always be friends.

We've also been through a lot together. Our friendship changed when we worked together because we wound up knowing and respecting each other in a different way. First of all, I admire her tremendously as a songwriter. She was definitely the catalyst for many of the songs that we've written. She's a great writer. She inherited that talent, and she's made it her own. She's just got it, and it's inspiring to be around her and collaborate with her.

But it was definitely hard on the friendship, especially when I was struggling with my own self-esteem issues. We developed this competitive thing in the group, and it put some distance between us, but we had to lean on each other for really heavy things, like being so physically exhausted and mentally drained from touring and promotion. We got to see our strengths and weaknesses in really chaotic situations.

It was difficult at times with the three of us. Sometimes Chynna did get more attention, and that was hard. But we always said, "Let's be honest with each other. Let's discuss what we're feeling." We did that, and it was better the second time around for sure. But there was also more pressure, so we fought more, and it seemed like we got a little more catty with each other.

Groups break up—in fact, most groups don't stay together. There are egos involved, and resentments build, and we didn't want that to happen. We didn't want our lifelong friendships to be ground up by being in the group. In a way, it made it easier to work together because we knew each other so well—and it made it all that much harder because we could push each other's buttons.

Wendy and Chynna were never mean about my weight. They saw me struggle from day one. Chynna told me my weight was cute, that it was part of my image—the chubby girl who was your friend. It was a friendly thing. It wasn't threatening. It was human.

I remember someone saying to me, "Don't lose weight. Don't change. You won't be you." Maybe that's what I told myself for years. Maybe that's why I stayed damaged inside.

There are so many reasons why things didn't work out with Wilson Phillips. Who really knows why? Maybe it really wasn't about my being fat. "You can't see my fat through the airwaves," I told myself. "You can't play the record and hear that I'm fat."

But it's natural to wonder, *Why this? Why that?*

In the nine years since we stopped recording together, every once in a while, Chynna, Wendy, and I get together. "Can you believe what we went through?" we'll say. "Can you believe the success that we had? We never got to enjoy it. We never got to feel it. We never got to really live it. We were just so tired that we didn't realize what we were doing and what we were accomplishing."

I'd give anything to be there again. They say hindsight is always 20/20, but it's more than 20/20. It was something that I still can't believe. I still have to pinch myself.

We felt like we were constantly trying to prove ourselves, and we did to the fans. They loved what they heard. "It all comes down to the music anyway," we'd tell ourselves. "It all comes down to what we're giving from ourselves and what our fans are getting out of it." And we gave everything.

We'll never, ever forget the bond that we all had making those records—Wendy and Chynna and Glen and Francis and me. What a beautiful experience it was, and how lucky we are that we got to ride on that bus, sing in those studios, and play to those crowds. We're just so fortunate.

Right now we're making demos, and by the time this book comes out, we might have our record deal all straight. But the bottom line is that we have to prove ourselves all over again. It's a different time, a different age, a decade later. Music, radio, record labels—everything's changed.

Every time your record is scanned by a cash register or played on the radio, the data adds up—that's how you get up the charts. It's Broadcast Data Systems (BDS) and Soundscan now—not pay for your hits anymore. Now, you have to struggle for every point and every spin.

We know it's going to be harder this time, but I believe there's still a following for us, and people are waiting for our record. There isn't a day that goes by—and it's happened every day for the past nine years—without someone asking, "When is Wilson Phillips going to make a new album? When are you guys going to sing together again?"

The three of us have gotten together recently, and we've been working with a great songwriter—Eric Bazillion. We've written this song called "Beautiful at Last." The lyrics say it all:

Don't listen to what you hear.
Don't speak of what you don't know.
There's nothing left to prove.
All you are is what you are.
You're beautiful at last.

That's the way I feel inside—like I've emerged from this cocoon. I feel that I've been beautiful all along, but now everyone can see it. It's the same for the group. We don't need to worry about what other people say. We just need to stay true to ourselves and make our music. It's always been beautiful, and it still *is* beautiful—our group, our music, our friendship.

My heart tells me we can do it again.

But when I look back to that day when we split, it was

something I didn't believe could really happen. I blamed myself. I thought about my fat, and I wondered if we didn't sell as many records because I was so heavy. I felt it was my fault, but there was nothing I could do.

I knew we all needed a break, but I was afraid it would be forever.

CHAPTER SIX

Larger Than Life

Sometimes Santa will send you a gift that's both naughty and nice. For me, it was an airdate with Howard Stern in November of 1993.

A year earlier, when Chynna started her solo project, Wendy and I were sort of left holding the bag. Each of the members of Wilson Phillips was signed individually to SBK. So we were all still under contract; we just weren't a group anymore.

After the split, Wendy and I decided that we wanted new management. A family friend recommended Mickey Shapiro.

Mickey is a Hollywood classic. As a young entertainment attorney, he represented Lenny Bruce during his struggles with the authorities over artistic freedom. He left his law practice to become a talent manager, and he worked with artists ranging from Eric Clapton to Wilson Pickett to Fleetwood Mac. He managed Fleetwood Mac at their peak, and if he didn't know someone in town, he knew someone else who did.

Wendy and I decided to go with Mickey as our manager, and for me it was the beginning of a relationship that would literally save my life. Mickey took me in like the daughter he never had. We came into his life after he had just lost his father, and he came into our life when we lost the group.

He's helped me through many things, and I've done the same for him. We've really stood by each other. He's always been very understanding about my weaknesses—my spending, my pot habit, my relationships, and food. He'd say: "I love you any way you are. I love you if you're 500 pounds or if you're 125 pounds. I just want you to be healthy and happy. That's what's most important."

I feel incredibly lucky to have somebody like Mickey guiding me in my career. He's always been really jazzed and pumped about getting my career going, and he's worked very hard for me. But more important, I feel fortunate to have him as a friend. He's shown as much devotion and belief in me as my own mother. I just love him so much for that.

I also love him because he's a bright, witty, sensitive man with a wild creative streak and a deep love of music. He has so many dimensions and such a huge heart. He's also the sickest motherfucker I know. You've got to love him for that. His twisted sense of humor is the mirror image of mine—and it's genius. We're two peas in a pod.

When Mickey started Spotlight Health, he asked me to come on-board to help people with obesity. He's the one who suggested I have the surgery. He's always made sure that I'm okay. Financially, he's helped me as well. If it weren't for Mickey, I'd probably be bankrupt. I'm extremely lucky to have someone like him in my life. I love him so much, and I want him to be happy, too.

With Mickey to help us, Wendy and I moved forward as a duo—the Wilson Sisters. After the New Year, the label gave us some money to make demos. So we went into the studio and started to write and record.

We were working on some wonderful things, including a terrific Diane Warren song we were sure was a hit, but in March we got the word to drop everything. The label wanted a Wilson Phillips Christmas album. Chynna wasn't into it, so Wendy and

I decided to do it ourselves. The record was called *Hey Santa!*

We started in the spring and were in the holiday mode for the rest of the year. Once we finished recording, we made a video and a VH-1 special, and we were really happy about our work together, especially the songs we did with Jack Kugell, Owen's husband.

It was really exciting to work as a duo with Wendy. We felt really powerful, and we discovered a lot singing two-part harmony together. It was a great experience, and we thought it sounded dynamite.

When it came time to promote the single, someone at the record company with a warped sense of humor booked us on Howard Stern's radio show. Howard's got a huge audience, but if you've ever heard his show, it's not exactly a perfect fit for the Wilson Sisters and a Christmas tune. We weren't strippers or porn stars, and Howard's taste in music back then was more like Pearl Jam or Stone Temple Pilots. I felt like we were being set up to be slaughtered, so I went in expecting the worst. Fortunately, we were scheduled to play the song, do about six minutes, and get out of there.

They put the record on, and Howard started talking non-stop, so no one could hear it. I was getting pissed off, and I asked him to shut up a couple times. Then he started in about my weight. He was harsh, but at the same time, there was some tenderness underneath those shades and that mop of hair.

"You have such a beautiful face," he said. "You have the face of an angel. Why are you so fat? Why do you do that to yourself?"

It was a question I'd been asking myself my whole life, but I didn't have an answer.

So I said something like, "I don't know. Why are you so ugly? Why do you have to be such a jerk?"

I wasn't taking any shit, and he loved it. We wound up going back and forth for more than an hour. It was fast and funny,

I made him laugh, and we had a great time together. He told me I was one of his favorite guests, and I've done his show six or seven times over the years since then.

Hey Santa! sold about 200,000 copies in six weeks, and then it was over. It still sells every Christmas, but that Christmas was history.

The New Year rolled in, and we thought we'd get back into our duo project, but the label kept stalling us. I began to get this bad feeling, but I trusted SBK. They had treated us like family during the Wilson Phillips projects. We'd sold millions of records together, and the Christmas project had been their idea. So I believed they'd always be there for Wendy and me. I never thought they'd let us down.

But days and weeks went by, and no news was bad news. Then we got the call that we were dropped. I couldn't believe it—and when I heard they were keeping Chynna, I felt like total dogshit.

The shock of being cut loose by SBK hit me much harder than the breakup of Wilson Phillips. I was devastated. How could the company we trusted throw us out into the street like we were yesterday's trash?

This was like a bad dream I'd been through before.

I felt totally disconnected from the music business. It was like, "My hope is gone." And I knew it was because of me. My weight had ruined everything.

All the old emotional memories came flooding back—the pain of rejection, the fear of abandonment, the shame of being too fat to be loved. I was angry and hurt and scared. What was I going to do? Where was I going to go? How was I going to pay my bills?

I felt like I was homeless, and no one gave a shit. I felt like maybe if I wasn't so fucking fat, they would have kept Wendy and me around. I knew I could write and produce and perform, but the industry wasn't waiting with open arms for a fat pop singer, no matter how talented I was. That was the sick truth, and I had to face it.

Suddenly I had no career, and I'd gotten myself into a horrible financial mess. The government was after me for $250,000 in back taxes, I had a house with a $12,000 mortgage payment, and I had a condominium that was $5,000 a month. I had expensive cars and owed thousands of dollars for clothes I had custom-made to make me look slimmer.

Just when I thought I couldn't sink any deeper into hell, I got a phone call from Warner Brothers Television.

A talk-show executive for Telepictures named Cathy Chermol happened to be listening to Howard Stern that day back in November. She had been the executive producer for Sally Jessy Raphaël and Jane Whitney, and she was looking for something new.

Cathy had called Warner Brothers Television and told them about me. "I don't know who this girl is," she said, "but anyone who can stand up to Howard Stern should have her own show." It had taken them months to get around to me, but finally they did. They wanted to know if I was interested in hosting my own talk show.

I was in total disbelief. This sounded like a miracle.

Mickey and I went in for a meeting, and we talked about doing a show that was different from the standard daytime talk show. It was going to be built around my personality, and I was going to sing and do comedy and have celebrity guests.

It was too good to be true.

We flew to New York to make a demo of two shows, but none of the variety elements we'd talked about were in the mix. Warner Brothers wanted the same old daytime question-and-answer thing. The only difference was that *I* was doing it instead of somebody else.

I had to go out into the audience by myself with a microphone and no experience, pushing a format that I wasn't even into. But the money was great, and I'd always been a good people person, listening to my friends' problems, trying to help them see the bright side, just the way my mother had taught me. And I'd been through years of therapy myself. I decided, "I'll just act like a shrink and talk to these people, give them advice, relate to them, and have a good time."

It turned out that this was just what Warner Brothers wanted. The demo blew them away, and the syndicators went wild. We got 90 stations almost overnight. They said it was the fastest-selling syndicated talk show in history, and production was scheduled to begin immediately.

The company wanted to do the show in New York, which meant leaving my home in California. That shook me up more than the earthquake we'd been through several months earlier. I'd never really lived anywhere else—except for Holland, back when I was a kid—and the thought of being separated from my mom and Wendy scared me the most.

But this was a chance to get out of debt, to build a new career, and I needed to make it work. So I picked up the dogs—Willie Wonka and Olive Oyl—took a $750,000 beating on the house and the condo, and moved clear across the country to start a new life.

Telepictures did everything they could to make me comfortable. I was an amateur in the talk-show world, but they treated me like a star. I had this awesome office in Manhattan, a lovely home in Connecticut, and they had $100,000 worth of beautiful clothes custom-made for me—everything I could think of.

But most of all, they gave me incredible acceptance and support.

"Aren't you worried that I'm fat?" I asked them.

"No, that's you," they said. "We love you. And the audience will, too."

Cathy Chermol was an extremely diligent executive

producer, always very positive and totally honest. We became close friends, and we still are. I had no track record in television, but she gave me a chance because she believed that none of the daytime talk shows ever had a host with real personality. She liked the fact that I was aggressive, had an opinion, and stood up for what I believed in. That's what the vibe was on Howard Stern. She thought a different kind of talk-show host would be a great spin.

Andy Lassner, the supervising producer, was one of the funniest, most talented people I've ever met. His crazy humor kept me relaxed and loose, and we enjoyed each other's perverted personalities. In addition to Cathy and Andy, there were six producers and their associate producers and assistants, cameramen, technicians, stylists, and the rest of the fantastic crew. It was a big team effort, and we all pulled together.

All I had to do was show up and be a good host, but I never had a tougher job in my life. It made traveling to five cities in one day with Wendy and Chynna seem like a breeze.

First of all, I was scared shitless. So much was riding on the show, and the level of expectation was extremely high. Telepictures and Warner Brothers were putting up a lot of money, and even though I had the best of the best to help me, when I looked around, it was *my* name on every wall.

I had to prepare myself for 90 stories every week, and I was constantly worried about my position, my cue cards, the prompter, the pacing, getting the questions from the audience, and pulling the answers out of the guests.

But everyone was telling me, "People love you." There were 15,000 letters pouring in every week, and the fans would write about how I reached them and touched them in my own special way. My confidence started to grow, and I began to feel this beautiful sense of power.

At the beginning of each show, something magical began to happen. I'd feel the adrenaline, just like the rush before a concert, and then I'd meet the audience, the nerves would melt away, and we'd share this amazing connection.

And it didn't matter how fat I was—they loved me.

Suddenly there were all these people coming up to me on the street, and they'd say, "You're such an inspiration because you don't let your weight get in your way." Just by being there, just by being me, I was sending out a message that was helping people feel better about themselves—and the sense of satisfaction was so good.

Guests would come on the show and say, "I'm fat, I'm nothing, I'm a worthless piece of shit."

I'd say, "No. You can do anything you want. Look at me. Look how big I am, and I'm standing here doing my own talk show. And I'm just as qualified as anyone else. I don't let my weight bring me down."

And I began to believe it.

The show actually boosted my self-esteem, because it told me, "Yeah, you might be fat, but you're worthy enough to be a host. It doesn't make any difference if you're 150 pounds or 250. You've got what it takes."

I loved to see the heavy women in the audience who'd come to the show over and over again. They enjoyed being there so much. They had such a good time. I'd stay out and talk with them during the commercial breaks, and I could feel how much the connection meant to them. I believed in my heart that this connection was coming through to millions of people across America.

I tried my hardest to win everybody over, even the young teenage boys in the crowd who were very judgmental at first. They'd be sitting in the audience, looking me up and down, and I knew they were thinking, *God, she's fat.* But then I would turn around and make them laugh, and by the end of that day, they were going "Go, Carnie." And I felt like I had accomplished something.

But it was probably the worst year in the history of television to debut a talk show. Rikki Lake had been this huge success the year before, and everybody was trying to make lightning strike twice.

I just wanted to be myself on camera, to let my feelings show and make the moments real. But whenever I let my personality show, they'd say, "Don't do that. You're too opinionated." Or "You're too sensitive. You cry too much." Or "You say 'Whoa' too much."

They had me work with a talk-show coach, which is not so unusual, but it felt really odd to me. I just hated watching myself on television because I'm very dramatic, and I could see how I was sometimes spastic and goofy—but at least I wasn't a clone like all the others.

People would say, "Hey, I love watching your talk show because you show how you feel. If somebody's an asshole up there, you give them a dirty look. Or if somebody's really cute, you gush about it. You told those wife-beaters to go fuck themselves. You didn't hold anything back."

But we found that when I said to a guest, "You're a jerk," or "You're an asshole for beating up your wife," the guests would get intimidated and clam up. That was the producer's nightmare and a ratings killer. When you flip on the channel, you want to see the *guest* going off, being psycho and trailer trash crazy. So they told me to tone it down.

None of the promises about music or celebrities or variety were ever kept. Every week the show became more tightly scripted—no ad-libs, no personality. Sometimes I'd sing during the warmups, and the crowd would beg me for more. But it never happened on the air, and the show began to turn into just another cheesy talk show—and the cheesier it got, the more uncomfortable I became.

The competition was intense, and the pressure to get ratings got heavier and heavier. Every morning Cathy would walk in with the numbers. "We only got a 2.8, and we need to get a 4. What can we do? What are we doing wrong?" She'd tell me how lucky we were to have the primetime slot after *Regis and Kathie Lee* in New York and on other stations across the country. So there was added pressure to deliver the ratings to keep them.

All the competing shows were rolling out the sleaze, and soon we started digging in the trash just like everyone else. We did one show that was just devastating for me. It was called "The Secret Show." Guests came on who had been hiding something from their spouse or a friend or relative. They were spilling these deeply personal, embarrassing secrets on the show in front of the whole world, and people were crying on the stage, screaming and running off because they couldn't bear the humiliation. I felt so sorry for them and was so mad at myself. I felt like this horrible person who was ruining other people's lives just to get a stupid rating. It ticked me off so much, I was furious.

When we wrapped that day, I went home, put on some music, sat by the speaker, and just cried. Then I got stoned and stuffed myself with junk food until I was sick. Pretty soon, it was happening every night, and I was crying myself to sleep, feeling guilty and ashamed.

As all this was going down, my weight was going up. When I hit 255, they called for an emergency meeting.

"What's going on?" they asked.

"What do you mean?" I said.

"You're gaining weight."

It was no secret. The seamstresses were letting out all my clothes because they didn't fit anymore.

"Look," I said, "the situation is freaking me out. Everyone's counting on me, but you don't want me to be me. It's hard for me to be neutral. It's hard for me to be non-feeling. I'm not this robot who just asks questions and gets answers."

I tried to lose the weight, but it didn't work. I gave it my best every day, but I felt like I wasn't doing a good enough job. I knew that I wasn't the best host. I knew I had weaknesses. I also knew that this wasn't what I was supposed to be doing any longer with my life.

Eventually I got a call from Jim Paratore, the president of Telepictures. "We're taking the show off the air," he said. "We're going to try a different kind of show with Rosie O'Donnell."

I knew in my heart that it was the right thing for them to do.

"That's great," I said. "I'm sure she'll be fabulous." I was a fan of Rosie's, and I still am. But when I saw her show, with the live band, the celebrity guests, and the showcase they made for her personality, I was bummed. I'm not saying I can do what she does. She's unique and that's why she's a success. But I felt that I never got the chance to show what's unique about me, and that was a huge disappointment.

But more than anything, I was feeling relief. We had taped 155 shows, and 150 had aired. It had been a tough year, but even so, it was really hard to leave. I felt like I was on this fabulous train that was going around the bend, and I had to jump off.

At the wrap party, everyone cried and told me how much they loved working with me. I felt so sad because we had the greatest group of people, and they'd given me so much encouragement. But I found myself confused, wondering if the show had failed because of me. Maybe I wasn't good enough. Or maybe it was cancelled because my image wasn't right. Maybe I was just too fat.

But I'll always remember those audiences and the lessons they taught me—that I could make a real difference in people's lives and help them feel better about themselves, and that I could tap in to my personal power and overcome my fears.

Now I had to do it on my own.

My show had solidified my image in a way that I had never really intended it to.

I'd always considered myself an entertainer, and thought that people would love me or admire me because of my talent and my personality—my singing, my songs, maybe even my acting if I got the chance—not to mention my ability to make them laugh with my brazen-broad bullshit and my in-your-face sense of humor. These had always been the things I counted on to draw attention away from my weight, to make people forget my body and remember me as funny and sassy or artistic and creative.

Now I could see that there were millions of people—especially women—who looked to me for inspiration because I was big and fat. They loved me because I was larger than life and I didn't let it stop me. I didn't apologize for it, and I made it work for me. I came across as proud of who I was, not ashamed to strut my stuff. And there were big women everywhere who wanted to feel the same way.

They were outraged at the way society treats the obese, with the definitions of beauty and fashion that left most women on the outside looking in. They wanted to feel accepted and attractive regardless of their size. They didn't want to be branded as lazy or overindulgent or weak-willed. They didn't want to put up with cruel fat jokes and insulting stereotypes and outright prejudice that made their lives miserable.

Ironically, I was one of them, but deep down I couldn't shake the feeling that I would be so much happier if I were thinner. I knew it wasn't healthy to be fat, and that was reason enough to try to lose weight. God knows I tried every way I could think of to get the pounds off and keep them off, but I couldn't do it.

And even though I made sure I always looked good and I was proud of the way I looked, I wanted to wear tank tops and shorts in the summer and show my bare arms and legs. I wanted to wear a swimsuit by the pool and not feel like a beached whale. I wanted to play the sexy femme fatale parts in movies instead of the funny fat friend or the brassy whore. I didn't want to be judged and rejected because of my weight.

Maybe society did this to me. Or maybe I let myself be a victim.

I found myself in the strange position of being an icon for a movement that I sincerely sympathized with, but that I never could really buy into for myself. I did the plus-size fashion spreads and the size-acceptance interviews. I made an exercise video for heavy women, and I went on talk shows and to the Million Pound March and said, "Fat is not a four-letter word."

But I didn't have the genuine feeling in my heart. I *did* believe that everybody should be accepted—fat people, thin people, tall people, short people—everyone should be accepted as people. I've always stood up for that. But I found myself at the Million Pound March feeling really out of place, even though I was almost 300 pounds.

There was something really beautiful about it. Everybody was walking around, all shapes and sizes, really proud to be who they were. But at the same time, I felt, "Aren't they uncomfortable with how heavy they are right now?" I just couldn't really believe that they were saying, "Fat is good. It's fine to be this heavy. It's okay." These are people who were 400, 500, 600 pounds. I just couldn't relate.

There was a part of me that was really afraid I was going to get that big. And I know that people will be hurt by my saying this. But the truth is that it's not healthy to be that big. We're not meant to be 300, 400, 500 pounds. It doesn't have anything to do with the kind of people we are.

When I got up to speak, I said, "I've been heavy since I was four, but I've never let my weight hold me back. I've always believed in myself as I am. I've always thought I was a good person regardless of my size. But I feel I'll always be an inspiration to people whether I'm 250 pounds or 150 pounds."

The crowd got really quiet when I said that. I could tell that some of them were annoyed by my comment. And I actually felt like I had to defend myself.

"I'm not standing up here saying that fat is good," I said, "because I don't think that it's good to be really overweight for health reasons." They didn't want to hear that, but I didn't care. I wanted to speak the truth—and that's what I'm doing now.

I can see how people might think, *Here she was speaking at the Million Pound March, and then she goes ahead and does the surgery.*

It's a betrayal.

But I'd love to be able to just creep into those people's heads and find out if they're truly comfortable with their size. They say they are. But many people are in denial, and I think they fool themselves.

I don't want to bash fat people. If you're reading this book and you're 500 pounds and happy the way you are, I want you to tell me how it feels when you can't go to a concert. How does it feel when you can't fit into a chair or an airline seat—when your thighs rub together, and you have a rash, and you're burning hot down there? When you're sweating every minute and you feel overheated? How does it feel when you can hardly make it up the stairs and your heart is pounding?

I know how it feels—and it's not good.

No one should have to feel guilty or ashamed or ugly because of their weight.

But what if you do?

What if you find yourself eating like crazy and you just can't stop?

What if you're discouraged and depressed when you see yourself in the mirror?

What if you tell yourself over and over that you're beautiful just as you are, but you just don't believe it?

What if you find yourself facing diabetes, heart disease, agonizing joint pain, shortness of breath, and maybe even cancer or the possibility of a stroke?

What do you do then?

I wanted to do everything I could to help obese people feel better about themselves. And I still do. I want to motivate and inspire people to love themselves and feel worthy of the love of others no matter what they look like. I want to stand up for compassion and respect and justice.

But I want it for myself as well.

I came out of Wilson Phillips and the talk show as a role model for heavy people. It was a role I honored because I know the pain so many are feeling. I know it's wrong for society to abuse the obese, and I want it to stop.

But I knew I wasn't happy, no matter how many people loved me for the larger-than-life example I was setting. I knew I was getting heavier, and it scared me. I knew my health was at risk, but I didn't know what to do about it. I was still trapped in a body I couldn't control.

The show was over, and I had to move on.

CHAPTER SEVEN

Sizing Things Up

My feelings of relief when the show was cancelled didn't last for long. I'd been able to pay back the government, so *that* financial pressure was off, but I hadn't saved much money, and I knew I needed to get something going.

After the grind of daily television and feeling like a fish out of water for a year, I was feeling like I really wanted to be back in music again—singing, writing songs, surrounding myself with harmony, doing what comes naturally to me. I wanted the sensation that life was going to be exciting again.

Mickey was on top of the situation. As soon as he knew the show was ending, he started shopping Wendy and me to the major music labels. Soon we had a record deal with Mercury for an album called *The Wilsons*, and the label was really excited by the idea of us working with our dad.

Basically, Wendy and I didn't see Dad for years after our parents divorced when I was 11. Once in a while he'd come to the house, and there was the time he came to see me perform in high school. But these moments were rare, and there hadn't been enough of them. There was a period for years where Eugene Landy wouldn't allow Dad to see us. Wendy and I had tried to work out our feelings about our father in therapy. We had missed him very much, and it had affected us both deeply.

I saw him at a Capitol Records party after the Grammys the year before the first Wilson Phillips record came out. I whispered in his ear, "Hey, I'd like to put away our past and become friends. I'd like to be your friend." He didn't really respond. I think he was taken aback by what I said, and I don't think he knew how to react.

So nothing happened. We started recording, the next year the album came out, and it was like a whirlwind. I still wanted to reconnect with him, but we were so busy that I just couldn't. I didn't know this, but he was following us, watching our appearances on television, buying *Billboard* and tracking our songs on the charts.

He was really excited for us, but he was doing his own thing, working on his solo album, and getting healthy again. He had gotten rid of Landy and was living on his own. There was a great guy named Jerry helping him, as well as a wonderful woman named Gloria who became his close friend, and who has lived with him now for 15 years. She probably knows him better than anyone.

Eventually, he met Melinda, his second wife, and she's really inspired him and cared for him for the last seven years. They live in L.A., and have adopted two beautiful girls, Daria and Delanie, my stepsisters. They are as precious as can be!

On the second Wilson Phillips album, *Shadows and Light*, we wrote "Flesh and Blood" because Wendy and I wanted to reach out to Dad, but we didn't know how. So we thought maybe we could do it with a song. But we didn't make the connection we were hoping for.

One night about a year later, I came home, and there was a message on my answering machine from Dad, asking me to call him back.

"Why is he calling?" I wondered. "He never calls." I was

sort of shocked and scared, and I wasn't sure I wanted to return the call. But Steven, my boyfriend at the time, said, "You really need to call him back. It's important. You've got to reconcile with him, because you don't know what will happen today or tomorrow or next month. You just don't know the future, and you may never get this chance again."

Steven had lost someone close to him recently, and there were a lot of things left unsaid. He knew about the issues I had with Dad, and he didn't want me to live forever with the same regrets he was feeling. He urged me to make that call, and that was one of the best things Steven ever did for me—and I want to thank him.

I took his advice, and I called.

"I'm doing a record with my friend Rob Wasserman," Dad said. "Would you want to sing with me on this song called 'Fantasy Is Reality?' I'd like you to sing the lead."

"I'd love to," I said. I couldn't believe it. I'd been waiting for this call my whole life.

The thought of going into the studio with Dad for the first time—of him producing me—was intimidating and exciting, all at the same time. When I heard the song, I thought it was fabulous, and it seemed like fate was finally bringing us back together. Father's Day was coming up, and the name of the song struck me as really ironic. This was a fantasy I'd had forever, and now it was a reality

I arrived at the studio, and I could tell that Dad was very nervous. So was I. He kept pacing back and forth as I sang. It was really nerve-wracking for him, and it seemed like he was uncomfortable watching me do it. But when I sang, he was blown away, and it was really cool. There was a wonderful connection. It was like our first real bonding experience, and it was beautiful that it came through the music.

We spent that Father's Day together—just Dad and Wendy and me. We had a wonderful dinner at the Chart House in

Malibu, and he was so sweet—it felt like the beginning of something.

Afterwards, I remember sitting on the porch in front of the ocean at his beach house. We were sitting really close together, and our legs and arms were touching. It felt so good to be physically close to him. He put his arm around me, and I was so happy that we could be comfortable with each other. It was awesome after 25 years to finally start getting to know my dad.

From that time on, we grew closer and closer, and every few months I'd ask him to work with Wendy and me.

I'd say, "Hey, Dad, do you feel like writing? Wouldn't it be great if we could write together? That could be so cool."

But he always said, "No, no, I'm not ready."

"Okay," I'd say, and I'd back off.

But we'd decided to work together on *The Wilsons* album, and everyone was so jazzed that we were going to be collaborating. Originally, the idea was that he'd be involved on the entire album, but we ended up doing four songs together.

I was over at his house, and we'd just been through a lot of things together—some beautiful moments.

He said to me, "I'm so sorry that I wasn't there for you. I'm so sorry that I wasn't the best dad, but I love you and I'm proud of you."

And then he said, "Carnie, you have the most beautiful face I've ever seen in my life." That was so sweet of him.

I really feel that I was ready to let go of my weight after I had healing with my dad. I had this little hole in me, and it had been empty for so long. I can't fill it completely. I never will. But at least it started to get filled up.

He acknowledged certain things, and I acknowledged certain things. It's like we were holding our breaths for all that time, and we finally started breathing again. Now we were in the same room in the same space, breathing together. So we were able to work together, laugh together, experience new things together, and to start a friendship.

I'd never thought it would happen. I'd feared that it wouldn't happen. But that day at his house, it did.

"Let's go to the piano," he said.

My heart started racing, and I thought, *Oh my God, this is it. I'm finally going to get to write with him. I envisioned this, and now it's going to happen.*

We went to the piano. He sat behind me and leaned back on his chair. "Play something for me, Carnie," he said. "I love to hear you play the piano."

It took me back to that day when I was 12. It was the one way we had always connected. I started playing this piece I'd been working on. It was just a few chords.

And he sang out, "Am I a fool to expect a miracle?"

I turned around and said, "What did you just say?"

"Am I a fool to expect a miracle?" he said. "Do you like it?"

"I love it," I said. It was like he'd tapped in to what I was thinking my whole life.

That was the beginning of the song "Miracle." And it was the coolest moment in the world. I remember that Melinda was so happy we were writing together. She was smiling, and Dad was really proud. It was like we had gotten over the hump.

When we finished for the day, I said, "That wasn't so bad, was it?"

"It was good," he said. "It was good."

"I love it," I said. "Isn't it great?"

"Yeah," he said. "It's great.

It was such a rush for me to be with him and to watch him work. It was surreal and a little terrifying, watching him arrange the songs, listening to him play. Part of me was going, "This is the great Brian Wilson, the great producer, the great songwriter. Am I going to be good enough to win his approval?"

And part of me was going, "This is just Dad. I've played for him, and he's played for me my whole life."

The moments we had together were magic, and I'll treasure them forever, especially singing the three-part harmonies in the studio. There was this physical connection between us that was really uncanny, all of us twirling the headset cords around our fingers and pacing back and forth in just the same way. When we moved at the mike, it was like watching triplets. And when each take was over, we'd look at each other and go, "Jesus Christ, did you hear that? Did you hear how good that sounds? Can you believe how good we sound together?" It was the coolest.

By the time we finished recording, Wendy and I thought the songs we did with Dad was some of the best work we'd ever done, but there were lots of bumps with the record company along the way. We had some creative differences, and things didn't end up the way we wanted them to. The label never really gave the record a chance, which sucks, because we loved the album.

It takes a lot of money and a highly coordinated effort to successfully launch a record. All the promotional pieces have to be in place, and the whole team has to believe in the project and support it. Otherwise you won't win because the competition is just too intense. Every week, new singles go to radio stations and video outlets around the country and the world. If the goods are in the grooves, the commitment behind the record can make the critical difference between success and failure.

Mercury didn't spend the money on us. They let us down, and we didn't get the promotional effort we deserved.

We did make a video for the first single, "Monday Without You," and I was so fucking fat, I felt like I totally spoiled the clip. I remember looking at Wendy and thinking, *Oh my God, she looks so good.* And then I looked at me, weighing 280 pounds, and the feeling was really, really bad.

I had thrown all my energy into writing songs with a lot of

different writers on the project, giving everything I had to the studio work. We were back in business, making money again, and under pressure to deliver. So I had celebrated each step forward and suffered through each step back the way I always had—by eating.

I wore this dress that had been made for me years ago, and I could barely fit into it because I'd gained so much weight. I'd put these big white streaks in my hair so that people would go, "Wow, what a cool hairdo," instead of "Oy, what a big ass."

In one scene they had me sitting in this car behind the steering wheel, and I could barely fit. My cleavage was enormous, and my boobs were practically up to my chin.

Everyone was telling me that I looked really good, but I knew they were just being kind.

Jesus Christ, I thought. *Here we go again. Now they're hiding me in a car.* But they couldn't hide the fat, and I couldn't hide from it either.

In another sequence, we were on this stage that was being driven through the streets of downtown Los Angeles. I was standing on this big moving platform with Dad and Wendy, trying to keep my balance, terrified I was going to fall off.

I was so heavy that my ankles had been collapsing under me lately, and I had been falling a lot and hurting myself. I was struggling to stay in the moment, to get into the groove of the song, and to feel the beautiful emotion of our reunion with Dad. But the fear of falling was sickening, and I felt like this big moose trying to move around, too scared to dance because I knew it would look ugly.

When I saw the video, I was so fat and so self-conscious, I knew it just wasn't working. We went out and did some touring. We tried, but it just wasn't happening, and I felt really down. I thought it was my fault again.

I thought that Wendy looked great, and we had these great songs, and if I had just been thin we probably would have sold a lot of records. But the record bombed, and I went into a heavy depression. Then the label dropped us, and it was a really big blow.

I was at my lowest, on the verge of turning 30, about 285 pounds, and totally unhappy. My relationship with Steven was crumbling. I was smoking lots of pot, and rarely exercising with Lisa because it just hurt too much.

I had sold my house in California, but I'd taken a huge loss. And instead of conserving what money I had, I was still living beyond my means. I was desperate to look as good as I could, so I was spending a lot of money on clothes.

I've always had beautiful clothes. I drove my mother crazy when I was younger because I was begging her to go shopping all the time. I remember always being so trendy and wanting to look good. I had this strong desire to present myself well, and I was proud of the fact that I was stylish no matter how big I was.

But it changed as I got morbidly obese, because it was harder to find clothes. Then it became a very emotional thing, and not in a good way. I was trying to cover up—like in Wilson Philips—trying to look as thin as I could and hide the fat. I started to wear big dresses and loose clothing and leggings with big, big shirts over them—anything that would fit me.

The plus-size fashion industry hadn't really exploded at that point, and finding clothes was hard. It was emotionally tough because nothing fit, and I couldn't shop at normal stores anymore. I started to get really upset about it.

I'd go to Lane Bryant, and I shopped for many years at a place in North Hollywood called Great Changes. They had beautiful clothes there for big women, and the owners, Idrea and Wendy, used to dress me in these gorgeous outfits. I always looked really good.

But as I got bigger, the choices became fewer and fewer, and it was frustrating because I didn't know what to wear. I got sick of the big dresses and huge shirts, and I simply couldn't hide it anymore.

Just when things were looking so bleak that I didn't know what to do, I got a call from Al Jardine, one of the original Beach Boys. He was putting together an act called Beach Boys Family and Friends, featuring himself and his sons doing Beach Boys music, and he wanted Wendy and me to perform with them. It was an offer I couldn't refuse. I loved the music, I knew all the songs, and I needed the money.

So I started doing gigs with Al, and I loved it. But we didn't perform enough to keep me busy full time. I had nothing else to do, so I stepped back and started looking hard at my life, reflecting on my childhood and my relationship with food. I asked myself why I couldn't lose the weight, why I really didn't really *want* to lose the weight. I knew that something had to change, and that the only one who could change things for me was *me*.

I remember saying to myself, "I need to be alone. I'm going to turn 30, and I need to get off the pot. I need to start doing something with myself."

So I decided to get sober. I quit smoking pot, and immediately it was clear that I was not going to stay in the relationship with Steven. We were not on good terms. We were fighting every day, and I knew in my heart that it wasn't going to work out. We were not going to be married. We were going to wake up and realize that we were over and that we didn't want to hurt each other anymore.

It was amicable at the end. I moved out and got a place of my own, and I lived alone for the first time ever for a good year and three months. I didn't have a man in my life, and I wasn't really thinking about that. I was feeling like I had to grow up and become a woman. I was actually just alone, crying myself to sleep a lot, feeling lonely and scared, out of control, and desperate in terms of eating.

I joined Jenny Craig and began to write a book called *Scared to Be Thin*, but when I look back on it now, I was venting my anger at my dad and the world because things weren't working out the way I wanted them to.

I remember people looking at me when I'd go down the aisles in the supermarket. They'd peer into my basket and stare at me and give me dirty looks. And I would say under my breath, "What the fuck are you looking at?" I was really bitter.

My mom would tell me, "Carnie, they're staring at you because you're pretty," or "They're staring at you because you're famous."

And I would say, "No, they're staring at me because I'm fat."

Then some musicians formed a band and called themselves The Fat Chick from Wilson Phillips. I thought, *Wait a minute. Is that because they like me? Or is that an insult?*

And I was angry at myself because I couldn't fit into a seat anymore, because I wanted to be active with my friends and do things for people, and I just couldn't because I couldn't breathe.

I started needlepointing to calm myself down, and I loved it because I could just sit still and stitch. It didn't require any physical activity, it was creative, and it replaced my craving for smoke. But I had stopped exercising, I was eating more, and I wasn't moving. So I was gaining weight.

Financially, I was in bad shape, so bad I almost declared bankruptcy. For the first time in eight years, I was paying my own bills, which I know sounds so spoiled, but previously I had accountants who had paid them. Now I couldn't afford the accountants anymore. So I wasn't keeping track, and I had a lot of late payments. And I was still racking up bills on custom-made clothes, doing everything I could to find an outfit that would make me look the thinnest.

I was also doing anything I could to bring in some cash, going on every audition I heard about for voiceovers and acting jobs. I had never taken acting lessons outside of school, where I'd had a personal acting coach for six years. But I knew I could act. It was just a matter of getting hired.

There aren't a lot of roles for someone who's pushing 300 pounds, but I actually got two parts. One was a role on an episode of *Silk Stalkings*. I went in for the audition wearing these spandex bicycle shorts underneath my dress. They kept my thighs from rubbing together so I wouldn't get a friction rash.

The director said to me, "Would you be opposed to showing your legs or wearing a dress?"

I said, "Are you kidding, honey?" And I lifted up my dress, flashed him my biker shorts, and said, "Look at these babies." I've always been proud of my legs because they were shapely, even though they were big.

He loved it. He loved that I was so free. They called two hours later and said, "You got the part." Later, when I saw the dailies, I remember thinking how big I was. I think if I saw that show now, I'd probably flip out because I was way up there.

The other part came a few months later, a character called Mama Earth in the NBC miniseries, *The '60s*. I was hired on the spot because I fit the role perfectly. It was a weird thing psychologically for me because I felt powerful, like I really owned the part. I played an actual person, a hippie who ran a compound up in Haight-Ashbury in the '60s. She took in all these people, cooked for them, and cared for them. They were strung out, tripping out on acid, and she'd calm them down and help them.

I've never felt such a connection with a part. I felt like Mama Earth. I felt like the person you'd go to if you were in trouble—this special woman, big and fat, larger than life. Yet I remember watching Julia Stiles, the actress who played the lead. *God*, I thought. *I just wish I were normal size so I could play that part.* I really wanted to be her, and I could feel the old pain welling up inside me.

But then I thought, *Fuck it. You know what? I'm not her. I'm three times her size. That's why I've got this part, and I'm going to play the hell out of this character.*

So I pushed the pain away, I acted my ass off, and I felt good about the job I did. They loved my work so much that they wrote more scenes for me.

But it was difficult to be an actress when I was heavier because I felt very limited. It was hard for me since I felt as if the only roles I could go up for were the fat-girl roles. I didn't like that. I thought I was being unfairly judged, and my talent would never get a real chance. That was very painful. I thought I was only good enough for certain things, and not good enough for others.

When I was heavy, I always dreamed that I'd get a role in a movie where Tom Cruise or someone really gorgeous was the leading man, and it was a story about a couple of girls and this guy, and he winds up falling in love with the friend who's overweight and not the typical beauty.

I always thought this would make a great story, because it would be so beautiful to know that somebody would look past someone's physical body and fall in love with their spirit and their soul. I just think it's such a great storyline. I still wouldn't mind being in a movie with Tom Cruise, I can tell you that.

But now it's different. Now I'm being sent out on roles that are much more diversified. Next week I'll be reading for a new Fox television show. The character breakdown is "mid-to late 20s to mid-30s, attractive." When I read this, I went, "Wow, they actually believe that's me!" And I guess I have to believe that it's me, too. I hope I get the role.

But in 1998, my role was to be heavy. In October, I went on the *Roseanne* show to plug *The '60s* miniseries and put in a few good words for size acceptance. Roseanne had recently had gastric bypass surgery, and it was the first time I had seen her since her operation. I couldn't believe how healthy and happy she looked.

During a commercial break, she leaned over and said, "Honey, if you ever want to get serious about losing all that weight, come talk to me." My doctor had mentioned weight-loss surgery to me several times, but I never really took him seriously. But for the first time, after being with Roseanne, I thought maybe I should consider this.

I knew that my weight was going up, and my situation in general was not looking good. I had become very introspective during this period, trying to figure out what was important in my life. I had decided that my health was number one on the list.

Now that marijuana was out of my life, I was feeling all my feelings, and the physical and emotional pain was tremendous. Because I wasn't covering up, there was only one thing I could turn to that would help me cope—food. So, I would eat and eat, because it was the only thing that made me feel good. And I started to become physically sick.

I was really slowing down, and I was getting very tired—I could hardly walk up a flight of stairs or around the block. It was impossible to exercise, and I was waking up over and over, maybe ten times each night, choking, out of breath, gasping for air, my heart racing, not knowing what was wrong. It was very frightening.

Maybe it's because of anxiety, I thought, *because I'm broke and staring bankruptcy in the face, because I'm lonely, and I've got no career.*

The discs in my back were throbbing, and jolts of sciatica were shooting down my leg. There was deep aching in my joints, and terrible pain in my feet all day long. My first step out of bed was excruciating.

My legs and my feet were hurting so badly that I called my doctor. "I can't feel my feet," I said. "They're going numb. I can't exercise anymore, and I'm choking in my sleep."

I went in for my checkup, and the news was bad. I was 298 pounds. My blood pressure was through the roof. My cholesterol was way up, and my triglycerides were sky-high. I was so stressed out that I had developed partial paralysis in the muscles of my face—a condition known as Bell's palsy—and the fat was closing my airway when I slept at night. It was called sleep apnea, and it could kill me.

I never thought of suicide because I've always had a strong will to live. I've always had this voice inside me saying, "You'll survive. You've survived this much in your life; you'll survive this."

But when I looked in the mirror, I heard another voice saying, "You're going to die young." I could see my death before me, and I had no vision of how I could stop it. But I still wasn't ready to save myself.

ON MY 31ST BIRTHDAY—April 29, 1999—fate gave me a terrifying present.

I was in Medford, Oregon, doing a concert with Al Jardine. We were getting toward the end of the set where we'd do this nonstop medley of the upbeat Beach Boys songs—"Surfin' Safari," "Fun, Fun, Fun," "Surfin' USA"—those great feel-good songs that just call for dancing.

I had been touring with Al only intermittently over the last 18 months, so I wasn't really used to performing. But as usual, I started jumping around on the stage because it's impossible not to move when you're singing those songs.

I wanted to put on an especially good show that night, because Tiffany Miller, one of my longtime best friends, had come to see me perform. The band and the crowd had sung "Happy Birthday" to me, they'd brought a cake onstage, and I was feeling so happy I had to dance.

I've always been self-conscious about my dancing—worried about my stomach jiggling, my double chin shaking, and all my body fat rippling everywhere. The thought of it embarrassed me, and I didn't want anyone to see.

But once I got up on the stage, something would always happen. The music would shoot through me. I would feel this rush inside my body and start dancing, and suddenly I wouldn't care.

By the end of the show, I'd be drenched with sweat and out of breath. I would ask Wendy, "Are you out of breath? Are you tired?" I suppose I wondered whether it was legitimate for me to be tired. Or was it just because of my weight?

Wendy would say, "I'm exhausted." And I would look, and she'd be sweating, too. I'd think, *Oh, thank God I'm not the only one.*

So on that night, I was thinking, *It's my birthday, and my friends are watching. I'm going to give this my all.* Even though I was 298 pounds—heavier than I'd ever been in my whole life—I was going to jump around if it killed me.

So I danced extra hard, and the stage began to bounce. When I jumped around, all the microphones would shake, and the thought ran through my head that I was going to make something fall over. I tried to block it out because I didn't want to get sad.

I'm going to break the stage, I thought. *Ah, fuck it. I'll just dance a little lighter.* But dammit, I wanted to dance hard. So I did.

After the show, it really, really hit me. Something was different this time. I didn't feel right.

I was talking to my friends, and everyone was very excited. But I felt unusually tired, hot, and sweaty, and I couldn't catch my breath.

Tiffany asked, "Are you okay?"

My heart was racing, and my pulse was pounding in my head. There was pain in my right arm, and I could feel my blood getting thicker and hotter in my body, especially around my ears and neck and chest.

"I have to sit down right now," I told her. She looked at me, and I could tell that she was scared.

"I'll be all right," I said. "I just need to rest for a minute."

I told myself to stop and breathe, to bring my blood pressure down by being calm, taking deep breaths, drinking a glass of water, letting the steam off. You see, I was literally *steaming*, sitting there feeling like this huge steaming pig, terrified in the frightening world of my own body, this world of pumping blood, on the edge and about to go over, afraid I was going to have a heart attack at any moment.

After a while, I began to cool down, my breath came back, and the pounding and pain went away. But I knew this was a warning I couldn't ignore.

CHAPTER EIGHT

You're in Love

D oing the shows with Al changed my life in more ways than one. It gave me the courage to just get my ass out on that stage, no matter how big I was. And it put me in touch with how far I'd let my health go.

I remember people saying, "You're so much fun to watch. You've got great charisma onstage." But I was very self-conscious about my size, and it was difficult and frightening to do those shows because I was so fat that my heart felt like it was going to explode.

But when I wasn't performing, I was working hard at just being by myself, which I think is so important. And I started to think a lot about what I wanted in a relationship—and what I didn't want.

I had always had similar patterns in my relationships, and those behavioral patterns were jealousy and insecurity. Maybe it was because I didn't get the attention from my dad that I needed as a girl. Not having that genuine affection and connection made it hard for me to believe that any boy or man in my life really loved me. I didn't feel worthy or deserving of that kind of love because I couldn't recognize it. I didn't know what it was, and I didn't know what to do with it.

It was difficult for me to let someone love me. I'd spent five-and-a-half years with Steven, and he was a very sweet person with a great heart. For some of that time, I thought I was in love, but I think we both deceived ourselves for a long while. He had some of his own pain that I felt responsible for, and I tried to solve everything, but I couldn't. I felt like I let go of myself because I was always worrying about him or us, and why things weren't right.

I was relieved when we both agreed it would be better if we separated and that we shouldn't get married. Finally, we realized that we'd be happier apart because we were so unhappy together. We fought all the time, and I smoked my brains out to keep from getting real with myself about our relationship. I can't speak for Steven, but it wasn't what I wanted it to be, and it didn't feel good anymore. I had known for a long time that it needed to end, but I held on to it because I just didn't want to be by myself. I was too scared to be alone.

I'd lost all my money. I had no job. I was 275 when we broke up, and then I put on another 15 pounds in the months after that. I felt like fucking shit.

I said to myself, "Maybe the relationship with Steven didn't work out because I wasn't happy with myself." But looking back on it now, I'm just so grateful for that experience with him, because it made me go deep into myself about my own problems with intimacy and trust, and it prepared me for something real.

I'm so grateful to Al, too, because if it weren't for him, I wouldn't have met Rob.

We were doing a show at the naval base in Willow Grove, Pennsylvania. It was a show for military veterans called VetRock. They had Steppenwolf, War, the Rascals, the Animals—all these '60s bands. Wendy and I were actually the only girls on the whole bill.

I was wearing these huge muumuus when I performed,

and I was feeling really big.

It was like, here's Wendy, looking so hot in her beautiful dresses and her beautiful figure, and then here's me—good singer, good charisma on stage, but just a fat blob. I was just feeling really yucky.

But the funny thing is that the day I met Rob, I remember feeling really pretty. One of my favorite things in the world is to dress up and put on makeup. I've learned so many great tips from world-class makeup artists over the years. I remember getting ready to perform and putting on these beautiful false eyelashes to make my eyes really big for the stage.

I was wearing these little butterfly clips in my hair, and I was happy with my makeup. I said to myself, "You're a big girl, but you're going to put on this outfit, you're going to do the best you can, and you're going to go out there and be proud of who you are."

I felt good that day.

I was backstage, feeling a little nervous as usual. The crowd was huge, and America—one of my favorite bands in the world—had just finished a really cool set. It was a while before we were due to go on, and I was hungry. So I said to everyone, "Let's go get something to eat."

We went to this huge food tent, and as I was on my way to the buffet line, I saw these two guys walking over on the other side of the tent. I especially noticed the one with the dark hair, and I thought, *Ooh, that is a really cute guy.* Then I turned my attention to the food.

So while I was standing in line, this guy with big frizzy hair comes up to me.

"Hey, hi, Carnie. My name is Ken Sharp," he said. "I want to thank you because I wrote you a letter on the Internet and you responded to me, which was cool. I really want to thank you for it." He told me he was a freelance writer, and that he'd be interviewing Al after the show.

"I think we're all going to go to dinner," he said.

I said, "Oh, great."

Then he said, "I'd like you to meet my friend, Rob Bonfiglio."

It was the really cute guy from across the tent. He had this big smile on his face, and I thought, *My God, this guy has the most gorgeous teeth I've ever seen in my life. What a great smile.*

He shook my hand and said, "Hi, Carnie, it's really great to meet you. I saw your talk show, and I want you to know that I really enjoyed watching you." I got a little tingle in my belly. I thought, *That was a really nice thing to say. What a sweetheart.*

"Thank you," I said, and I felt really shy and didn't know what else to say, because that's the way I really am. I can be totally bold and brazen when I want to, but underneath I'm this totally fucking shy girl—a *perverted* shy girl, if that makes any sense.

Rob asked, "Hey, would you mind if I had my picture taken with you?"

And I thought, *Oh, how cute.*

"Of course," I said. "Of course I wouldn't mind."

So Ken took a picture, and Rob put his arm around me, and his arm was shaking. *Oh my God,* I thought. *He's so nervous. What a munchkin.*

And that was it.

They said, "Have a great show. We'll be out in the front, and we'll see you later." And they walked off.

I thought, *How sweet,* and we ate our lunch.

When I went onstage, I saw all these people in the front row, and there was Rob. I couldn't keep my eyes off him. Some of the time he was standing, or he'd be sitting Indian-style.

And he was staring at me.

I was thinking, *Wait a minute. Is he staring at me?* Because

I was so used to all the guys checking Wendy out. I looked over at Wendy, and I looked back at Rob, and I thought, *No, he's not looking at her. He's looking at me.*

I was so excited, it made my day. He stood there with the biggest smile on his face I've ever seen, this enormous grin from ear to ear. He was mouthing the words, and when I sang "Dar-lin'," he just lit up like the most precious thing.

He is such a sweetheart, I thought.

So I sang the whole concert to him because I was just thrilled. I didn't know anything about him. I thought he was Ken's assistant. I had no idea he was a musician.

So we finished the show, and when we went backstage, Rob was there. I was out of breath, and I felt like this sweaty pig.

"That was a great show," Rob and Ken said. "That was so much fun. You did a great job." And they wanted to give me a hug.

Oh my God, I thought, *I'm sweating really bad. I hope I don't smell bad.*

Later on, Rob told me that one of the first things he noticed about me was how good I smelled and how much he loved the smell of my perfume. It's called *Happy* by Clinique, and I still wear it every day because I know he loves it—and I love it, too. It makes me happy because it reminds me of when we first met.

After the show, I had forgotten that Ken was interviewing Al and we were all going to be together at dinnertime. We went back to the hotel, and there was Rob waiting in the lobby. My heart skipped a beat when I saw him, and I got really nervous. I started to notice that there was something almost magnetic going on with us. I was really attracted to him physically, and I was feeling like he was this adorable shy guy, totally the type I'm attracted to.

I changed, put my hair in a ponytail, and felt really cute as we walked to dinner, but I was too shy to walk beside him. When we sat down to dinner, I didn't have the nerve to sit next to Rob. Al, Ken, Rob, and Wendy sat at one table, and I sat at a separate table with Ritchie Canata and Adam Jardine, staring at Rob's back. The entire dinner I kept telling them, "I've got a crush on that guy right there."

The evening sunlight was coming through the window, and Rob was wearing glasses and a magenta sweater. He was so gorgeous with those beautiful eyes and the sunlight on his face. I was getting horny and thinking, *This guy is so hot. I wonder if he'd be interested in me?* It was just fabulous.

But I didn't know what to do. I didn't know how to approach it. So after dinner, we walked back to the hotel, and I remember just saying, "Nice to meet you guys. Bye-bye." And it was over.

I went home, and I didn't really think twice about it. I just thought he was a cutie that I'd never see again. In my heart, I didn't have the self-confidence to believe that there was any way he'd come after me. I didn't have the self-esteem, and I'd never really dated before. Someone had always set me up or I went out with someone I already knew. I'd never been asked out on a date, and I'd never asked anyone out on a date. I had no idea how to go about it, or if anything would come of it. But I knew I liked him.

About a week later, I was on the Internet checking out the Wilson Phillips message board, and I saw a letter to Carnie from Rob Bonfiglio. *Rob Bonfiglio?* I thought, *Who? Who the hell is that? I don't know a Rob Bonfiglio.*

Then I read the letter, and it said, "I'm Ken's friend. I met you backstage, and you were so gracious and kind. I really enjoyed meeting you and watching you onstage. It was a great show, it was really fun, and by the way, I think you're really beautiful."

My heart just melted. I mean, flatter me and forget it. I'm yours. That's just it—especially from a cute guy.

I thought to myself, *You know what? I'm going to have*

some balls here, some chutzpah. I'm going to write this guy back, and I'm going to ask him if he's single. Why the hell not?

He had asked in his e-mail about my interests, so I wrote him a nice long letter, and I said, "P.S. Are you single?"

He wrote back and told me all about himself. He was a musician and a writer in a group called Wanderlust that had just made a record. He loved jazz and had graduated from Berklee College of Music in Boston.

I was getting really turned on. *Wow, this guy, he's made records, he's been on tour, he even opened up for The Who. This guy's so cool. He's like this rock guitar player!* And I was getting really excited because I'd never been out with anyone like that. I wondered if we were going to start any kind of dating, or if we were going to see each other, because he lived in Philadelphia.

At the end of his letter, he wrote, "Yes, I am single."

I wrote back, "Here's my phone number if you ever want to call me."

And he called me that day.

We started talking over the phone, getting to know each other. I loved his voice and how gentle, delicate, and very sweet he was. It was the beginning stage of a relationship where you're really nervous talking to each other, but it's really fun to get to know that person.

And I loved it because he knew what I looked like. He knew my whole deal, and he was still interested. He was really excited to get to know me over the phone, and then we realized that we'd been talking every day for two hours. My phone bill was a thousand bucks a month, and I was getting excited because I thought, *I think we're going to start dating.*

We had spent about a month on the phone, when we decided it was time to see each other again, even though we lived on opposite sides of the country. I flew him up to Portland, Maine, in July for our show there, and I got him a hotel room because I figured we were really getting close on the phone, but there's no way that we were going to sleep together.

I still have *some* values, for fuck's sake.

He'd been telling me how excited he was about giving me a kiss—and I was just as excited about being kissed and kissing him. So when he got off the plane, it was the cutest thing I've ever seen. He gave me this quick little peck, kind of like the way you kiss your grandmother. He was totally shaking, and my palms were so sweaty, I swear to God they'd been sweating for three months straight.

I was so excited just to walk around with him. We went for our first meal together at this little place where they served Armenian wraps. I remember walking down the street thinking, *My feet are going to kill me by the time we get to this restaurant*—and it was only one block away. I had only one pair of shoes that were comfortable for me to wear at this point because I was walking on the sides of my feet. I was so heavy I couldn't keep my ankles from rolling over.

Rob was walking at a normal pace—maybe a little fast—and I was really struggling to keep up with him. I was huffing and puffing, my nose was flaring, and I was sweating. I was so ashamed and embarrassed, but I didn't want Rob to know.

This was only the second time I'd been with him, and I didn't want him to see me like this. *He's going to be turned off,* I thought. *He's not going to want to be with me because I'm such a sweaty pig.*

We got to the little restaurant and ordered our food. I remember being so careful to take small bites. I didn't want it to look like I was inhaling my food. I wanted him to think that I wasn't as hungry as I really was, that I always ate slowly and gracefully, and that I was delicate, feminine, and attractive.

When I was really fat, I thought that if somebody saw me eating, they'd feel that I was a glutton who didn't deserve that food. "Why should *you* be eating? Why should *you* put food into your mouth? Look at your body!"

That's how I was feeling. I was very embarrassed eating in front of him, but it was our first meal together, and I could see that food was very important to Rob. He loves to eat, and I do, too. I still do. So it was a very special thing, and I didn't want to do anything to spoil it.

Rob recently asked me if I remembered our first meal and how special it was.

I told him I did, but in the back of my mind, I was also thinking about what an intense emotional experience it was for me. So I have such compassion for overweight men and women who feel self-conscious about putting food in their mouths in public. I understand why there are so many closet eaters—because people are just so fucking ashamed.

I did the concert, and we were together every moment we could manage. After the show, the airline sponsoring the tour put on this beautiful lobster dinner. As we were eating, I said to him, "I want you to kiss me right now."

"But everyone's watching," he said.

"I don't care," I said. "Kiss me right now."

So he gave me this soft, open-mouthed kiss—not like Frenching—but nice, gentle, and very sensual. I felt like a different person from the fat blob who could hardly walk that afternoon.

It was the first time I'd ever had clams, and of course, I was making jokes.

"I hear these are aphrodisiacs," I said, "so let's just keep shoving 'em in." We were thrilled because we knew that after dinner we were going back to the hotel together. I didn't know if he was going to sleep in his room and I was going to sleep in mine, but we both knew we were going to make out for the first time.

It was so exciting and so nerve-wracking. He was feeding me clams, and it was so romantic and so much fun. They were delicious, and the lobster was amazing.

We went back to the hotel flushed with that great feeling you have after a wonderful meal.

I went to my room, took a nice bath, lit candles, put on my pretty perfume, and Rob walked in wearing tortoise-shell glasses. I thought it was the cutest, most sophisticated thing ever. He was in plaid pajama bottoms and a T-shirt—and I just about wet my pants.

He was so cute, so strikingly good looking. We were totally nervous, but it was the most romantic couple of hours ever. He spent an hour and a half touching and kissing my face. It was like nothing I've ever done, so sensitive and delicate and sweet. The rest of the details are private, but we didn't go all the way. We kept it pretty clean, but it was just so special, I was a goner from that moment on.

WE CONTINUED SEEING AND TALKING TO EACH OTHER as much as we could, but he was in Philadelphia and I was in Los Angeles, so most of our moments together were over the phone. A couple of months after we met, I mentioned to Rob that I was thinking about having weight-loss surgery.

He told me I was beautiful just the way I was, but if my weight bothered me, then it bothered him.

"This surgery is really drastic," I said, "and it's a permanent thing. It would be changing the way my organs are inside. What do you think of that?"

"Is it safe?" was the first thing he wanted to know.

"Yes," I said.

"Then I think it's a great idea," he said. "If you're going to help yourself, and it's going to make you feel better, then I totally support it."

"That's great," I said, "because I'm really going to need your support for this. I'm really scared, and this is extreme."

He said to go for it, and when I heard him say that, it

definitely validated something for me, because I had this feeling I was going to be with him for a long time—and I wanted to make sure I'd be around to love him and be loved by him.

Rob was curious about the surgery. He wanted to know exactly what it was, how it worked, and what it entailed. I told him what I knew, and together we looked more and more into the procedure and the recovery.

In the middle of the summer, I spent ten days with Rob in Philadelphia. He was really eager to show me his hometown, and it was great to meet his family. I had a wonderful time, but I was very embarrassed and sad because I was so heavy. I had only two pairs of shoes I could wear that didn't hurt my feet. It wasn't really the shoes, but my feet, that were killing me. They were so big and wide and fat, it was like they couldn't get enough room to breathe.

Rob took me to a quaint place called Peddler's Village, with cobblestone streets and little hills and a big outdoor shopping mall. I was sweating so badly, so overheated and winded, so sloppy and so yucky. I could barely make it up the hills. I was huffing and puffing, trying to keep up with him, trying to slow him down, turning my head to exhale so he wouldn't see me gasping for air. I smiled at him and tried to breathe through my nose, but I knew my nostrils were flaring like a racehorse because I was suffocating. I was miserable.

Here I was with my new boyfriend, wanting desperately to be fun and to enjoy myself with him, just trying to do something so normal, and struggling with it every minute. In my heart, I was ashamed of myself and so frustrated and afraid he'd be disappointed and disgusted.

"I'm really embarrassed," I said. "I'm sweating like a pig."

"So what?" he said. "So am I." He was so kind and thoughtful, and he knew I was having a very hard time, but he didn't want me to worry.

"How are you doing?" he'd ask. "Are you all right?"

I'd say, "Yeah." But we both knew it was really difficult for me. And all I could think about was, *I've got to have this operation. I've going to start taking care of myself. I'm doing it. I'm finally going to do something about it.*

I was in love, and I had to protect that love. I couldn't let anything stop me.

I never really imagined that I would fall in love like that. I'd had loves before, and I'd never want to hurt anyone by saying that they weren't the real thing. But I'd never felt this kind of beautiful connection with anyone in any relationship in my life. Rob was my true love, the man my heart had always longed for, and I couldn't risk losing him and the life we could share together.

I knew that it was more than just about my health or my career.

Now it was about love.

Decision of a Lifetime

N ot long after the *Roseanne* appearance, Mickey Shapiro called me. "Would you be willing to talk about your obesity and your struggles with it on the Internet?" he asked. "I'm starting a Website called Spotlight Health. We'll make some streaming videos and do some online chats. You'll be able to help a lot of people."

Wow, that's great! I thought. It was sort of along the lines of what I'd been doing, but on a bigger scale—no pun intended.

A few weeks went by, and Mickey called with another question. "Would you ever consider weight-loss surgery?" Little did he know I'd already been considering it. Roseanne had piqued my interest, and now after discussing it with Rob, I had decided to seriously investigate the procedure. Mickey's partner in the Website venture, Dr. Jonathan Sackier, explained it to me.

It seemed so radical, stapling your stomach to reduce its size, making it impossible to overeat, rearranging your intestines. But I was so apprehensive about my situation, and I didn't know what to do anymore.

I'm going to die if I don't do this, I thought. *This is the only way I can save my life.*

It's hard to put it into words, but when you're ready, you know you're ready. And I was ready. I was ready to help myself, and this was the way.

Another factor that helped me make up my mind was Rob. When I met him, I was at my heaviest, and he made me feel so good about myself because he didn't care that I was 300 pounds. He wanted to know me, and love the person inside.

People are so afraid to be themselves, but I've never had that problem, no matter what I weighed, and it's been a wonderful thing. I attribute that to my mother, because she'd say, "No matter what you look like or how big or small you are, you're still who you are." That was the quality that Rob saw and loved about me. He told me so.

So I did feel attractive to him, but I knew in my heart that I didn't feel attractive to myself. I knew I'd be physically happier if I lost the weight, because I knew it was going be a permanent thing. I knew in my gut that this was the answer for me.

But I was scared shitless. This wasn't like deciding to go on a new diet. They were going to cut me up and change my insides all around, and I wasn't sure if I'd ever enjoy eating anything again, or if I was going to have an upset stomach for the rest of my life.

Mickey wanted to make all the arrangements and get going, but I was waffling.

Dr. Sackier took me into Mickey's office. "Listen," he said. "You're 31 years old. If you don't do this, the odds are you'll be dead in ten years. You'll have diabetes by the time you're 35. Your risk of developing breast cancer is 50 percent higher than normal. Your joints are going to break down, and you could suffocate in your sleep from the apnea, or you could have a heart attack at any time."

All these things frightened the living daylights out of me, so I made my mind up for sure. I knew it was time. I was actually scared I was going to die, and these feelings of doom were with me constantly. Knowing what I was headed for, I had to do something.

People are so afraid of change, but I've always thought of myself as the type of person who takes risks, who goes after what she wants in life. But the one thing I really wanted, I could never achieve. I'd tried so many times to lose the weight. I tried every single diet there is, and I feel like I *did* make the effort. But there was always that part of me that wasn't ready. And that's what's really important here—people have to be ready, ready in their hearts to make it happen for *themselves,* not for anyone else.

When you're fat, everyone is always saying, "You better lose weight or you're not going to be healthy." I'd heard it since I was six years old. You appreciate the fact that people care about you. You know the consequences. But you're in so much pain inside that for some reason at a deep level you feel comforted by the security of being fat. The fat was my cushion, my safety blanket, my armor. I was protected by my fat. Nobody could get to me. Nobody could hurt me. My size gave me power. It made me feel strong. It made me different, the big girl, the one you remembered.

So I felt like I was sabotaging myself by having the surgery. I didn't truly believe that I deserved to feel good. Emotionally, it was easier to stay fat. But physically, I was at such a desperate point that I started to think seriously about how I was going to do this.

Making the commitment to do the programs with Spotlight Health got me moving. Over a series of weeks, we made the videos that told my story as I prepared for the surgery. They created an online support group for me and others who were weighing the surgical alternative.

The great thing about the Internet is that you can be as public or as private as you want to be. You're in your home, you're on your computer, and you don't have to be anywhere or see anyone you don't want to see. It's wonderful to read e-mails, to chat back and forth with people, and to see their pictures and share everything from the physical to the emotional. It's not the same as being with them in person, and that takes a lot of the pressure off. There's a comfort in the space between you, and you can get as close as you want or back off into your own privacy when you need to.

People who had already undergone the operation began to post their experiences on the site, and it was incredible how open they were and how much they wanted to help each other. I read them all, and I started e-mailing people back, talking to them online about how they felt before they had surgery. "I'm so scared," I was saying. "What if something happens? What are the side effects? How do you eat afterwards?"

And the postings came pouring back in by the hundreds. Some of them were horror stories. People told about botched operations, bowel leakages and intestinal obstructions, busted sutures and ruptured staples, infections, and hernias. There were warnings about aftereffects—constant indigestion; nausea; diarrhea; hair loss; and ugly, sagging skin.

Some of my fans felt betrayed. How could I, the poster girl for fat acceptance, buy into the idea that my body had to be mutilated so that I could be happy? Didn't I know I was beautiful just the way I was? How could I let myself be manipulated and brainwashed by a sick society that persecuted overweight people?

But many more of the e-mails were overwhelmingly positive and inspirational.

I kept reading the same thing over and over:

"This is the best decision I've ever made."
"I feel like I'm a new person."
"I never felt better."
"It's magic."
"I have a new lease on life."

"I would do it again in a heartbeat."
"I can't believe this. It's a miracle."

There was such a beautiful vibe about these stories of people just like me who had suffered their entire lives, and how the surgery had given them a way to save themselves from certain death—either from the complications of morbid obesity or the desire to just end it all by killing themselves.

These were people who knew firsthand the frustrations and the fears of living in a body that was out of control. They knew the deep soul ache of never being able to love yourself or to let yourself be loved by others. They knew the twisted agonies and ecstasies of being obsessed by food. They had lived with the shame and discrimination that gets cruelly heaped on the obese—and they had been set free.

I related to these people in ways that I had never felt before. I began to think of them as sisters and brothers who were there to help me when I needed help most. From across the country and all over the world, they were chiming in to give me their courage and lend me their strength, opening their hearts and baring their souls to share their most intimate memories and emotions.

And they convinced me more than ever that by doing this, I would be helping others, too. I wouldn't just be helping myself, but all those in private pain who needed to know that there was hope, all those who were struggling with this relentless burden I knew inside out, all the women and men who were staring at an unbearably bleak future when they looked in the mirror every day.

So now that I was going to do it, I decided to get all the details about the operation. Originally, I was thinking of just going to Roseanne's bariatric surgeon in Los Angeles. But as Dr. Sackier helped me understand more about the surgery, I changed my mind.

It's important for people to know that there is more than one kind of weight-loss surgery. There's the gastric bypass, which is considered the gold standard, the best of the procedures because there have been more successful outcomes with this procedure than any of the others. That means that more people have been able to lose a greater amount of unhealthy weight and keep it off with fewer complications than with the other procedures—such as vertical banded gastroplasty, biliopancreatic diversion, or the duodenal switch.

There's an interview with my surgeon, Dr. Alan Wittgrove, in the Appendix of this book that explains the differences between these procedures. But Dr. Sackier, who's a surgeon himself and an expert in minimally invasive surgical techniques, explained everything to me. He convinced me that gastric bypass was the best option for me.

Then he told me that there are different ways of doing the gastric bypass—either "open" or "laparoscopically." In the open method, they make an incision through the muscles in the center of your abdominal wall. The incision starts just below where your ribs come together and goes down to your belly button. Then they open you up and the surgeon operates on your stomach and intestines while looking straight at them.

The laparoscopic technique is the minimally invasive alternative, and it's a more high-tech way of doing it. Instead of a big central incision, they make five or six very small incisions—maybe an inch long, two at the most—at various positions off the midline in the abdominal wall, so all your muscles aren't cut and pulled apart at once. Then they insert plastic tubes called ports into the small incisions.

Specially designed surgical instruments, including a small telescopic televison camera with a light, are then inserted through these ports into the abdominal cavity. This camera is called a laparoscope, and it broadcasts pictures from your abdominal cavity back to the surgical team. They see the pictures either on big color television monitors in the operating room, or through these space-age headsets that the surgeon and assistant surgeon wear.

The headsets have small television screens in front of each eye that give the surgeons a three-dimensional view of everything, just as if they were looking at your organs through the air like they do in the open procedure. One of the advantages of the laparoscope is that it can magnify the view up to 1,000 times, so they can get a much closer look than if they were doing it open. The laparoscope is manipulated by a computerized robotic arm that's programmed to the surgeon's voice so that it moves precisely whichever way he tells it to.

It's really an amazing bunch of technology, and the beauty is that they don't have to cut this big hole in you, so you have a faster recovery with less pain and fewer chances of complications.

One of the most frequent complications is called an incisional hernia. This happens when either your intestine or your stomach bulges through a weak spot in the incision after it's been closed. This can happen 10 to 20 percent of the time with the open procedure, but very rarely with the laparoscopic technique.

Once they're in—either open or laparoscopically—they make a small pouch out of the top of your stomach using a double line of staples. Then they cut between the staples, which separates the new pouch from the rest of your stomach. The remainder of your stomach stays in your abdomen to produce enzymes your intestines need to process the nutrients from the food you eat. (See illustrations, pages 248–249.)

About 18 inches from where your intestine attaches to the bottom of your stomach, they cut your small intestine in two. The limb on the right is hooked up to the new stomach pouch, and the limb on the left is attached back into your intestinal tract a little lower down. The new arrangement is in the shape of a *Y,* and that's why the procedure is known as Roux en-Y. It was developed by a doctor in France named Roux, and it looks like a *Y.*

Not everyone can have the laparoscopic procedure, especially if they've had other abdominal surgeries. There may be other anatomical reasons as well that might make someone a poor candidate. But Dr. Sackier didn't think there would be any problem for me. He recommended minimally invasive surgery because he believed it was the best method, and he told me that the surgeons who developed the laparoscopic procedure, Alan Wittgrove and G. Wesley Clark, had their practice right down the interstate in San Diego.

So Spotlight Health arranged a meeting for me with Dr. Wittgrove. He's a handsome guy and very mellow. I was nervous at first, but he put me right at ease.

I told him my story, and in five minutes, we were both crying.

"So society's put all this on you to the point where it makes you feel like this is a last-ditch effort," he said.

"Yeah," I said.

"In fact, it's not. This surgery is really the best treatment there is for obesity. When you think about what diets are able to do or not able to do, diets are really not designed to be successful for morbidly obese individuals. You can lose weight, absolutely. It's an equation—how much food goes in versus how many calories you expend. On the other hand, keeping it off, that's the problem. So this surgery is able to give you a tool to help you with that."

"What about safety?" I asked.

"Is it risky? Sure," he said. "There are risks for any surgery. But the benefits, that's what we look for."

"So what are some of the risks?" I wanted to know.

"The risks are similar to the risks of almost any surgery," he said, "except when you add to the mix the problems with operating on someone who's morbidly obese, somebody who's already had a heart attack because of their obesity, or has diabetes, hypertension, sleep apnea—all those health-related illnesses—they have more risk. On the other hand, they have more benefits to gain, too."

Dr. Wittgrove asked me, "What's the main problem that you see as a result of your obesity? What do you hope to get out of this the most?"

"I hope to just shed the pounds," I said, "and be more free and not so inhibited, and just physically feel lighter so I can do what I want to do. I also want to avoid future health problems."

"I don't think that most people who know you would think of you as inhibited," he said, smiling.

"In a lot of ways, I'm not," I replied, laughing. "I've always had boyfriends. I love men, and I've had great sex and great love. But physically, the obesity limits a lot that you can do. I think that being thin, I would feel so much freer and less inhibited. You know, I'd like to wear tank tops in the summertime, show my arms and wear shorts, because I have good legs."

He smiled again.

"There are a lot of reasons for desiring surgery," he said. "Some medical, some physical, some psychological. They're all valid reasons. You don't have a lot of other medical problems, so you're probably a perfect candidate for this. You don't have a lot of illness yet, but you're overweight enough to need the surgery.

"That doesn't mean that people who are sick from being overweight aren't good candidates," he said, "because this surgery can give them so much more benefit. It can eventually remove the cause of their weight-related illnesses, so they're good candidates as well.

"But it's good for you, because we know the natural history of obesity," he continued. "We know that diabetes, hypertension, sleep apnea—the likelihood of all those problems increases as your age and your weight increases."

"I've already got high blood pressure and high cholesterol and sleep apnea," I said. "And my joints are aching a lot, and my endurance is poor."

"After the operation, as you lose the weight, all of those conditions will naturally improve," he said.

"That's great."

"Let's talk a little bit about the operation itself," he said. He started to get excited, probably because he's a surgeon and he loves the thought of surgery.

"Okay," I said.

"The bypass procedure we do has been around since the 1960s."

"Wow," I said. "I thought it was more recent."

"No," he said. "There's an extensive history with this procedure. We do about half our operations open, and the other half laparoscopically. We've been doing the laparoscopic procedure since 1993. Whether we do it open or laparoscopically, the procedure inside the abdomen is the same. The only difference is access. But we've found that people do better with the smaller incisions."

That made sense to me.

"The open incision is hard to get over," he continued. "It's pulling and it's painful, at least for the first several days. But then you have to worry about the tension that's on the facia, the gristle there, and incisional hernias. They're not that risky, but you still have to go through another operation, and there's the expense of the second surgery, and more time off from work or whatever your normal life is. It's just more pain and inconvenience."

"Well, I don't want that," I said. "I'm a baby when it comes to pain."

"That's why we developed it laparoscopically. There's

almost no chance of incisional hernia and a lot less discomfort."

"Cool."

"Now, when we do it laparoscopically," he went on, "if for some reason there's a problem, we always have the option to switch and do it open."

"So if I'm on the table and something goes wrong or whatever, then you'd have to cut me open down the center?" I asked.

"Right," he said. "But we prefer not to do that."

"Me, too."

"Well, it's important to understand that there's always a potential risk of complication. We never know until we get in there. But laparoscopically, we actually have a better view of what we're doing because we can use the telescope to get right down close to the site.

"But it's a smaller field of view than looking at the whole thing open. So, for example, if we have a lot of bleeding all of a sudden, our field of view can get obscured fairly easily. A lot of bleeding is one of the reasons that we may have to change from a laparoscopic to an open operation. But so far, that hasn't been a problem.

"Knock on wood," I said.

"Absolutely," he smiled. "Anatomic problems are another reason. Everybody's anatomy is a little different. The spleen, for example, is right next to where we do the dissection of the stomach. So if your spleen is very large or lives up over the top of the stomach instead of over on the side, then it's a little bit more in harm's way."

"How do people know who's good at this?" I asked.

"It's important to know that different surgeons do gastric bypasses a little bit differently," he said. "People need to check out what the outcomes are from the surgical group they're considering. We feel very strongly, for example, that people need a very small pouch. Otherwise they might not lose all the weight they need to. We feel that way because of our outcomes.

"We size the pouch at 15 cubic centimeters, and we have a specific measurement on the length of intestine that we bring up, and the dimension of the opening between the intestine and the small stomach pouch. All these parameters are based on the outcomes of our patients."

"Do some surgeons make the pouch bigger?" I asked.

"Yes," he said. "And that can affect how much weight you lose. We've followed our data for five years, and longer on our laparoscopic cases, and I can tell you with confidence how well I think you'll do. I think you'll lose three-fourths of your excess body weight. That's what our numbers show when the operation is done the way we do it. Small pouch. Set length of incisions. The intestine being this long, brought up this way, with that type of pouch. If any of those components are changed, people really need to know how good the outcomes are for their particular surgical group.

"So outcomes are important, not only for you as an individual, but for society as a whole," he continued. "Outcomes are not just about weight. How about diabetes? Diabetics make up 20 percent of my patient population. And diabetes is such a devastating disease. It's the number-one cause of blindness in adults. Over half of the amputations of the lower extremities every year are from diabetes."

"Both my grandmothers had diabetes," I said. "They had problems with their eyes and their kidneys."

"Diabetes is the number-one cause of going onto kidney dialysis machines," he said.

"My Grandma Audree was on dialysis before she died," I said. "It was bad."

"There's really no other process that can put diabetes into remission the way gastric bypass can," he said. "We've done a lot of research on that, and it's so gratifying.

"It's so neat to take folks with a whole constellation of medical problems, and then follow them through their recovery.

Cooling off in blue waters.

Me, Mom, and Wendy (left to right) in Hawaii in 1992
on our first vacation after Wilson Phillips's breakup.

My mom, Marilyn
Wilson-Rutherford.
I love you, Mom!

Wendy and me—all grown up!

The *Carnie* show executive producer,
Cathy Chermol—"my little Cath."

My 29th birthday on the set of the *Carnie* show.

Having some fun in the studio
while making *Shadows and Light* in 1992.

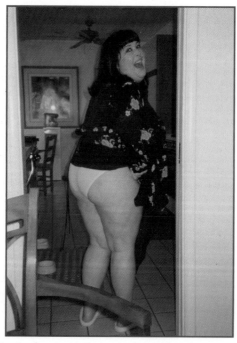

Two months before surgery in 1999 (and never ashamed).

(Photo: Henry Diltz)

Singing with Al Jardine in Michigan.

Here I am, singing at the VetRock concert,
moments after meeting my future husband, Rob.

Tiffany and me—Road Warriors 1995.

The five girlfriends together—Tiffany, Julie, Jenny, me, and Wen (below).

My best friend Owen Elliot-Kugell at my 30th birthday party.

Me; Mom; my stepdad, Daniel; and Wendy (left to right).

My future husband, Rob (left), with Ken Sharp (the best man at our wedding) watching me onstage. Look at that smile!

Shaking it at the VetRock concert.

Backstage after
the VetRock
concert feeling
the post-gig glow.

Moments after
meeting Rob
. . . who would
have thought?

Our first date in Los Angeles.

In the studio
with Wendy and
Dad, making
"The Wilsons."

Here I am
singing at the
First Annual
Carl Wilson
Tribute in 1998.

Me (at my
heaviest) with
Mom and
Wendy on
Mother's Day
1999.

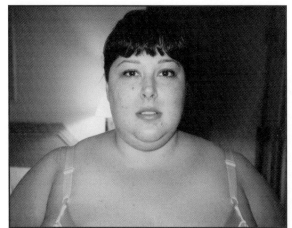

I'm in my hotel room the night before surgery, August 1999.

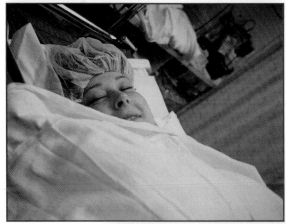

Me, pre-op. I'll be dreaming of bikinis.

My heroes, Dr. Wittgrove and Leslie Jester, R.N.

Four days post-op, chatting on SpotlightHealth.com.

My 21st meal of Jell-O and chicken broth . . . ugh!

Eight days post-op.
My first piece of toast
with butter—*Yum!*

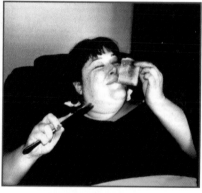

The Weight Loss Surgery (WLS) celebration cruise to
Ensenada, Mexico, with surgery graduates.

Three months
post-op and
45 lbs. lighter.

Dr. Wittgrove and me
on the WLS cruise,
eight months post-op.
Good-bye 114 lbs.!

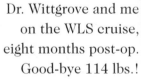

Dad (Brian Wilson) and me: Coming full circle.

Rob and me. Isn't life grand?

Me, moments before the wedding ceremony started.

From left: Mom, me, Auntie Dee Dee, and Wendy. The day we've all been waiting for!

Dad; me; and my stepmom, Melinda.

Rob and me after saying "I do!" Dreams *do* come true.

Dad and me during our "father-daughter" dance.

(Photo: Allison Leach)

Book photo session:
I feel just like a model!

Dr. Wittgrove
(left), me, and my
manager Mickey
Shapiro (right).

(Photo: Terri Sharp)

Philadelphia
freedom—my
photographer friend
Terri Sharp's style
(September 2000).

Obviously, it's great to help them through the process and the risks of surgery. But then to be able to follow how it's changed their lives—that's really exciting.

"So what other questions do you have?" he said.

"Well, first of all, how long will the operation take?"

"Laparoscopically, it takes a little bit longer than it does for us to do the open operation. Right now, we try to do the open operation with a shorter incision as well, so it takes us about an hour, sometimes an hour and a half to do an open operation. After doing 600 cases or so, it takes us about an hour and a half to two hours to do it laparoscopically. We try not to waste very much time in an operating room."

"So you're not gonna stop for a coffee break or something?" I asked.

He laughed. "No, we don't do that."

"Another thing I'm very concerned about is the pain," I told him. "What sort of pain can I expect with this surgery?"

"There are several different parts to that," he said. "Of course, the most important part is the anesthesia. During the time you would experience most of the pain, you're anesthetized. We use the same group of anesthetists that we've used for ten years. We're very concerned that it's done exactly right. So you can rest assured about that."

"So I'm not going to wake up in the middle of the operation?" I wanted to clarify this.

"No," he smiled. "There's no chance of that."

"Well, that's good," I said. "I'd rather watch it on video."

"Yeah," he smiled. "Now after the anesthetic wears off, we do several different things. We have what's called a PCA unit, a patient-controlled analgesia machine, so you're able to control how much narcotic you give yourself for how much discomfort you have."

"So if I'm feeling like I want more, I can have more." This I understood. "But what will it feel like?"

"Laparoscopically, the pain and discomfort are certainly less. The first 24 hours are the most uncomfortable, and then it drops off dramatically after that."

"Is it like cramping, or a stomachache, or what?" I inquired.

"Cramping is a good description. Although I haven't personally gone through it, that's how people describe it, because it's a muscular kind of thing. We go through the muscle, especially laparoscopically. When we do it open, we put sutures in the muscle to hold things together. So oftentimes, it's kind of a crampy type of pain. And there's muscle soreness."

"What about the narcotic?" I asked. "It's not going to be addictive or anything weird like that, is it?"

"No, and that's the importance of your being able to control it," he said. "Along with that, we give you another drug called Tordol every six hours intravenously, even if you don't ask for it. It's not narcotic, but it decreases the pain. It doesn't necessarily take it completely away, but it makes it more tolerable. And it does this without really messing with your head. The problems we have with narcotics are the psychiatric effects."

"Like what?" I said.

"You can't concentrate the way you normally would, and some people actually experience more pain with narcotics because of that. You're having a big surgery, so it's rational to expect some pain. A lot of people can manage their pain when they know what to expect. But if you give them a narcotic that affects their mental process, they can't rationalize the pain away."

"I don't have a lot of tolerance for pain," I said. "I'm a baby, remember?"

"Well, after the first day or two, the pain drops off dramatically. We did a study on that two-and-a-half years ago, where we looked at laparoscopic patients. The survey showed that after the patients leave the hospital—usually in two to three days—half of them didn't even fill their narcotic prescription. So we don't expect that you'll have a lot of lingering pain."

"Good," I said.

"So laparoscopic patients stay in the hospital two days," he went on. "Open operations generally stay for three days. Then people are out of the hospital and doing things. We want people to get active as soon as possible afterwards. We don't want you to think of yourself as sick or ill, and we don't want you staying in your hotel room or at home in bed. We want you to get out and get going. Even while you're in the hospital, the nurses will get you up and walking on the first day."

"I'll be so raring to go," I said. "I know me. I'm going to be like, 'Come on! Let's go!'"

"That's what it's like with this kind of an operation," he said. "The patients are motivated, because once they see that the potential benefits so far outweigh the risks, they want to have this surgery. It's not like any other surgery there is."

He paused for a moment, and there was this smile on his face that was so calm. "Any other questions that we need to cover at this point? We'll have plenty of time to talk more about it."

God, he's so confident, I thought.

"I know you're the expert at this, and I'm just so grateful and so thrilled. I know you're going to change my life, and I really look forward to that. Oh, God, I'm not going to start crying again, but I really appreciate it, and I can't wait. Thank you."

"You're welcome," he said. "It's going to be very exciting."

CHAPTER TEN

Going Public

It was Mickey's idea to broadcast the surgery over the Internet.

"Are you crazy?" I asked.

"I think it would be a very brave, bold, and generous thing to do," he said.

And then I thought, *Wait a minute, that's the best idea I've ever heard in my life. That's the best idea ever. Why not share what I'm going to go through with other people?*

So I said, "Okay, let's do it."

People said to me, "Why the hell would you do something public like that?"

And my answer was, "Why not? Why not be open? Why be ashamed? What for? Why be embarrassed? Because I'd be *judged?*"

Who cares what people think? You know, who cares? I don't care if someone thinks that I'm a nutcase because I did this. I know that for every 5 people who think that, there are 100 people who got something out of what I've gone through. Maybe they started a new diet and they lost the ten pounds. Maybe they joined Weight Watchers and dropped 30. Maybe they went for the gastric bypass and lost 150. Maybe they decided to get married or take charge of their life.

That's why I decided to do it in public, because I knew it was going to help people. I'd say, "Hey, I've shared everything else in my life so far, why not this?" It wasn't really a big deal to me. Why not stir up a little excitement? Why not be the person who admits that I have a problem, that I need to get a handle on this, that I need help and support?

I wanted the audience. I wanted to be cheered on. I wanted to know from people who had been there that I was going to be okay.

I knew I was in really good hands, and I was going to have the most modern technology available. But as the surgery date got closer and closer, I was wondering, *Oh, God, do I really want to do this?* At night when I was trying to fall asleep, I kept thinking, *I just want to make it through. I just want to survive this operation.* I kept thinking of my chances of dying on the table, of getting a blood clot in my leg that would travel to my lungs. I was afraid, and I was having second thoughts.

So when we were doing the Spotlight Health video pieces, Dr. Sackier asked Karen Metzfield, a neighbor of his from Washington, D.C., to fly in and help me deal with these feelings.

Karen is a registered nurse who had a gastric bypass several years ago. It was an open procedure. Dr. Wittgrove could say, "This is how you're going feel," but Karen had done it and lived it. I wanted to hear from her about the pain and the recovery and what it was like to eat after you've had the surgery.

We took a break to eat before her segment, and I was really interested to see her plate. She had a little bit of fruit, a little bit of turkey, and a little bit of cheese—that was it.

I thought to myself, *Is that all you're going eat?* But she seemed perfectly happy, and Dr. Wittgrove just looked at her plate like everything was normal. Mine was piled as high as possible with everything the catering truck had to offer—but so was Dr. Wittgrove's. We both packed it in, but I don't think he gained an ounce.

Talking to Karen helped me feel much better. She was a grandmother, but one of the hippest-looking grandmothers you've ever seen. She had short spiky hair and a slender body, and she just radiated health and contentment.

She told me her story, how she'd been heavy for years, losing and gaining, going up and down. She talked about the embarrassment and the shame and all the things she missed out on with her husband because she was so obese.

One day they were riding in the car and there was a spot on the radio about weight-loss surgery. She turned to her husband while he was driving and said, "Honey, maybe I should look into that."

"Why not?" he agreed.

His response really surprised her, because she knew her husband loved her even though she was big. But she decided to go for the surgery, and her husband was very supportive. As the weight came off, he encouraged her with gifts and flowers, and he told her that for him it was like making love to a new woman each month. They were both so thrilled about her weight loss, and they began planning all the things they were going to do together and the places they were going to go when he retired in the months ahead.

Then suddenly he died of a heart attack.

He never saw her reach her goal weight, and there was a sweet sadness about her that really touched my heart. I felt so sorry for her, but *she* wasn't sorry. I could see how much she loved her husband and how much she missed him. But she was happy to be alive, to be there for her daughter and her grandchildren—and to be there to help someone like me.

I told her I had fears about being thin. I'd never been thin, and this person at 298 pounds was me. Even though I was uncomfortable with all this weight, it was *me*. On the other hand, I was so depressed about the point that I had gotten myself to. I was very angry with myself, mad that I had let myself go. I was proud I was sober and that I was finally going to do something about my weight, but when I looked in the mirror, all I could think was, *Look at what you've done.*

Karen was very understanding. She knew exactly how I felt. And she said something that stuck with me from that day until the surgery and even after: "The best part about this surgery isn't losing the weight," she said. "It's knowing that you'll never have to be afraid again that the weight will come back."

That same day, we taped the interviews with Mom and Wendy, and it was very emotional. Spotlight Health had chosen a beautiful house in Hancock Park, right on the golf course of the Wilshire Country Club, for the location. In the backyard, they shot some video of me in a blue dress that captures for all time what I looked like at my heaviest. They let *20/20* and *Oprah* and many other shows use the shots, and you can see them on the Spotlight Health Website. But when I look at that sequence, I see someone so sad and so incredibly obese that it makes me shudder. I was remembering a whole lifetime that day, and you could see in my face that I was miserable and frightened, and struggling with myself about the surgery.

Mom had cried when they asked her about it. "Of course, as a mother you're worried whether everything will go well," she said through her tears. "But I just know it's going to be the best thing, and I wish her all the happiness because she's just the greatest person and she deserves it."

My mom was just so wonderful that day. She's been such an inspiration to me always, and knowing she was there for me even though she was so afraid meant so much.

The same goes for Wendy. She really didn't want me to do it because she thought the surgery was unsafe. She was completely terrified about it, but she was just as terrified of what might happen if I didn't do it.

When the cameras rolled, she said she wished I could try

again to lose the weight the "old-fashioned way" like I had before. She thought the surgery was strange.

"But who am I to say that it's strange?" she said. "It's been great for so many people, and they're doing miraculous things now in medicine, so maybe it *is* the answer.

"If Carnie's at a place where she's throwing her hands up in the air and saying, 'I'm out of control and I can't do this on my own,' then she should definitely get the operation. And I'll be right next to her holding her hand, because I want her to stay around. That's the bottom line.

"Obviously, the risks of the surgery are less extreme than the risks of her staying this weight. The ultimate goal is to be healthier, and I know this will bring her there more quickly. I'm sure that she'll feel better, and that will motivate her, and she'll be able to get to her goal. There's nothing more that I want for her than to feel good about herself and be healthy."

Having support from the people you love is so essential when you're facing a life-altering thing like this. Otherwise, you just want to walk away from it, even though you know you're going to kill yourself if you don't do something.

I knew my mom, Wendy, Dee Dee, and everyone in my family were behind me, and my dad and his wife, Melinda, were very excited for me. Of course, Rob was really wonderful. He'd say beautiful things to me like, "You're going to do so well. You're going to get through it, and you're going to make it. It's going to be the best."

When I told Lisa about the surgery, she was surprised and very concerned, and I knew she wouldn't love the idea because she feels so strongly about doing the right thing for your body and protecting it. "To alter your physiology, to actually cut open your body and change the way it works is so intense," she said. "But I know you wouldn't make such a dramatic statement like this if you didn't have a huge need."

She told me she respected my decision, and that she

thought it took a huge amount of courage.

"Making a decision like this has a certain amount of finality to it," she said. "You're taking on a whole new way of living life because your stomach's smaller and you eat less. But that doesn't mean that your problems will go away."

We both knew that there were issues that would come up, and she promised to help me learn how to sit in the middle of the storm long enough to figure out how to react to things when they happened and figure out what I could do to make it different.

"Carnie, I love you," Lisa said, "and I hope that you get everything you want from this—especially some sense of peace. I'll be there in any way I can to help make this a great experience for you."

I do think there's a lot of courage involved, and I don't make decisions lightly. I consider my choices carefully, and that's something Lisa helped me learn to do. She taught me to take it step-by-step, to make a list of things, to write down my feelings, and to evaluate the pros and cons. Her acceptance and encouragement were so important to me.

My therapist, Marc Schoen, was terrific help to me as well.

"I know one of your biggest wishes from day one has been to be thin," he said. "This is something you've always wanted, and I think you'll have tremendous motivation to do all the things that will help preserve this change. I also believe that all the energy that's been wasted on weight control for all these years is now going to be released to be applied in much more positive, beneficial ways in your life."

It made me feel so good to hear him say that.

"By preparing pre-operatively with hypnosis, I believe we can dramatically affect your post-surgical outcome, not only in terms of pain, but in terms of recovery and healing and your mood state. A very important part of the preparation will be giving lots of suggestions in terms of your recovery—in terms of dealing with weight loss, dealing with food differently, eating differently, making better choices, and knowing that there's no going back.

"You're also going to have to deal with feeling very excited by the change. When you lost weight before, it was wonderful and exciting. But at the same time, it was frightening, because you received a tremendous amount of attention for being thinner, and it made you feel uncomfortable. It made you feel more than ever that you were judged by your appearance and not your talent or who you were as a person.

"There are different expectations of people when they're overweight versus when they're thin. When you're overweight, people have a certain expectation, a certain view of you. When you're thinner, all of a sudden people have different things they expect you to do, expect you to be.

"When someone who's been heavy all their life loses a lot of weight, some of the tools they've used to protect themselves through the years don't work anymore. The weight's not there to perhaps soften your uncomfortable feelings about esteem or abandonment, but the struggle still will be. Now you're going to have to create new tools and prepare to deal with things in different ways."

I told him I was concerned about sticking with the program after the surgery, that I still might want to eat my way through my problems.

"People who go through this operation don't usually challenge the limits of it," he said. "Because of the extreme nature of this intervention, people tend to be fairly respectful of it. In the early stages of recovery, you have to be very careful. But certainly as you become more acclimated and comfortable with it, you'll become more relaxed, and there will be a natural tendency to relax some of the limits that the follow-up program sets. Later down the road, we'll have to watch what you do and see if you're tempted to stretch it a little bit too much. But I'm optimistic that this won't be a problem," he said.

Marc prepared two tapes for me—one for pre-operative preparation, and the other for post-operative recuperation so that I could heal quickly. I wanted to heal fast, and I told myself that I needed to be mentally prepared to make that happen. Having these tools gave me real comfort, and I began to use them to get ready.

But what really put the cap on it for me was my dad. He was incredibly upbeat about the surgery because he was so scared about my health. He told me that he cried every day worrying about me. "You know I love you, and I don't want you to die," he said. "You have to do this surgery. You've got to do it. This is going to change your whole life," he said. "You'll be able to get up onstage and be proud—proud of your body, proud of the way you look. This is the greatest thing I've ever heard of." He even made a little video at the piano where he sang a couple lines from his song "Don't Worry, Baby."

"Don't worry, Carnie," he sang. "Everything will be all right."

He pleaded, "Please, please do it for me. If not for yourself, then do it for me."

Having that validation from my dad had a huge impact on me. When I heard that from him and I felt that from him, I knew that I had to do it.

So I was determined to go forward. Every single day I kept saying to myself, "You're doing the right thing. You're brave. You can do it. Keep it together. You know you've got the support. You've got the best doctor. Everybody's pulling for you. This is going to be the best."

I kept myself very, very positive. I would get together with my therapist, and we would do hypnosis with positive affirmations about how wonderful this experience was going to be, how helpful and lifesaving and life-changing this metamorphosis was, and change was good.

My mind was at ease about the operation itself, but I was still concerned about the recovery. So I went to San Diego to meet Leslie Jester, a nurse on Dr. Wittgrove's team, and I started to do a lot of the pre-op work with her.

Leslie is one of my favorite people. She's one of the most energized, positive, real, and wonderful people that I've ever met. She had weight-loss surgery herself, and when I went to the office for my blood work and glucose tests, I was blown away because all of the women who work there have had the surgery.

I met Queenie, who had lost 100 pounds. Pam showed me her pictures, and Leslie showed me hers. Aimee Johnston, who runs the whole program for the weight-loss center, also had the surgery, and I was just knocked out that everyone was so jazzed. Everybody had so much energy.

I think a lot of gastric bypass patients seem wound up like little dolls. They've spent so many years dragged down by their fucking weight that they feel physically and mentally like they've been set free from a cage.

Leslie is very serious about her work, and she's very confident. She knows exactly what she's talking about, and every single thing she told me came true—how I was going to feel, how much weight I was going to lose, how fast it would be, what it was going be like physically and emotionally losing the weight. Leslie was my guide through the entire process, and I'm very grateful to her.

What I also liked about Leslie is that she didn't kiss my ass. None of the people in the office did. That's what I loved about everyone there. They were all so real. They didn't treat me any different from anybody else, and that was just what I wanted. They helped me get ready, and as the days got closer, I was very calm.

My mom was still freaked about the operation, but after Jonathan Sackier explained to her exactly what was going to be done, she felt a little more at ease—and that made me feel better.

I was preparing to be really mellow, mentally saying to myself, "For the next month—or at least the next ten days—you don't know how you're going to feel. You know you're going to be a little bit sore." But I had no feelings of uncertainty.

I was totally confident going into it, thinking to myself, *Yes, yes, yes. I'm doing it. This is going to be the best. Keep that positive feeling going.*

Each night at bedtime, I did my pre-operative hypnosis with the tape. The words of encouragement calmed my nerves and helped me sleep really well. The nurses all told me that people who went into the operation with a big smile and a good attitude were the ones who came out the best and healed the fastest. I was determined to make myself one of those people.

I have a low tolerance for pain. I fear death. I fear being uncomfortable. I want to be healthy, and I wanted to do whatever I could to make everything as easy as possible for myself. So I listened very carefully to everything the doctors and nurses said, and I really tried to follow all their rules, because that was the best way to maximize my chances of doing well.

I wasn't smoking marijuana or drinking alcohol. I was trying to keep myself very clean that way. I followed the directions very carefully, taking my vitamins and drinking my water. Two weeks prior to surgery, I stopped taking Advil.

They gave me a breathing apparatus to strengthen my lungs before the surgery. Because they operate near your left lung, it partially collapses during the procedure, so you have to get it working again or there's a chance you'll develop pneumonia.

The breathing exerciser was kind of like a bong in reverse. You blow into a flexible tube that's connected to a plastic cylinder with a little ball in it. The harder you blow, the higher your air moves the ball up the cylinder. There are numbers on the side to gauge how well you're doing.

I won't make any of my usual jokes here about blow jobs, because I took this preparation very seriously. I'm a singer, and I need to take care of my lungs.

In the weeks leading up to surgery, I blew into that tube like a wind machine, because I wanted to cut my chances of pneumonia down to zero.

My mind-set was very focused, but I had one major distraction—food. Big surprise. In the last week before the surgery, I didn't know whether to eat my fucking heart out or not. I was sort of feeling like this was my last chance to pork out. So I'd go to Burger King and get the Double Whopper with the double bacon and double cheese and the fries and onion rings and a shake, all in one sitting. Believe it or not, this was not overeating for me at this stage.

I basically ate whatever I wanted. I'd have desserts, but I didn't go crazy. Actually, I was trying to lose a little weight because Dr. Wittgrove and Dr. Sackier told me that would be better for my heart. I was taking slow walks on the treadmill, thinking that if I got my heart pumping a little bit, maybe I'd do better on that table. Maybe my heart wouldn't be shocked by the anesthesia. Or maybe my circulation would be stronger so I wouldn't get a clot in my leg. That was my main concern.

DRIVING DOWN TO SAN DIEGO with Wendy, Dee Dee, and Mom, we had the car packed. It kind of reminded me of the trips to fat camp, only this time everyone was going. Leslie had told me, "Bring really loose sweat pants and big T-shirts and big robes. Be comfortable, because you're going to be in San Diego for ten days."

Spotlight Health got us a suite at the Marriott with three adjoining rooms. It was incredibly luxurious, and I know that most people don't get this kind of treatment.

I was starting to feel the pressure of the media. There

were a lot of cameras and reporters asking, "How do you feel? Are you scared?" And I felt like saying, "Fuck you, of course I'm scared. How the fuck would you feel?"

I was scared—and annoyed. But I knew what I'd gotten myself into. I had to be open. I had to talk about it because I'd made that commitment. So I was willing to do the media thing. But at some point, I said to Mickey, "No more cameras. I'm done."

It was my time to center myself.

The night before surgery, I was pretty scared. I spent quite a while in my mother's arms, hugging her, and she was very loving.

I didn't want Rob to be with me because I was embarrassed to have him see me that way. If he had been there, all my attention would have been directed toward him, and I felt like I needed to really focus on myself and be with my family. I wanted to wait a couple of weeks before I saw Rob.

I did a lot of meditation that night and a lot of praying. I asked God to take care of me and to let me survive the operation. I was on the Internet speaking with people in the support group. I was making postings. I was doing interviews. And I was feeling very spiritual, calm, centered, focused, encouraged, and brave.

And very ready.

When I got up the next morning, something very peculiar happened to me. When it was time to go, I went out on the balcony, and I was looking out over the skyline of San Diego toward the ocean. It was a beautiful morning. I took some deep breaths and said to myself, "Take it all in right now. Breathe the air. Feel the body. Take in the air. And when you breathe in, take in beautiful, positive thoughts about strength and being strong. Then breathe out all the negative thoughts."

At that moment, a bee flew up to me.

Normally, I'm terrified of bees. But the bee came right up

to my face, and for some reason, I wasn't afraid. I just stood there, very still, looking at this bee suspended in the air. And it seemed like the bee was looking right back at me.

Immediately, my mind was filled with images of my Uncle Carl, who had died of cancer the year before. He was the sweetest man I've ever known, and at that moment, I could feel his love surrounding me. Maybe I'm nuts, or it sounds stupid, but I thought that bee was him. I thought, *He's telling me I'm going to be okay.* And I was filled with this deep sense of calmness.

And then the bee was gone.

Then like a soldier, I walked downstairs, and it was like, "Here we go."

IT WAS A SHORT DRIVE TO THE HOSPITAL, but it seemed like time was warping. The blood was rushing through my head, and I could hear it in my ears. I could feel myself breathing, but the sensation was weird, like I was disconnected from my body. I blocked everything out, trying to keep my focus.

When we got there, the cameras were on me as soon as I stepped out of the car.

I was feeling like, "Okay, I'm not really digging the cameras being on me right now, but they have to be here. I'm sharing this."

I walked with Mickey and the Spotlight people down the driveway. The sun was shining in my eyes, and the video crews were crowding around, walking backwards, the reporters holding out their microphones, asking questions, trying to get a sound bite.

But there was nothing to say. This was it.

We walked up the stairs and into the building, down the hall, into the elevator, up to the second floor, and into the pre-op room. There was a video crew following us, and a still photographer and some other people, but I wasn't paying attention to them.

"No more cameras," I said. And suddenly I was absolutely terrified.

My mother was there with her fiancé, Daniel; and Wendy, Dee Dee, and Karen Metzfield. Karen gave me a little keepsake photo album for pictures of the "new me" when I lost weight. But the pages in the album were empty when she handed it to me, and it hit me that I had no idea what my future would bring.

I broke down, sobbing, very afraid. My mom put her arms around me and said, "It's okay, baby, it's okay. You're gonna be okay."

I cried, "I'm scared. I'm so scared."

Tears were streaming down my cheeks as they shaved my stomach and put these compression stockings on me that pump your legs to improve the circulation. It was very scary, and I was crying hard.

They started me on a small IV, and I began to feel better. Then, out of nowhere, I heard this small voice from inside me saying, "What are you worried about? You're going to be fine."

And I just said, "Fuck it, man. I'm done. I'm done crying. I'm done being scared. I'm gonna do great. Here we go. Welcome to my new life. Here we fucking go, man."

And they wheeled me out the door.

The feelings were overwhelming. I was flat on my back on the gurney, rolling down the hall in my little nightgown, feeling awesome. There was a whoosh of automatic doors, and in a few moments, I was in the operating room.

The whole team was there, in their scrubs and masks, ready to go. I was feeling very calm and loving. I looked up at the anesthesiologist, and he had these beautiful blue eyes.

"I know you're going to watch me," I said, "and do a good job."

"Don't you worry," he said. "My eyes will be on you the whole time. You're going to be just fine. Would you like me to give you something more to calm your nerves?"

I said, "Fuck yes."

Almost instantly, I felt so good. I was really loose and high, and all I wanted to do was sing. I started singing "Kentucky Rain," one of my favorite Elvis songs. I remember wanting Wendy to harmonize with me.

I was feeling all this love, and I wanted to kiss everyone—the nurse, even the reporter from *People* magazine. I made them all kiss me. Everybody had to kiss me.

"No, you can't kiss me on the cheek," I said. "You gotta kiss me on the lips."

And I wanted to get everyone's love, as much love as I could.

Then Dr. Wittgrove came in.

"Come here," I said, feeling higher than a kite and very giggly. "I just have one question to ask you."

"What's that?" he asked.

"I just wanna know, will I be able to swallow semen?"

He looked at me with this twinkle in his eyes, and even though he was wearing a surgical mask, I could tell he was smiling. "You know, you're the first person who's ever asked me that. I'm going to leave that up to you."

We laughed together.

And then I went out.

I CAN'T RECALL DREAMING DURING THE OPERATION. But I remember a vision from my sessions with Lisa Roth.

"How do you see yourself?" she would ask.

And I imagined myself running through a field of yellow poppies, kind of like the Wizard of Oz, wearing a short-sleeved white T-shirt and 501 jeans. My arms were bare, and the fat was gone, and the jeans fit like a soft glove on my slender body.

It wasn't so much the clothes or the situation—it was the feeling inside that I remember most. I was strong and alive and light as a feather, so healthy, so happy, so free.

I remember looking at a model in a magazine in a black sleeveless dress and thinking about the way it clung to her body, how you could see the contours of her kneecaps and her collarbones through her skin. And I dreamed that one day I was going to wear that dress, and how much better I was going to feel when I was thin.

I also dreamed about making love to Rob, feeling like a sex kitten, totally uninhibited, and not afraid that I was going to crush him.

Chapter Eleven

Getting Down

Even though I wanted to share my surgery with the world by streaming the operation over the Internet, I wasn't comfortable having my guts on the screen. I thought I was being open enough by letting the world go through the procedure with me live, knowing that I was in there, that it was happening, how I was progressing, what I was doing, who I was doing it with, and what type of procedure I was having done.

But for some reason, I did not want my guts to be shown. Everyone kept saying, "Well, guts are guts. Everyone looks the same inside." But I just felt like it was too much to be revealed.

After the operation, some people criticized me, because from time to time, when we wanted to show the laparoscopic view of the procedure, we used a videotape of another operation that was exactly synchronized with mine. We didn't keep it a secret or try to deceive anyone. Dr. Sackier explained exactly what we were doing at the top of the Spotlight Health Webcast and several times throughout the program.

But I really don't care if a few people were disappointed that they didn't get to see my stomach or my spleen or my intestines. Just the fact that I was letting everybody know that I was doing it, when I was doing it, and everything about it—before, during, and after—was enough.

I brought the gastric bypass procedure to the attention of millions of people. That was the idea. I showed my guts in a different way.

IT ACTUALLY TOOK ME LONGER TO COME OUT of anesthesia than everybody anticipated. I think it was more than an hour before I came to after the surgery. I've always feared not waking up, so I was nervous when they told me that, but happy that I'd made it through.

Mom had called Rob during the surgery and told him that I was okay. She called my dad and everybody else in the family who wanted to know.

I had all these tubes hooked up to me—a little pulse monitor on my right middle finger, a tube going down my throat, and a tube up my nose. I had a catheter in my bladder and tubes to drain the fluids from my body. And while some were going out, there were IV fluids going in, and tight compression stockings pumping my legs over and over and over to keep any blood clots from forming.

Even though my ass was numb, the hospital bed had a mattress that seemed like it was only an inch thick. I was really uncomfortable, but not for long.

The first day, they keep you on morphine in case you experience some pain. After all, they've cut six small holes in your torso, pumped you full of gas and fluids, cut up and rearranged your organs, stapled and sutured everything together, and stitched up all the incisions. So obviously you'd expect some pain after major surgery like that.

But I really wasn't feeling pain. I was just very out of it, groggy, in and out of consciousness, and sore. Of course, Mom and Wendy were there, and Dr. Wittgrove and Dr. Sackier came to visit. But I wasn't into talking, which is really rare.

I was trying to do as little as possible.

The soreness in my abdomen was what I was feeling most, especially when I tried to move. I had a wonderful nurse named Rosemary who told me to pretend that everything was happening in slow motion, and that's what I did. Dr. Wittgrove had mentioned earlier that many nurses don't want to work with gastric bypass patients because we're too heavy to move around or just too much trouble. Bariatric nurses like Rosemary are very special and extremely attentive. They're always ready to help you whenever you need it. And you *do* need help, believe me.

I had told myself before the operation, "Okay, you're going to be really excited after this surgery, and you're going to want to recover really quickly and get back to work." But after the procedure, it was, "Whoa, slow down. You want to heal. You don't want to rip your sutures or pull out those staples inside."

I would say, "Oh, Rosemary, my butt hurts. I feel numb. I've got to turn over." But I couldn't. I was so tubed and wired up, I didn't dare move. I've always slept on my stomach, so the challenge was getting used to sleeping on my back. Of course, the first day, it wasn't too much of a problem. I could give myself a dose of morphine anytime I needed it just by pushing this little button on my personal anesthesia machine. You bet your ass I was pushing that thing as often as I could.

You're warned that the first ten days after surgery are really critical. That's when infections can set in, especially in your lungs. Blood clots called pulmonary embolisms can also form if you don't get your breathing going. These can cause you some serious problems, but they minimize the odds by giving you blood-thinning medication before and after surgery

As I lay there hooked up to all these machines, listening to the constant beeping and clicking, I was very aware of the risk factor, and it was kind of scary. But I'd done my best to get ready, so what else could I do?

Wendy was totally freaked out by all the tubes. When my IV fluids would run out or it was time to check the oxygen levels in my body, an alarm would go off on one machine or another. Wendy would just completely flip out and go, "What's wrong? Is she okay? Is something happening?"

Rosemary would come in saying, "No, no, no. Everything's fine." She'd take the readings and reset the machine or hook up a new bag, and we'd be back to the clicks and beeps that were starting to drive me nuts.

In the pre-op sessions where they prepare you for recovery, they tell you how important it is to get the patient up and walking as soon as possible after surgery. "You're going to have to walk on the first day," they say. "You're going to be on your feet, and you're going to be walking."

It seems like a reasonable idea at the time, but after the operation when Rosemary came to get me up, it was a different story. "Are you crazy?" I said. "I can't get up. I'm too tired, I can barely keep my eyes open, and I'm so stiff." Even going to the bathroom was unthinkable. I had the catheter in, so I was peeing in a bag, but I wasn't eating, so fortunately there was nothing coming out the other end.

Even though I was hooked up to all these things, Rosemary said, "All right, it's time. Get out of bed. Let's go." She was like this little drill sergeant, and there was no way I was getting any slack.

She helped me get up, and I don't think I've ever felt so sore. It was like someone had whacked me in the stomach with a baseball bat. I was hunched over like a little old grandmother, and I found it very difficult to stand up straight. "Just take it really slow," Rosemary said. "Walk very slowly." I wasn't going to argue, because I didn't want to move at all, but I shuffled along as best I could.

We walked down the hall and back to my room, and that

wiped me out. I was ready for a nap. Every time we did it, we went a little farther, and eventually I made it all the way around the floor, sometimes with Rosemary or another great nurse named Ralph. They were both very patient and accommodating, and I felt extremely well cared for.

When the catheter came out, it was a huge relief, and when they took the oxygen tube out of my throat, I felt so much better. But after 24 hours, I started to itch all over my body. I think it was a reaction to the morphine.

I actually hated the feeling of being on the stuff, so I switched to Tylenol with codeine, but I didn't like that either. It gave me headaches and made me constipated, which didn't help at all. They want you to have a bowel movement while you're in the hospital because the anesthetic shuts down your colon during the surgery, and it's important to get your elimination working again as soon as possible.

I was so damn thirsty after the surgery, and my throat was so dry with this tube going down it into my lungs. At first they'd only let me suck on ice chips. Then eventually I started to sip water. They told me that the more water I could drink, the faster I'd heal, so I went for it more and more as time passed.

Every few hours, I'd feel a little bit better, and I'd sit up in the chair for a while. That's where I was when they brought in my first meal—a little cup of chicken broth and some Jell-O. It was exciting and frightening all wrapped up into one, because I knew that my new tummy pouch was tiny, and the opening into it was very small—about the size of the hole in a toothpaste tube. So naturally I was scared to chew anything and swallow it. I wanted to be sure that my body was going to respond well.

Eating was like an experiment. I took a small sip of hot broth, and it felt really good going down. I waited for a moment to see how my stomach was reacting, and everything was fine. The next sip tasted so flavorful and delicious that this warm, cozy feeling spread all over me. It was great.

Then I had some Jell-O. Jell-O has sugar in it, and sugar is something gastric bypass patients want to avoid because it makes you "dump" (when too much sugar is "dumped" into your small intestine). But right after surgery, your glucose levels are so low that they want you to eat some sugar. For some reason, you don't dump like you will if you eat sugar later.

I took the tiniest little bite—it must have been a quarter or an eighth of a teaspoon—and I chewed it and let it melt in my mouth before I swallowed it. That Jell-O tasted like the best dessert I'd ever had in my life. I was thrilled that my body was handling it and that I wasn't throwing up or feeling sick. Everything was working so well.

I took maybe three little bites of Jell-O and about five little sips of broth, and I felt full. Then I put my spoon down, just like Rosemary and Leslie had told me to do. "As soon as you start to feel satisfied, stop," they said. "Put your fork or your spoon down, and stop."

I stopped. I felt satisfied. I was done.

It was the most incredible sensation. And I took that with me for the next six months. As soon as I started to feel satisfied, I stopped. I never, ever pushed it. But at that moment, it was just great to know so far so good.

But the rest of the routine was getting on my nerves. They were checking my blood pressure every half hour, and the stockings were pumping and squeezing my legs so tight. I couldn't get comfortable no matter what I did, and there was always something going on that kept me from getting any rest.

The tabloids kept trying to sneak up the stairs to get in my room and snap a picture. They'd abused me so often that I wasn't surprised they'd want to invade my privacy when I was helpless in the hospital. We had to keep a security guard outside the door the whole time I was there. I just wanted to vomit all over those disgusting rags.

I was like, "Get me out of here. Get me off these machines. I just want to go home and heal." So little by little, they removed the tubes, and then my stitches. Finally, after two nights in the hospital, they told me I could be discharged. But I wasn't ready to go.

I was still feeling very sore and bone-tired, and I didn't really have the energy to face the move. Plus, I felt very safe being looked after by the physicians and nurses. It's not that I didn't trust Mom, Wendy, and Dee Dee, who were going to take care of me at a hotel nearby for the next eight days, I just needed an extra day in the hospital, and I was fortunate that I could stay.

For the final night, we rented a recliner and had it brought to my room. I'd given up on trying to get comfortable lying flat, so I slept in the chair, and it was the best rest I got since the surgery.

When I was discharged the next morning, Rosemary wheeled me out in my little white terrycloth grandma gown. I said good-bye to her, got into Mom's car, and we rode over to the Marriott.

It was the same trip I'd made only a few days before, only this time in reverse. But the feeling was so different. On the way over, it had been like in the movies when suddenly you don't hear any sound, and things are moving at strange speeds, and you're so deep inside yourself that nothing else can get in.

Now, even though I was on painkillers, I was sensing everything—the warmth of the sun, the smell of the breeze off the ocean, the sounds of the cars on the freeway.

I still felt like I'd been hit by a truck, but I knew my life was moving in a different direction, and there was no looking back.

My body was aching, and I was still the size of a small house, but it seemed like the world was so much bigger now, so wide open. I wasn't hungry. I wasn't desperate. I was in a whole new mode.

I didn't feel like dancing or jumping for joy, and I wasn't ready yet for that field of poppies. I just wanted to get to my room and lie down, to make it through the days ahead, to start feeling normal—whatever that meant—and to get on with my new life.

But life at the hotel was a continuation of the never-ending struggle to get comfortable. I'd hoped that a big soft bed would make it easier, but even with 14 pillows between me and the mattress, I couldn't fall asleep on my back. No matter what adjustments Mom would make, nothing worked for very long, and I was very irritable. Thank God we brought the recliner along, because it was my only relief. I could get a couple hours' sleep in the chair until the soreness would come back, and then I'd hit the Tylenol and codeine again.

Next, I got my period, which really sucked. My mom, bless her heart, took care of me in the bathroom like a born nurse. She slept on the couch in the room right nearby, because I took up the whole goddamn king-size bed with all my pillows and my big butt.

She never got a good night's sleep because I was always calling her to shift a pillow for me this way or that. I was bitchy, short, and snappy—but she never complained. She was amazing, and I could never thank her enough for everything she did. She's truly a saint.

I was so relieved that the surgery was over. "Thank God I made it," I kept saying to myself. "I did it. I'm on the road to recovery." And every night I would listen to my healing hypnosis tape and fall asleep with this beautiful, peaceful feeling.

Meanwhile, the post-surgery menu was getting pretty old. We had this big dining room table in our room at the hotel, and Mom and I would sit across from each other at mealtimes. Five or six days into this ordeal, she ordered a big salad with pieces of broiled chicken.

"Oh," I said, "I can't wait to eat that. It looks so good. How is it?"

"Oh, it's good," she said. "But it's not that good," trying to make me feel better.

I was staring at my 18th meal in a row of broth and Jell-O. I was just about ready to go insane. I took my spoon, looked at her with a face filled with disgust, and said, "Bone appa-fucking-teet."

We started laughing so hard, we cried. My mom didn't stop laughing for three days. At night, when I was in bed, I'd hear her suddenly giggling hysterically in the next room. It was so contagious, I couldn't stop myself from laughing, too—which was a bitch, because when you've got six incisions in your stomach muscles, laughter hurts like hell.

On the seventh day after surgery, I went to a meeting at the hospital about what to expect physically during the next phase of recovery. The class included instruction about the exercises we needed to do to keep our circulation going.

It wasn't exactly aerobics. We'd circle our ankles to get the blood flowing and lift our arms very slowly—no fast or jarring movements—taking it very easy because we didn't want to rip the stitches.

We also learned what our new eating regimen was going to be like. After seven days of water, broth, and Jell-O, we were moving on to solid food—a hard-boiled egg.

I'll probably never eat Jell-O again as long as I live. After 21 meals in a row of the stuff, it's hard to get excited about lime instead of cherry. It doesn't matter what flavor it is— lemon, strawberry, watermelon, or kumquat. It's Jell-O, and you're sick of it.

But that first little hard-boiled egg and piece of toast with butter was like a Thanksgiving dinner. Nothing ever tasted so good. It was just so delicious that I had to take a picture of it to commemorate it for all time.

I ate maybe four or five itty, bitty bites of egg yolk and a tiny taste of the egg white, maybe two or three very small bites of toast, and I was full. And of course, I stopped. I didn't feel hungry. I didn't feel deprived. I felt totally satisfied—and I was shocked and amazed. It just blew my mind. I couldn't get over it.

I remembered eating a Big Mac, super-size fries, a milk-shake, onion rings, and all that stuff in one meal, and feeling stuffed like I was going to vomit. Then there'd be extreme feelings of guilt and shame.

Now after these few bites of an egg and a piece of toast, I felt proud and stoked and very relieved. Dr. Wittgrove had done a great job with the surgery. No problems, no complications. It was perfect, and I was on the road to health. It was the best.

The next day, I had the cutest piece of salmon I've ever seen in my life. It was about the size of a peppermint patty, grilled plain with just a little salt and pepper. I probably ate about half an ounce, and it was a delicacy beyond belief. My mouth's watering right now as I think of it.

I was determined to get my fluids and take four to six little walks every day, because I knew that the more I walked and the more I drank, the faster I would heal. So I'd fill up on water, get up out of the chair very slowly, and walk at a snail's pace down the hall and back to the room—and I'd be exhausted. I don't ever remember feeling so tired. But I just kept listening to what my body told me, and I rested and slept as much as I could.

Everything seemed to be going well, except for one thing. A few days after they took the drainage tube out of the larger incision on my left side, I started to notice some redness and swelling. I was tender there, and it was kind of hard when I pressed on that one spot.

I asked Leslie what it was, and she told me it was probably a seroma.

"A seroma?" I said. "What the hell is that? What's wrong with me? Is this a complication?"

"No," she said. "It's not a complication. It's just an annoyance that happens to a few patients when a small amount of bacteria gets into the wound and causes an infection." It was a pocket of pus under the incision, and it sounded disgusting. But when she told me I'd have to have it opened up to drain the pus out, I was so pissed off I almost lost it.

Goddammit, I thought. *Why does this have to happen? Why do I have to go through this?*

Leslie had to take an orange stick and reopen the wound every time we had to drain it. She would insert the stick about three to four inches, poke around the pocket, and push out the pus and the blood. It smelled like hell—like rotting, decaying flesh—and it had to be drained two or three times a day for a week straight.

This was probably the worst thing about the whole surgery experience. It's at the top of the list, and I'm a baby, but it was awful. I'd be crying so hard before we even started that Leslie would give me novocaine shots in the wound to numb the pain, and that would help a lot. But Dr. Wittgrove took a look at it once and just opened it right up and poked the stick in before I could say anything. This guy is used to working on someone who's under anesthesia, but I was in total agony.

I started thinking, *God, what's wrong with me? Everyone in my group seems to be healing faster than I am. I've got a seroma. I'm hunched over, and I'm walking like a 105-year-old.*

Then I told myself, "We all heal at our own pace. Don't be so hard on yourself. You're healing the way you're supposed to, and you're doing everything right, everything you can. Just know that God's going to take care of you, and you're going to heal."

So eventually, after ten days of going back and forth from the hotel to the hospital, that ordeal was over, and it was time to go home. "I'm so proud of you, baby," said my mom. "You're doing so well."

I had already lost almost 20 pounds, but my weight had actually gone up on the day after surgery.

Prior to the operation, I was nervous and I didn't eat much. So I'd gone down from my peak of 298 to about 290 when I went into the hospital. But when I got on the scale the day after the procedure, I weighed 304.

"What the hell?" I said. "I just had weight-loss surgery and I gained 14 pounds?"

"It's normal," Rosemary told me. "When you have the gastric bypass laparoscopically, they have to pump your body full of fluids. So, you're retaining a lot of water."

By the third day after the operation, 7 of those pounds had come off, then 10, then 15. After two weeks, I had lost 20 pounds. It was really quick, and I loved it.

I never once regretted having the surgery—even in my most uncomfortable moments with the seroma or the soreness. I never regretted it for a second. I told myself that everything was in Divine order, and everything was happening the way it was supposed to be. God was testing my patience, my endurance, and my strength—and the test was far from over.

At home, I weighed myself every day even though they told me not to. Some people can get discouraged if they see their weight fluctuate. They can lose their confidence in the program and go back to the wrong habits, but I was obsessed with the scale. Every time I'd get on it, it was moving in the left direction. I was blown away, because throughout my entire life I'd watched the needle go the other way. Now, every day another pound was gone.

I was completely committed to the four rules of the follow-up program:

1. Eat protein first.
2. Drink plenty of water.
3. Don't snack between meals.
4. Get regular daily exercise.

There's actually a fifth rule, too: Take your vitamins. Your body won't get enough nutrients from the reduced amounts of food you eat because of your smaller stomach, so you need vitamin and mineral supplements to stay healthy. I found that it was best to take them with meals, because on an empty stomach, they can make you feel queasy.

I drank tons of water—probably 70 ounces a day. And every time I'd pee, which was often, I'd get this great feeling knowing that the fat was flowing out of my body and down the toilet.

I'm not going to lie. Sometimes I'd snack between meals on a little bit of cottage cheese or string cheese. But most of the time, I wasn't hungry, and I wasn't craving all the fats and sugars that used to drive me crazy.

As for exercise, every day I tried to do a little bit more. I was still very tired, but I wanted to get moving. I got bored just watching television, doing the circulation exercises, and walking around the house. So as soon as I could, I started going to the market, or I just walked around outside for half an hour. I was still moving very slowly, but I could feel my strength increasing. And the pounds kept coming off.

One of my first meals outside the hospital and the hotel was at Taco Bell. The staff recommended the Bell's refried beans as a really good source of protein. They re-fry their beans in water, and a lot of their patients found that the beans went down smoothly. So I tried it, and it was great—just a few bites, maybe a quarter of a cup with a side order of chicken cut up into really small pieces. I felt perfectly fine, and I stopped when I felt satisfied.

But it was also at Taco Bell where I had my first experience with "dumping." As I mentioned earlier, dumping happens when too much sugar is "dumped" into the small intestine. The body reacts by producing a surplus of insulin, which makes you feel really ill.

I went to Taco Bell one day for the refried beans and decided to order them with cheese. *I'm allowed to have cheese*, I thought. *It's good protein.* But the cheese at Taco Bell must have had sugar in it, because as soon as I ate it, I felt this nauseous sensation. My heart started racing, I was sweating, and I felt very nervous and anxious for about 20 minutes—and then the feeling passed.

"So that's dumping," I said to myself. I knew what it was because I'd heard the doctors and so many bypass patients describe it. But I'd wondered what it would feel like for me, and now I knew. It was intense, and I didn't want to go through it again. So from that day on, I've been on the lookout for sugar in any food I eat. Just a little is okay, but too much and it's definitely bad news. Dumping is no fun. (I never actually tasted a Krispy Kreme donut until after the surgery. I had a little tiny bite and nearly shit in my pants, it was so good. But I knew that such delicacies weren't for me anymore.)

IN OCTOBER, JUST TWO MONTHS AFTER THE SURGERY, we went to Napa Valley for Wendy's 30th birthday. We stayed at a charming bed and breakfast and toured the local wineries there, which are some of the best in the world. I was afraid to drink the wine because I knew it was wrong for me. First of all, wine is loaded with sugar. And when your stomach size has been greatly reduced, your body absorbs the alcohol so quickly that you can get a toxic reaction.

But this was a special event, so I'd take a sip of the wine and then spit it out. What's classic is that you're supposed to do that anyway when you're tasting wines. They actually have these little spit bowls in the tasting rooms so you can try a variety of different wines and not get too loaded.

Of course, everyone else on the trip wanted to get a buzz going, so they were drinking theirs down. But even without the buzz, it was lots of fun for me, and I loved seeing Wendy having such a great time.

At this point I was very committed to my dietary rules, and I'd learned that if I wanted to experiment with food, it had to be one bite at a time. Then I'd wait sometimes as long as ten minutes to see how I'd feel. I wouldn't make the mistake of trying to eat a whole hamburger, bun and all. I'd eat the meat—protein first!—but never if it was fried. Maybe I'd have a little part of the bun, and that would be it.

But my discipline was constantly being tested during this trip. For dinner one night, we went to a restaurant called Mustard's, which was simply fabulous. Everybody's meal was incredibly delicious, and for dessert they brought out this banana cheesecake with a graham cracker crust, covered with a caramel sauce.

I thought I was going to fucking fall over.

I took a bite, and I just closed my eyes, and I chewed as slowly as I could. The temperature in my mouth melted it instantly, and I was pissed because I wanted the flavor to last forever. But I put my head back and told myself, "Okay, this is probably the best thing you've ever tasted, and you're very lucky to be eating just one bite. Enjoy it, because this is it. You're not going to push it. You're not going to have another bite. This is all you're going to get."

Part of me felt sorry for myself. Everybody else could have a whole piece, but I had to stop. But there was another part of me that was really proud because I had the willpower to say no. And I knew I really didn't want it for all the right reasons.

I tasted it, it tasted great, and that's all I needed. I told myself, "This is going to be my new mentality. This is going to be my new approach. Take a taste, and that's all you need."

Throughout my whole life, I'd never deprived myself of anything that I wanted, and I still don't have to. I can enjoy the finest quality foods in the world. It's just with the quantity that I have to set boundaries.

After I had lost about 50 or 60 pounds, I began to notice some hair coming out in the shower as I shampooed—and I got scared. I've always loved my hair. Even when I was at my fattest, I could look at my hair and know it was beautiful. It was thick and healthy with this gorgeous sheen, and I've always been proud of it no matter how I wore it or colored it.

Now it was going down the drain.

I called Leslie. "What's going on?" I asked. "The hair loss is starting."

You don't have to talk to very many gastric bypass patients or read more than a couple of Internet postings to know that hair loss happens to many people who have the surgery. But I'd hoped that I could avoid it, like the other complications and side effects that had passed me by.

"Are you eating your protein?" Leslie asked me.

"Of course I am," I said.

"Well, the more protein you eat," she said, "the less hair you'll lose."

So I focused on eating more protein, and I tried not to worry about my hair, because I began to notice other things that were so positive. I was losing all this weight and feeling so much better. Walking was easier because there was a lot less pressure on my feet. Getting in and out the car or a chair took much less effort getting up and down. And I was really getting off on these changes.

I was going down in pants sizes so fast I couldn't believe it. One week I was size 24, and then I was a size 22, and then a 20. I'm thinking, *Oh my God, I'm almost in the teens. I'm going to be a size 18 soon!* I couldn't remember the last time I'd worn an 18, so I was really overjoyed.

But I began to notice that I was hungry for more food. At first I started to crave a little something tasty in between meals—like peanut butter. I knew that it was a good source of protein, so a spoonful of sugar-free peanut butter became one of my vices. But it didn't completely satisfy my hunger. I was definitely feeling the need to eat a larger amount of food, and I was concerned.

"What's the matter?" I asked Leslie. "Why do I want to eat more? Is my stomach stretching out? Is it getting bigger? Does this mean I'm going to slow down or stop losing weight?"

"It's normal and it's healthy," she said. "Your stomach is actually becoming more comfortable with food. You've always had the room for more, but your tummy was sensitive, like a little baby's."

So it was okay for me to increase the amount of food I was eating, but it had to be done gradually. For breakfast I might cook an egg and roll it up with a bit of cheese in half a tortilla, then heat it in the microwave. I'd always eat the egg first, and most of the time I wouldn't finish the rest.

I found myself looking at carbs as taboo, and I'd say to myself, "You don't want that. Don't think about bread. Don't think about pasta or rice or potatoes. Think about protein."

Everyday on the Internet I'd compare notes with other patients. "How are you doing? How much have you lost? How do you feel?"

People would say, "I'm throwing up a lot," or "I can't keep chicken down," or "Steak makes me sick." But I was eager to try different foods, and I was craving protein like crazy. I just wanted beef, turkey, chicken, fish—and nothing made me sick. My senses had become so heightened that everything was smelling and tasting fabulous.

Food was tantalizing to me again, but there was a difference this time. I didn't have the obsessive drive like I did before to eat as much as I could and just shove it all in. Now I couldn't wait to eat, because I knew I was going to enjoy the flavor so much. And I knew that when I ate just a few bites, that would be enough, and I was going to feel great.

It was fantastic.

I really wanted to try sushi because it's always been one of my favorites. It's very clean food, a good source of protein, and Rob and I really enjoy it. So about six weeks out of the hospital, we went to have some. After five small pieces, I was sick. I didn't throw up, but I was so full it was extremely uncomfortable. It was my first post-surgery experience with overeating, and I really learned my lesson. You have to take it very slowly.

I had another experience with a certain food that really shook me up—Alaskan king crab legs. Leslie had recommended them. "Get some crab legs," she said, "dip them in butter, and enjoy." Just imagining the flavor got me so wound up I couldn't wait to try it.

I bought these gorgeous crab legs at the market and went over to Owen's. I was going nuts thinking about them while they were cooking, and when they were ready, I was so thrilled that I took too big a bite and didn't chew the food enough. With my small pouch and its narrow opening, I'm supposed to take little baby bites and then chew everything completely before I swallow.

But I didn't. When I swallowed the crab, I knew it was too much, because I could feel it lodge and stick in that little hole at the top of my stomach. And for the next ten minutes, it was the weirdest sensation, like there was an alien crawling back up my esophagus. It was moving up and then back down, and then back up again, pushing back and forth because it couldn't fit through the hole. Eventually I got it down, but it scared me so much that I never forget now to take small bites and chew my food thoroughly.

I've never thrown up once. I've never had any food come back up out of my mouth—not ever. That crab was the closest I've come to barfing.

One time I dumped hard after eating some Carbo-lite yogurt with these chocolate chips that were supposed to be sugar-free. It was a tough lesson. I felt really nauseated, but I didn't throw up. I put a cold washcloth on my head and laid down for 20 minutes. It was like cheating on a test and getting caught, and you feel bad about it. But I took the risk of eating too much instead of testing it with just a couple bites.

So I suffered the consequences, and I dealt with them. But the sacrifices I'm making now are so much less substantial, because look at the result. That's what I'm thinking. You can't even compare dumping to bingeing, and the tremendous feelings of guilt that would follow. It was unbelievably overwhelming.

Bingeing would take over my whole being, my whole day, my whole week, every moment. It's so much better to know that I can't overeat anymore. But there are still moments when I *want* to binge. I just want to keep eating. I want to have a bite of this and a bit of that and a bite of that over there. And before I know it, I've had a piece of string cheese, a teaspoon of peanut butter, some beef jerky, a handful of nuts, and all of a sudden, I'm full. I realize that I've just had a meal without thinking.

I WANT TO MAKE SURE THAT PEOPLE KNOW THE DETAILS of my eating history from the time I came out of surgery in August of 1999 all the way up to now. It's not like you eat five peas and you're full, and that's the way it is for the rest of your life. The beauty about this surgery is that you gradually eat more and more until your stomach can hold about two cups, or eight ounces, of food. I guess that's the average. That's what I can hold.

How full I feel depends on what I'm eating. A big plate of salad might look like a lot of volume, but you don't feel so full. Five ounces of swordfish can make you feel really full because it's solid bulk protein. It's interesting how my stomach will react to different foods.

But problems with food have been really few and far

between. The weight kept going down, and my energy level began to skyrocket. My skin cleared up completely, and I began to see the bones and muscles in my body.

Every month we made a new tape at Spotlight Health to document how things were going. We'd shoot me at the gym or eating a healthy lunch, taking a walk or going shopping. Shopping was just sensational. Finally, I could go to stores that never carried clothes in my size when I was big, and it was just so cool getting into things I could only have worn before in my dreams.

Even though fashion has come a long way for big women in recent years, there's still no comparison to what's available in the smaller sizes. Many of the best designers simply don't make clothes for larger women. It's a sad thing, but that's the way it is. As my body morphed into a more fashionable shape, a whole new world of style opened up to me, and I had to resist the temptation to go wild with clothes, especially because I was changing so rapidly.

But one temptation I couldn't resist was sex. Sex has always been great for me, and I've never been inhibited or shy about it. I've always wanted satisfying sex in my life, and I never let my weight stop me. If it was there, I went for it. If it wasn't there, I wasn't totally happy. But it was difficult for me to feel sexy at 300 pounds, and hard for me to believe that many guys would find me sexy when my weight was way up there.

I think I always had confidence with men in general most of the time because I'd just rely on being funny. I found ways to turn them on spiritually and mentally. I could turn them on sexually just by feeling free and being free about my sexuality, no matter what size I was.

I could always say, "Hey, I love pleasure. I love to feel good, and just because I have a big stomach doesn't mean I can't be sexy." Just making love and having sex openly is a beautiful thing—and everyone should experience it. It doesn't matter what you look like. When you love someone, you love them for who they are as a person. That's what you're making love to.

That was a wonderful thing about Rob. He had fallen in love with me when I was the heaviest I had ever been. He saw beyond my weight and connected with me on so many different levels, and I'll always love him for that.

He was a tremendous inspiration to me during this period. Every time we'd see each other, I was down another size or even two, and it was thrilling to see his reaction.

Eventually I moved to Philadelphia to be with him all the time.

Around that time, I wrote this in my journal:

How incredible. Oh boy, I love to fantasize about Robbie and me. The thought of feeling sexy around him makes me happy in my heart. I want to wear black lace for him and make him crazy. I want him to be attracted to my body. I want him to crave me and tell me that. There isn't anything I wouldn't do for him. I'm in love with him. He is so fascinating to me. I've never met anyone like him. There's so much ahead of us.

I know he has a million emotions in his head just like me. We really do make a nice match. I hope he feels the same about me. All I know is that I feel better and better. As I feel better and better, my confidence will improve. I want to feel good about myself. I can't wait to make love with Robbie when I'm thin. Major fucking on the way.

I'm skipping the next part.

Anyway, I'm getting tired. Of course, I'd wind up talking about sex. I can't help it. I'm in love. I'm in love with him and also my new life.

I wrote something really, really interesting. This is sort of personal, but I feel that it's important to read because it's part of how I've been dealing with feelings of insecurity after feeling so vulnerable.

I need to keep a strong reality and identity with myself. It's just that I've never really been, truly been in love until I met him. The thought of him leaving or having him being taken away is such an overwhelming threat. I need to try and stay positive and enjoy our life together.

I'm so grateful for meeting him. He makes me want to be a better person. It will take time, but I will trust him and let him trust me. Love has to be unselfish, not selfish. There needs to be a promise made. I promise myself to trust that he loves me for who I am and that I deserve that love. I accept how he loves me and expect no more than he can give. I will be grateful for every moment we share from now on. I will let him enjoy the feelings he has, whether he thinks someone else is pretty, or if he wants to be by himself. This is the best way I can love him.

It seemed like I got hornier with every pound I lost, and I found myself feeling more and more sexual and just so fabulous. I don't know if it was a release of hormones from the dramatic weight loss or just feeling so good about myself. I was madly in love with Rob, and all I could think about was being with him and having sex.

I remember making love with him for the first time after the surgery and being so excited that I was slimmer and shapelier. I wondered as he put his hand on my waist or my hip if he was turned on or off, and if he would be more excited as I lost more weight. I was eager to see his reaction every time I was with him, and how it would be each new time we'd make love, how it would be in different positions we hadn't tried before, how it would be as we became closer and closer and I felt sexier, more sensual, and set free.

CHAPTER TWELVE

Be My Baby

The one thing that was so beautiful about connecting with Rob is that he's extremely musical. I was very excited by his talent, his musicality, and his performing ability. When I saw him play guitar onstage, I thought I was going to collapse. I felt like a groupie watching the Beatles. I was just blown away, and it turned me on so much that I knew I wanted to marry this adorable guy.

It was so cool that we related on that level. I had never connected with anyone like that—and he hadn't either. This was new for both of us, and it was really fabulous. He was so intelligent, so thoughtful, and so considerate—not to mention that I just think he's the most beautiful man I've ever seen in my life.

We both knew it was getting serious and that we didn't want to live apart any longer; we wanted to share life together. So we started talking about getting married. We weren't in a big hurry, but it seemed like a nice idea to both of us.

On November 15, 1999, we went to dinner at The Ivy, our favorite restaurant in Los Angeles. We were sitting outside, eating pasta with lobster. At one point I excused myself to powder my nose and freshen my lipstick.

When I came back, Rob pulled at his shirt and said, "Honey, this shirt is really weird. Is it screwed up? There are all these strings hanging off it. Look at this string. Can you pull this out?"

I started to pull on it, and the string was really thick and satiny. *God, that's a thick string for this shirt,* I thought. I kept pulling and pulling, and all of the sudden, dangling in front of my eyes was this beautiful engagement ring.

"Oh my God!" I gasped.

"I love you, honey," he said. "Will you marry me?"

I said, "Yes, yes, yes, yes, of course I will."

I was so overwhelmed that I didn't even cry. I was so happy—and so surprised.

I had suspected that he was going to ask me, but not until the next week. I was performing with Al Jardine in Las Vegas at the MGM Grand, and I thought Rob was planning this big engagement party and my whole family was going to be there. But instead, he did it romantically—just the two of us—at my favorite restaurant.

It was so perfect. The people around us were clapping, and I was thinking, *This is just so surreal. I've met the man of my dreams.*

It was like I was swept away, envisioning our life together, our happiness, everything we were going to be sharing, and I was thrilled to be heading toward such a healthy lifestyle. I'd already lost about 75 pounds, and it was such a load off my back, literally. I was feeling so much better already, and I was looking forward to so much more. For the first time I could remember in so many years, I was excited about the unknown.

Wow, I thought. *My dream of being married and spending my life with someone special is really coming true. I'm losing weight, I'm working, I'm singing, I'm getting married. I've got everything I want.* It was a very fulfilling, beautiful time, and everybody was so happy for us. Rob's family was thrilled, and my parents, Wendy, and all my friends were just ecstatic.

We all headed into the holidays on this fantastic high, and I felt like my life was one wonderful gift after another.

AS THE YEAR ROLLED INTO DECEMBER and everyone was counting down to the end of the millennium, *I* was counting down to the loss of 100 pounds (it had now been more than four months since my surgery). I'd never dropped that much weight in my life, and I was really looking forward to it.

I was eating pretty much everything that I wanted, sticking to very clean foods—a salad with chicken breast for lunch, always eating the chicken first. Little bites of vegetables like carrots, squash, zucchini, and spinach were working well for me. Other protein options were ground beef, steak, turkey breasts, and ground turkey patties.

I stayed away from fried foods, although occasionally in the morning I'd make eggs with a little olive oil. Whenever I'd try something like this, it wouldn't settle right in my stomach. I didn't dump, but it didn't feel good, so I knew that fried foods were just not right for me.

A couple of times when I went out to dinner, I would have a piece of bread with butter and a few bites of salad before the meal. Then when my plate arrived, I'd eat a little bit of the protein, and that would be it. This left me less satisfied, so I kept telling myself to pass on the salad and the bread and stay focused on the protein.

As I moved closer to the 100-pound mark, the feeling was very unusual. I couldn't believe that I had actually lost 100 pounds, but my face and figure had changed so dramatically so fast that it was shocking to people. I would see someone I hadn't seen for a long time, and they'd say, "Oh my God, you look so different. Wow! You've lost so much weight."

These reactions began to scare me a little. I started to feel like an object. I didn't feel like a person, but more like a machine or a piece of wood that was slowly being carved into something else. People were looking at me like this round ball that had been chiseled away, like they were admiring a sculpture. And it was very strange, really weird.

But it was actually a good feeling because who doesn't like a compliment? It was beautiful, and I was thankful for the attention and the appreciation, and the feeling of accomplishment was so satisfying. But I found that when I was with a group of four or five people who were all talking to me at the same time, it was a bit overwhelming. This had never bothered me when I was heavy. I tried to be comfortable with it, but I realized that what Leslie had told me was true: The emotional part of the experience really didn't start to catch up with me until I lost 100 pounds.

I think that subconsciously I was telling myself that losing 100 pounds would be such a feat that it would be a real high. But because of my experience with highs and lows, I was nervous about how I was going to feel when I did hit the mark.

Would I feel great for a few moments and then like shit after, like having a hit record and then coming off tour with nothing to do but be bored and depressed? Or would it be like going to a fast-food restaurant, eating all this food that tastes so good, and then feeling extremely guilty and miserable?

So I was anxious, and I started to take out some old "before" pictures and look at them every day. I carried them with me wherever I went. I started to feel sad and depressed, and I didn't know why. I would look at an old picture, and I would recognize myself. Then I'd look in the mirror and say, "That's not me."

But it *was* me in the mirror, and it was still me inside no matter what was on the outside. In a way, it was like a strange twist on what my mother used to tell me when I was teased as a child (that people would love me for what was inside, not outside).

I was very confused and disoriented, and there was a lot going on for me. I was away from home, living in Philadelphia, preparing to get married, flying back and forth to Los Angeles setting up a wedding, trying on wedding dresses, and doing a few shows now and then with Al.

There was a ton of media around keeping everyone updated on my story. It seemed like every week I was being interviewed by a magazine, or I was on the radio or television—*20/20* had covered my story since before the surgery, and every so often we'd do an update. I was on *Good Morning America* seven times, and the reception from the people on the show and the live audience was so positive and encouraging that it made me feel great.

I did *The View*, *Entertainment Tonight*, *Extra*, *Leeza*, and so many others. It was fun to go back on *Roseanne* and *The Howard Stern Show* to talk about how my life was changing.

But perhaps the most gratifying of all these appearances was when I was on *Oprah*, because I knew that she wasn't a fan of weight-loss surgery. I wasn't sure how she would receive me or what she would say and how it would make me feel. She was warm, but very somber as we talked about the procedure. She wanted to make it clear that my choice was not for everyone and that it was serious—even radical and controversial.

I agreed with everything Oprah said, and I told her audience the same thing I tell everyone else about gastric bypass surgery. It's not a solution. It's a tool to help you control what you couldn't otherwise control. It's not a quick fix. You have to stick with your protein-first diet, drink your water, take your vitamins, and get your exercise. And you can't snack in between meals if you want to get all the weight off.

They had a taped interview with Wendy on the show that touched me so much I started to cry, but I was so excited to be there because Oprah reaches so many women who struggle every day with their weight. I hope my story gave those who were suffering from morbid obesity the prospect of a healthier, happier life. As I left, Oprah hugged me and asked me to come back again. She seemed sincere, and I'd like to go on again because so much has happened to me since then.

My story's been everywhere—in *TV Guide*, *USA Today*, the *New York Times*, even the *London Times*. I think I've been in every major newspaper in the country. And I don't mention this to brag, because I know why people are interested. It's not really about me as much as it is about the weight and the surgery and the decision to go public.

When I crossed the 100-pound threshold, they gave me a cover story in *People* magazine—but not the main feature. That came about nine months later when I had lost 150 pounds—half my old bodyweight.

But while all this was happening, inside I was really becoming terrified of my new body. I didn't know how to feel. I would call Leslie, crying, and say, "I'm scared. I'm scared inside. I don't feel like myself. I'm feeling all these bones in my body, and I feel like I'm getting closer to the core of me."

It frightened me because I was so used to having that thick security and padding, and it was dwindling away. I didn't want my heart and inner self to dwindle away as well. I didn't want to lose who I was. I wanted to hold on to my old identity.

I told myself, "It's just weight. It's just fat. It's just skin. You're changing inside because you're becoming stronger, and the more you accomplish, the stronger and better you'll feel."

But that wasn't what was happening. The more weight I lost, the more vulnerable I felt.

The feeling of accomplishment was always in the front of my mind, but at the same time I was trying to just deal with what I felt. One day I would feel like Leonardo DiCaprio in *Titanic* at the bow of that ship—the queen of the world. And then the next day I would feel like a scared little girl who didn't know what to do.

After I lost the 100 pounds, I started to smoke marijuana

again. I started because I didn't want to feel these strange, upsetting sensations. I wanted to numb out. That's when I called my therapist, Marc.

"I need to talk to you," I said, "because I'm starting to refer to some old habits again."

Marc asked me, "How do you feel when you look at pictures of yourself?"

"I feel scared," I said. "I feel scared for her."

I started referring to myself in the third person. I'd say, "God, you know, she was really unhealthy. She was really unhappy. Look at her."

It was really weird, like I wasn't myself anymore.

We started doing some hypnosis, as well as some of the cognitive techniques that had been really helpful for me in the past. We focused on self-acceptance and becoming comfortable with change.

I said to myself, "Hey, change is difficult, it's a challenge, and it's hard. But you've got to look inside and remind yourself why you're doing this."

I'd ask myself, "Why *are* you doing this? Why do you want to lose all this weight?"

The voice from my gut came back to me loud and clear: "I want to lose all this weight because I want to live a long life. I want to lose this weight because I know I'm going to feel better about myself. And I want that feeling of putting on those 501 jeans."

So with Marc's help, I let myself fully experience my feelings. It was a phenomenal experience, grieving for the death of my old body and the parts of my personality so deeply associated with it.

Marc helped me put things into perspective. For me, my weight had actually helped me become dynamic. Over a lifetime, I learned to compensate for it by being very extroverted, and I did well with it. But on the other hand, it was torture for me for most of my life, and it caused me a great deal of pain.

For many people, weight is a way or an excuse to explain why certain things have not worked out well. "It's because of my weight," or "It's because I wasn't attractive enough." If you take the weight away, you can't use it anymore as a reason for your failures. It's like starting your life over without any kind of defenses, without the tools that you've become dependent on using to protect yourself.

Some overweight people feel lonely or isolated because they hold themselves back from meeting people. They limit their own opportunities because they're afraid they'll be rejected. Thanks to my mom, I was able to overcome a lot of these fears, and I just put myself out there as a fun-loving fat person. But it was still an effort on the inside to feel good about myself, and often it didn't work.

Everyone wants to meet people, or feel accepted, or be able to connect. There's a certain rejection factor that anyone has to deal with in terms of making connections, no matter what they weigh. But overweight people can sometimes unconsciously or indirectly use weight as a reason for why these connections don't happen. If you take away the weight and all of a sudden there's no excuse, we take it much more personally. Now it's not about the weight, it's about *us*.

When you're overweight in this society, which values thinness and attaches personal weakness to people who are heavy, it's like wearing this badge that everyone can see, and everyone attributes a certain negativity to you. If you have a headache or a stomachache, which people *can't* see, it's a very different story. But when everyone sees that you're fat, it's a great source of attention, disappointment, and anxiety.

Weight has ruled many aspects of my life and has dictated how I've spent so much of my time—trying to exercise more and eat less, going on numerous diets, searching for special clothes, going to different people for treatment. And then there's all the time I've spent being disappointed that all this effort didn't work, or the time spent doing drugs or stuffing myself to make the unpleasant feelings go away.

Now I was wondering what to do with myself.

There were many nights that I would lie in Rob's arms, crying my eyes out, saying, "I don't feel right. I feel funny. I've lost all this weight—and I'm proud of it—but I'm sad, and I'm scared."

I'd tell him, "This is all new. What am I going to do when I'm done? I'm not going to have a challenge. I'm going to meet my goal, and then what the hell is there to do after that? I've spent my entire life with this burden on my shoulders, this load of bricks: 'How the fuck am I going to lose 160 pounds?' The question's always been there: 'How am I going to do this?'"

But I never thought it would happen. I just didn't believe it could be true. And all of a sudden, it was a reality. It was like a shock, and it happened so quickly.

So I went through the stages of grieving—shock, denial, anger, sorrow, depression, and finally acceptance. Rob really helped me through this period of emotional adjustment. He would hold me and tell me I was going to be okay, that these feelings were normal, and that it was just going to take time to accept my new body.

The support from my mom; my sister; and my friends Owen, Katrina, Terri, and Leslie Jester also meant so much. And as the months passed and my weight continued to drop, I was dealing with all these feelings as the most important day of my life approached—my wedding day.

Like all brides-to-be, I was nervous about getting married—not about *being* married. I was so in love with Rob—I'd never felt anything like it before—and the thought of being together forever was like unbelievable bliss. I just wanted the wedding to be the wonderful day I had been dreaming of since I was a little girl. And I was extremely stoked because my dad was going to be walking me down the aisle.

The planning of the event was very smooth. You know how people talk about the nightmares of planning a wedding? Well, this was just so easy. I was in Philly for most of the process, and my mom handled most of the details in California. She did such an amazing job, and my father's wife, Melinda, helped us, too. We all kind of planned it together.

Wendy was my maid of honor, and my best girlfriends from childhood were my bridesmaids—Owen, Tiffany Miller, Jenny Brill, and Julie Siegel. We all met at the bridal shop, and it was unreal. People get married on television shows, and you see them in their gowns, and you're just so happy for them. But this time, it was me getting married, and I almost couldn't believe it.

The scene was just hysterical—we were laughing uproariously. It felt so much like our days growing up together, when we'd laugh so hard that Julie would go to the hospital with asthma attacks. The laughter I shared with these girls at that time was my savior. It helped me put away my pain, and it strengthened my faith in humor as a central feature of the "me" I showed the world. Everything seemed so much better when I could laugh and make others laugh.

Now I wasn't laughing to keep from crying. We were sharing sheer joy.

I tried on lots of dresses, and finally I found the one I wanted. It was ivory in color, off-the-shoulder, really poofy on the bottom, with a huge train and Battenberg lace everywhere. It was a size 16, which was really like a 14 or 12, because wedding dresses run two sizes bigger.

I was blown away to be in the teen digits. Since the surgery, I had come down from a size 28. *I can't believe this,* I thought. *I'm getting married, and I'm going to be a size 16.*

But what happened in the weeks ahead was even more unbelievable. By the time Rob and I got married in June of

2000, I had lost more than 130 pounds. We had to keep taking the dress in until it was down to a size 12. Then with only a few weeks to go, I completely changed my mind and went for a simpler beautiful white matte satin with a high waist, lace sleeves, and a tighter round scoop neck. It didn't poof out too much—just enough—and I just felt so good in it.

I wore two veils—a cathedral length, and another on the top with flowers. My friend Daniel styled my hair back in a Spanish bun with gardenias. Another friend, Avril, did my makeup. Even though I was as nervous as I can ever remember being, I was so delighted with how I looked that I was floating on a cloud. It was all like some surreal fantasy, only it was so real that I was thrilled every moment.

I weighed 165 pounds, still 25 pounds from my goal weight, but I wasn't thinking about that. I was thinking about my dad, my mom, Wendy, my best girlfriends, and all our friends and family who were there. Most of all, I was thinking about Rob, my future husband, and how beautiful our relationship was and how much I loved him.

We were married in the garden at the Bel Air Hotel, just like a dream, absolutely gorgeous, so fabulous. We were so lucky. I would have gotten married skydiving. I wouldn't have cared. I just wanted to be married to Rob. We felt really privileged.

It was a lovely June day, and everything was perfect. We celebrated, we danced, we ate. I wish we could have invited everyone we wanted to, but we only had room for 200, which was still quite a party. Dr. Wittgrove, bless his heart, flew in on a red-eye and then flew right back out.

It seemed like every moment of the day was precious.

When Daddy walked me down the aisle, I never felt more beautiful or special in my life. All those years when we were out of touch, it made me so sad to think that this day would never happen—but now it was.

"I'm so happy for you," he told me.

It was like a gift from heaven. And it only got better from there.

After the ceremony, Rob and I danced our first dance as husband and wife to my dad's song "Warmth of the Sun." It was so romantic, we felt surrounded by so much love, and the music was so right. Everyone was crying to see us so happy together.

But the most tender moment for me was the father-daughter dance. When the music started, Dad went, "What? Are you kidding? Who chose this song?"

"I did," I said. "I chose it just for you."

It was "Be My Baby," my father's favorite song, the one I'd heard him play every day when I was a child.

"Oh, Carnie," he said, "that's great." And my heart was full of so many feelings.

We slow-danced for a while, then all of a sudden Dad started rocking out. He grabbed me and swung me around, then he stopped, held me, looked straight in my eyes, and said, "Ah, Carnie, I love you so much."

I couldn't help it, I just burst into tears. I was so overwhelmed with emotion, I didn't know what else to do.

"Are you crying? Don't cry," he said with the sweetest smile.

But I cried out of such happiness and joy and relief.

So many times in my life I had longed for my dad to be there, and now my heart was overflowing because he was there with me to tell me he loved me. It was something I had been waiting for my whole life. I knew in my heart he wouldn't have missed it for the world.

After our dance, I went right over to Rob and just sobbed in his arms. He cried, too, and I went to Mom, and we all cried. It was just a beautiful, beautiful moment.

Later, Wendy made the most genuine, touching, sweet, loving, maid-of-honor toast. No one could get over it. It was classic, just incredible. And she was so lovely.

She said she'd never seen me this happy. She talked about us as little girls and sisters, how we had shared so many things in our lives, about how proud she was of me, how I'd come so far, and how thrilling it was for her to see me overcome the obstacle of weight.

She talked about Rob, and told him how she wanted him to take care of me. It was just the ultimate.

But at the end of the day, there was one person to thank more than anyone else—my mom. Just like everything else she's ever done for me, she went overboard to make sure that every aspect of our wedding was filled with beauty and tenderness and love. That's how she is and how she's always been. There's no one like her in the world.

In so many ways, this day would never have happened without her, and my love for her is at the center of my soul forever.

CHAPTER THIRTEEN

The Weight Is Over

After the wedding, we were still living in Philadelphia, which for me was away from home, and that was a little hard. There were lawsuits about the name of Al's band, so the shows were rarely happening. I was newly married, still losing weight, and a lot was going on for me mentally.

I was feeling anxious and out of sorts, and I wasn't sure what was next for my career. So I decided to slow down and spend the next few months with Rob just enjoying each other's company.

In July, we went to Italy for our honeymoon. It was 16 amazing days and nights of beautiful sights, wonderful food, and best of all, just being together. Rob's father's family originally comes from Italy, but Rob had never been there. So it was a thrill for us both, but there were also a couple of challenges that my new lifestyle put on my plate.

It was a ten-hour flight to Rome, and I became very dehydrated on the plane. The result was my first experience with serious constipation, and I can't remember too many times in my life when I've been more uncomfortable. It's really important for everyone—and especially gastric bypass patients—to drink your water every day, and extra when you're traveling.

The way they serve meals in Italy also makes it difficult to get your protein first. They bring out course after course—salad, soup, pasta, appetizers, and lots of bread—and finally, the entrée. I did my best to pace myself, but my system wasn't used to this style of eating, and it took a few days to settle down.

We did a lot of walking—which helped to burn off all those carbs—and one of the things we enjoyed doing most was rollerblading. Skating around was so much fun, but one day, I fell on a curb and hit my hipbone. I was really in pain, but secretly I was kind of pleased. "Okay," I said to myself, "you've fallen, and it hurts like hell, but goddammit, there's a bone in there. You hit the bone!"

In spite of my excitement, that was it for me and roller-blading, but I still managed to lose five pounds on our honeymoon, while Rob put on eight.

BACK IN THE STATES, ROB AND I TOOK LOTS OF WALKS together in Philadelphia, and I did a tiny bit of weight training. I regret that I didn't do more, because I think my arms and stomach would have shrunk down a little better.

I started to notice my skin really changing. It was starting to hang. On my arms you could see the definition of the muscle and the bone, and then underneath was this big sagging piece of skin. I could swing it forward and back, and it was disgusting. I would look in the mirror and just shudder.

My stomach at the bottom had that weird apron thing and wrinkly skin, and my inner thighs at the top had a couple of ripples. My legs and my butt were in good shape, but my stomach and arms and underneath my armpits—it was gross. And my breasts were really hanging. They just shrunk down to nothing. I lost ten inches in my bust and went down two cup sizes, from a tight 44D to a 34B. But I was really thrilled that I was down to a size six.

At 18 months out of surgery, I hit 148 pounds, and I've been maintaining that weight within a few pounds ever since, only eating when I'm hungry. For me, this is quite an accomplishment, because I've never been able to maintain a certain weight limit in my life. It's always been up and down, up and down. So it's been a real relief to see the scale stay steady.

When I look in the mirror, my skin might disgust me, but then I look at my size, and my body is still changing every two weeks. The skin around my belly button looks different than it ever has, and all of a sudden, I have no hips. I'm getting really small at this point, and people are saying, "You're so petite, you're so little." I've actually started to feel little. I've gone from feeling like this elephant that would shake the ground as I walked, to this tiny thing, as light as feather. It's a feeling that I've shared with some of my new friends.

For the past three years, Dr. Wittgrove and Dr. Clark have had a Carnival Cruise for their patients. I went for the first two cruises, and they were amazing experiences. The first year we had about 40 weight-loss surgery patients, and then the second year we had about 80.

It's so amazing to watch everyone get up there and tell their stories. I had to have a big box of tissues next to me, because every time somebody would get up to talk about their accomplishments, I'd just burst into tears. I was so proud of every person. You could see the joy on their faces and how their lives had changed and what they've accomplished.

It was such a beautiful bonding experience, and we all found such a kinship because we knew what it was to be really heavy and limited by our weight, so unable to do the things we wanted to do. Now it was like we were all let out of prison. It was an incredible thing to see.

The first year, I met Katrina and Marty Zucker. They're two of the wackiest people, just like Rob and I are, so we get along great. I instantly related to Katrina. It was like we're the same person. But she's 5'10", and I'm 5'4", and it's very funny when we walk around together.

We have this total understanding of each other because we know what we've struggled with—we've had the same surgery, we've lived every detail of it, and we support each other. We eat together. We dump together. We feel good together. We feel bad together. We can share so many things that other people can't. Maybe you're meant to meet people when you do, but we wish we'd met each other earlier in our lives because we've had so much fun together.

The second cruise was great, but I was moving from Philadelphia to Los Angeles, flying back and forth, and trying to find a house to buy. I was traveling so much that I became severely dehydrated. It didn't really affect my energy level, but constipation became a real problem. It was becoming frequent in that six-month period, but it became very serious when I pushed too hard and tore a muscle in the lining of my rectum. It's not pleasant to talk about, but nature calls every day, and we've got to do our business. I hurt myself, and I'll never forget the pain. The surgery was minor, but it was no fun, and I learned a lesson the hard way about how essential water is.

When you travel, every hour you're on a plane you lose a pint of water. No wonder I got constipated when I went to Italy on my honeymoon. The flight was ten hours long, and I didn't drink enough water to replace the ten pints I lost. That's enough to dehydrate you for the whole trip.

This was my first major problem after surgery. I wouldn't call it a complication, but it was another surgery, and it could have been serious. So my advice to everyone is drink that water and get that fiber. Now I get up every day and brush my teeth, take my vitamins, eat my bran, and drink my water. Everything thing works better that way.

There are a lot of people who blast this surgery, especially on the Internet. They think it's bullshit, and they have statistics that are scary. The numbers show that many people who have this surgery only lose 50 percent of their excess body weight. But I truly believe that unless you have something wrong with your hormones or your thyroid gland or something that requires medication, it's up to you how much weight you lose.

If you go to a surgeon who makes your pouch small enough, you're going to lose a lot of weight in your first six months. The average weight loss is 100 pounds. That's why it's so crucial to work on your head. Dealing with your head at the same time you're dealing with your body is very important. It's what made us heavy in the first place.

When I went on that second cruise, I saw people I remembered from the first year, and some of them had put on weight. When I was taking my walks, I'd see them snacking, walking around eating ice cream.

I don't want to be one of those people, I thought to myself. *I don't want to revert back to my old habits.*

Everyone has weaknesses, and I'm going to admit that I snack. I probably snack every single day, and I haven't been able to control that in the last six months. That's why I've been maintaining rather than losing. I know what I can eat for my meals. I try to make the protein-first choices. But if I snack, I'm only going to maintain—and if I snack on bad foods, don't exercise, and don't drink enough water, I'm going to gain weight.

There are other risks involved with that, too. But it was really scary to see those people on the cruise lose control like that. I just had to wonder, what's going on with them? They're probably happy and proud because they've lost 100 pounds and saved their lives. But it's sad to be stuck with 40 or 50 pounds you still have to lose. Even with the surgery, getting to your goal is hard work. That's why support group meetings are so important.

It's important to find a support group where you can feel you can be heard. The support group in San Diego has now grown to about 200 people, and now it's basically a lecture that Leslie Jester does. That's okay, but I went to a support group meeting last week that was wonderful because there were only seven people, and we really got to talk about things. I've noticed that a lot of us who have had this surgery love to take off our clothes and show each other the scars from plastic surgery or how we've lost weight here, or how we hate this part or love this part.

I'm really looking forward now myself to reconstructive plastic surgery. I've hit a point where I'm feeling pretty satisfied with my size—but this skin has just got to go. I've been feeling extremely self-conscious about it, and I don't want Rob to look at it. I turn to the side and cover the bottom of my tummy, and I'm getting more and more uncomfortable with it.

When I hit 155 pounds, everyone started asking me, "Are you done, or are you going for plastic surgery?" So I went for a consultation with my friend Dr. Steven Zax, the plastic surgeon who is probably the best-kept secret in Beverly Hills.

He told me that because I'm young, some of my skin has retained its elasticity, but some of it hasn't. He explained that skin is like a napkin designed with little ridges. If you pull apart the napkin and stretch it to a certain degree, when you let go, the napkin is not going to go back to that original shape. That's what my skin is like.

I'm looking forward to not being ashamed of my skin. It's the same type of feeling as being ashamed of fat. But it's different because I'm proud at the same time.

I look at it and say, "Hey, remember what you used to look like? All this skin was filled with fat, and now it's not. They're going to cut it off—and it sounds gross—but the results will be beautiful."

I'm going to have a big scar almost from hip to hip on the bikini line, but it will be very thin, and eventually almost unnoticeable. Dr. Zax told me it's important to get down as

close to your goal weight as possible before you have the surgery, because the less you weigh, the easier it is to remove the
skin with less scarring.

So my goal is to be between 140 and 145 when I have the
surgery. I'm going to have a tummy tuck, a breast lift, and the
skin removed on my arms, under my armpits, and possibly a
tiny bit from under my chin.

Some people don't choose to have plastic surgery after
they lose a lot of weight, even if their skin is hanging—and
that's perfectly fine. It's all a matter of individual preference,
and everybody needs do what will make them happy.

I personally believe that lifting my breasts and removing
the skin at the bottom of my stomach and on my arms will help
me feel a lot better. I stand in front of the mirror and pull up
my stomach or pull it in and down. I look at my arms, and I
pull the skin aside, and I think, *Wow, you already look so good.
You're going to look so amazing when that's done.* I'm really,
really looking forward to it.

But I'm also fucking terrified. I'm terrified of the results.

I've never had any type of reconstructive surgery for my
appearance, and it's very scary. To me, it's scarier than the
bypass surgery itself. But the skin needs to be removed for medical reasons as well as aesthetic ones, and I'm confident I'll prepare myself well in exactly the same way I did for the weight-
loss surgery—positive thinking, hypnosis, healing tapes, and
healthy eating.

As I write this today, Rob and I are celebrating our first wedding anniversary. I can't believe a year's gone by. We both can't.
It's been a year that's been both wonderful and difficult.

A lot of trust issues have come up for me, and Rob has been
very patient and supportive. Living with someone, sharing
everything with someone, can be hard—especially when you're
in your own headspace. I'm not easy to live with, and I've been

feeling very needy. Rob is really honest with me. He's quick to say, "Honey, I need space, I need to breathe, and I've got my own stuff to deal with, too."

It's really important to acknowledge the contributions of partners, spouses, friends, and family as loved ones go through the gastric bypass experience. *They* go through a tremendous change, too. They've known you one way, and all of a sudden, they blink and you're another way.

It can make them feel insecure as well. I think that Rob actually was sort of blown away by it. He's told me that. He's also told me so many times how well I've done, how proud he is of me, how good I look, and how much healthier I am.

I've needed this constant reassurance. "How do I look? Do I look fat? Do I look thin? Do I look pretty?" I drove him fucking nuts, and he's been so compassionate and so concerned.

When we'd go out to eat, he'd say, "How's it feel going down? Does that taste good? Are you doing okay?"

If I'd eat two or three bites of dessert, he'd worry. "Okay, honey, don't do that. You don't want to dump." Or "Are you sure you can eat that?"

I'd have to remind him, "Baby, look. I know what I'm doing. I've lost over 100 pounds. It's working."

And he'd say, "Okay, okay, okay." But he's always been coming from such a helpful place.

Sometimes I feel guilty that so much attention has been focused on me because of this operation and my weight loss. It's just another side of how preoccupied our culture is with appearance and weight. Gain too much weight, you're a loser. Lose a lot of weight, you're a hero.

It is an achievement to drop 155 pounds no matter how you do it, and I don't mind getting a pat on the back for it. But to me, the real achievement is being and staying in a healthy relationship.

Rob's feelings and aspirations are just as important as

mine. This whole weight thing has been an emotional roller coaster for both of us, but our relationship has grown so much stronger. Marriage is everything that I hoped it would be and more. I've learned more from being with Rob than I've learned from anything else in my life.

What I love is how he's helped me learn so much about myself. I've never had the desire or the ability to look at my faults, my idiosyncrasies, or my attributes. But I've had to be real with Rob, and it's been an eye-opener for me. The hardest part has been learning to trust and let go. That's where I'm at right now—trusting Rob, letting go of the fear of abandonment and the feelings of not being worthy of love.

You can talk with family, friends, other patients, or anyone who's struggling with issues like this. But to have that support from your husband and to count on a friendship like this is so incredible.

More than anything, I want to give that support back to him, whether he's struggling about his band, striving to get a record deal, or writing songs. I want to be there for him to inspire him when he's feeling frustrated, to give him encouragement and say, "You can do it. You're talented. You've got it in you. Get your butt in that studio right now."

Rob's been working hard writing and recording, both when we were back on the East Coast, and now in Los Angeles. We've moved to a cute little neighborhood in the Valley, and he has his own studio in the backyard. I've been working with Spotlight Health, making appearances, doing television shows, and writing this book. I've also been shopping, making dinner, taking care of the dogs, exercising, focusing on my weight-loss program, and socializing with my gorgeous husband.

One thing that's hysterical is that Rob gained 15 pounds since we met.

"I'm getting fat," he says, with this worried look on his face.

"No, you're not," I say. "You were just too skinny before."

But he does have this cute litle belly I just love to kiss. However he *is* down seven pounds now that we're exercising together.

I LOOK BACK NOW TO THE WAY I USED TO BE, and I try to learn from my past. I try to help myself relax and feel content. But the echoes of the old feelings are still with me.

I felt like I couldn't get ahold of something. I couldn't get control of something. And even though I felt really pretty at times, or even really healthy at times, it wasn't until I was morbidly obese that I knew that I had to change something. It seems like I was coasting along for a long time and denying myself true happiness.

But what *is* true happiness? I weigh 145 pounds now, and I have more anxiety than I've ever had. I feel sort of aimless at times. It's kind of like the movies where the devil is on one shoulder and the angel is on the other. I've got a big doughnut on the left side and Leslie Jester on my right. I just keep hearing Leslie's words, "It's emotional. You've got to be real with yourself. You're not perfect. Don't beat yourself up."

I realize now—and Rob has helped me discover this—I always play the victim. I blame myself for a lot of things. I almost thrive on feeling guilty. This is something I've discovered in my therapy, and I'm working on it. It's all about deserving to feel better, and maybe that's why I kept myself heavy. I kept myself heavy because I needed to complain about something, and now I look for other ways things to complain about.

But I know it's time to stop complaining and just enjoy my new life.

My relationship with Dad is the best it's ever been. Now I can just call him up and tell him how much I love him, and he does the same for me. When we travel and don't see each other that much, sometimes I get those panic feelings that I'm going to lose the relationship. But I know in my heart how he feels about me, and he knows how I feel about him.

I really admire my dad's strength, and the way he's turned his life around. It's been an inspiration to me—he's such a rock. He gained control of his weight, and his discipline now is awesome. He runs five miles each morning, he eats healthy, and he writes every day. It's like breathing for him.

He's out on the road, and he blows my mind. Every time I see him in concert, I can't believe he's up there. And he loves it. He thrives on it now, and he's finally getting the praise he deserves. In the past five years, *Pet Sounds* has been appreciated like it never has been. I also got to learn the album and appreciate it myself. I think Dad's really proud.

There are still things that I wish could be different or better or stronger. I wish I could see him more. But I'm so grateful that he's in this positive mind frame. I'm happy that he can feel happiness and enjoy his new daughters and be in love. Maybe my mom and dad shared that together in the beginning, and I know that they still love each other and they always will.

I'm so proud of him, and it's so ironic that of everyone in his family, he's the survivor. You'd think he would have been the first to go—but he's the true strong one. And now that I'm thinking of it, perhaps I got a lot of my strength from him.

I had an amazing experience doing a show recently in Seattle, Washington, called *Northwest Afternoon*. They told me that most of the people in the audience were gastric bypass patients, some were members of my online support group, and most were going to be women. They were so excited to see me, and they all had flowers and cards.

I was excited, too, but I wasn't prepared for what actually happened. It was really overwhelming. It was one of the most beautiful experiences that I've ever had. I'm going to put it right up there with my wedding day, and going number one with Wilson Phillips.

All these people that were standing up, crying, and saying,

"Because of you, I've lost 200 pounds, and I'm healthy again, and I'm happy." And I was crying, too.

Every time somebody would say, "I lost this much weight," I was so thrilled for them, and I related to them in such a big way—it was the most satisfying feeling. My heart felt like a butterfly—so light and free and lovely.

After the show was over, everybody wanted to take pictures. But the producer of the show said, "You're going to miss your flight."

"It doesn't matter," I said. "I'm taking these pictures with them." So we took about 50 pictures, and it was just so neat, hugging everyone. I left feeling really great, and I even made my flight.

But I don't know if it's Jewish guilt or what the fuck it is, I started to feel responsible. I started to think about the impact that I actually was having on human beings I don't even know. That is a really heavy-duty thing to take in.

I'd had a touch of that with Wilson Phillips when people would say, "I listened to your songs, and I didn't slash my wrists." Or "I saw your video for 'Hold On,' and heard you singing those words 'Hold on for one more day,' and that's what I did. I didn't kill myself."

That's pretty fucking heavy when someone says that to you. So I started to feel this incredible sense of responsibility. *What if they gain the weight back?* I thought. *What if they have serious complications and get physically sick? What if somebody has this surgery because of me, and then they die?* I feel like I'm responsible for them.

So I called my therapist. I was crying very hard. "I feel so responsible, I don't know what it is," I said. "I'm so happy for everyone, and everyone's doing so well. But what about the small percentage of people who won't do well? What if they have the surgery because of me, and it's my fault?"

Marc said, "Carnie, you can feel like a motivator, and you

can feel like an inspiration, and that's a good, healthy feeling. But you're not responsible for other people. You're only responsible for yourself.

"Everyone makes their own decision for their own benefit," he said, "and you can't control other people's destinies, fates, futures, successes, or failures. It's their path, and that's it. So you have to take that off your shoulders."

And after I really thought about it, I felt better.

But a while later, I took my car to be serviced, and one of the girls who worked in the dealership said, "I have a friend who saw your surgery, and she decided to do it. She had the operation, and she became very sick. Her sutures busted, and she had obstructions and bowel leakages. Then this infection spread throughout her body, and she almost died."

I was devastated. This was the first time that I'd ever experienced this kind of negative response to the work I'd been doing with gastric bypass. I'd read about these complications on the Internet, but this woman had the surgery because of me. It was a terrible feeling.

Rob did his best to comfort me. "Honey, it's not your fault," he said. "It's not your fault that she didn't recover well."

That woman is doing better now, and she's okay, but I'm going to have to deal with this issue forever. I'll always be working through that guilt and responsibility versus the motivation and encouragement I can give to others.

THE OTHER NIGHT, ROB SHOCKED ME TO THE CORE. I was serving dinner when he looked up and said, "Honey, are you going to die in five years?"

"What the hell are you talking about?" I said.

Rob had read some articles on the Internet about weight-loss surgery. The articles were about intestinal bypass procedures, and the prognosis for patients who had this operation. The doctors presented data that the life expectancy for these people was 5 to 15 years, and that many had died of kidney failure.

"That can't be true," I said. But there it was.

I started to panic. For the first time since my operation, I began to question if I'd gotten all the information. I began to think that I'd made a terrible mistake. I got nervous and scared, and I started to cry.

By the time I called Leslie Jester, I was hysterical. This time it wasn't about someone else. I was afraid for *me*.

Leslie explained that this was an old malabsorptive procedure—not the operation I'd had. Medical science had moved on precisely because the old procedure didn't work well. The body couldn't absorb the nutrients, and the patients got ill.

But my body *does* absorb food. And if I'm not careful, I'll gain weight. And if I don't take my vitamins, I can become malnourished or get osteoporosis. If I don't drink my water, I could develop kidney problems. And if I don't watch my alcohol intake, it could harm my liver.

But I know these things, and I am on top of it.

Leslie made me think about my situation.

I believed that if I had the surgery I'd survive—and I did.

I believed that if I followed the rules, I'd lose the weight and reach my goal—and I did.

Now I needed to believe that I would live a long life—and I will.

There is no data about how gastric bypass patients will do in 20 or 30 years. But there is data going back 15 years that supports the benefits of the surgery. There's also data that shows what will happen if you stay morbidly obese. You won't make it 20 years without serious illness.

There are people who don't support this operation, and they'll do what they can to scare you. But if you want to be really scared, just think about your health if you don't get your weight down.

That's been the challenge and the reward for me—accepting the changes in myself and the role I've taken on to help others. That's what I've gone through, and I've kept moving forward. I'm proud of myself, and grateful, and so relieved. And now I have such hope, not just for myself, but for others, too. I just want to share it with everyone.

When I see someone who's really, really overweight, I want to ask them, "Have you been struggling a long time? Have you tried everything you can to lose weight?"

If they said to me, "Yes, I have," then I'd want to say to them, "Let me tell you about what I've been through." I don't care if I sound like an infomercial, because I'm going to be a living infomercial for the rest of my fucking life. It's not about money, it's about health and personal satisfaction. That's it.

That's the reason for this book. I want to share how wonderful it is to have a goal, to accomplish it, to be scared and proud and happy and sad and thrilled all at the same time. Sometimes I feel like I'm getting my revenge on the people who would tease me when I was fat. They were such losers, and now I'm a winner. I took charge. I saved my life. I saved my health. But it's not about revenge. It's about the lessons of karma that my mother taught me way back when. I've tried to be a good person my whole life. I've tried to make people feel better by making them laugh or singing them a song or telling them a story.

When I was one or two years old, my mom and dad went to this very old psychic who prepared a ten-page chart on Wendy and me. The first sentence was "Carnie is put here on earth to help people."

That's how I feel. That's my purpose.

Recently in New York, I was out to dinner with Rob the night before I did the *Montel Williams Show*. I looked at Rob and I said, "I know how much you love to play music, and how it's in your soul, and that's what you love. But you know what

I love? I love to help people. That's it."

The next day on the show, there was a lady named Paula. She's very active in my support group, and she even has her own Website. She's lost about 150 pounds, and she looks so good. She just kept hugging me and thanking me, and I appreciated her thanks, but it was the joy and elation in her eyes that made me feel so special. I didn't choose to share my life because I wanted praise or gratitude. It wasn't really about me. It was knowing that somebody else is going to feel better. If they can share what I feel, there'll be more and more people feeling good. That's the world I want to live in.

So when people thank me, I say, "You're welcome, but *you* did it. You took charge, and you did it. You should thank yourself. Give yourself a high five."

I've had blessings in my life because I've chosen to believe that miracles can happen. There's always been an inner fire inside of me that I've been able to just tap in to. I feel like my body is a rocket, and I just turn on the engine and I go. I don't know where the hell it comes from. For some reason, people just don't believe that good things are there for them. I've never understood why. Nothing is guaranteed, and nothing is permanent. One day you're going to feel great, and another day you're not. But I've always been optimistic, because the bright side of things is just better.

I've been down so low it was hard to get up. But you can't *get* up unless you *look* up. You don't have to do what I've done—just follow your heart. I'm not a doctor. I'm just a 33-year-old human like you, and I can't tell you what's right or wrong for you. But I know that if you're going to get anything out of this book, it's going to be this: If you don't like the way something is, look within yourself like I did, and make the choice to change it.

I feel so incredibly lucky. I thank God for my whole life, for everything I've been through. I thank God for every high and every low I've felt, the depression, the pain, and ballooning up to the edge of death. I thank God that it got to that point.

I think it was a blessing that I hit rock bottom, because it made me take control. It made me do something about it.

Weight-loss surgery is the best thing I've ever done in my life. You can take the hit records and the TV show and anything else I've accomplished. I'll live longer now, there's no question about it, and knowing I've prolonged my life is the greatest. It's the greatest feeling in the world. My tummy is my new little friend, my best friend next to Rob. And I feel like I'll be good to it, and it will be good to me.

I want to keep my weight off, and I don't have the fear that I'll gain it back. For the first time in my life, I can honestly say that. I may put on a few pounds during pregnancy, and I'll deal with that when it comes. But I won't psych myself out or make myself nuts with it.

I've always wanted to have kids, and I know I'll be a great mom. I look forward to that. Now I'm much less frightened of the idea, because it's harder to get pregnant when you're heavy, and there's the risk of gestational diabetes, which I don't have to worry about now. When you're really heavy, your hormone levels are out of whack, and it can be difficult to have a healthy pregnancy.

People ask, "Are you able to have kids if you've had a gastric bypass? What's that like?" The answer is, "It's totally fine. You can get pregnant. You actually have a better chance than if you're heavy." They ask you to wait between a year to 18 months because you're not really eating enough for two people. The average birth weight for a gastric bypass pregnancy is a little lower than average—between five and six pounds, rather than between six and eight. Everything else is exactly the same. You might gain 20 pounds, but you're not going to gain 50 or 60.

I'm not worried about that. It's just going to be a natural

thing. I'll deal with it then, and hopefully I'll be all right. But I look forward to motherhood, and to loving my children the way my mom loved me. It's such a beautiful thing, I can't wait.

A lot of people will read this and think that I came from this rich family in the limelight. How has she really suffered in her life when she's had everything given to her? She's just a glutton, a spoiled, gluttonous pig.

I did have all that. I did have money. I was spoiled. I was a glutton. I was that way. I've always loved to eat too much and shop too much and maybe even talk too much. I've been so fortunate that life has given me the riches, opportunities, and successes I've squandered. But really, I was empty inside—and people need to know that.

Go ahead, change positions with me, and you'll see how it feels. It doesn't mean shit that you come from a famous family. It doesn't mean shit that you have money, or that you're able to get this or that. It's what you make of yourself. It's what you set your mind to doing, what you want to accomplish, and how you direct your will. That's what's important in your life.

People have criticized me, "Oh, I don't have the kind of money it takes to get that surgery, and she's never had to worry. She took the easy way out. She just had her stomach stapled, and it's done for her."

Well, that's a bunch of bullshit. That's the kind of thinking that will keep you from getting anywhere in life. That's the kind of excuse people use to keep themselves from checking out their options, from seeing what their insurance will cover, from risking a serious operation with potentially fatal complications, from embracing a tool—not a solution—that can help them change their lives forever.

I'm not Mother Teresa. I still want to be famous. I want to be a big success. I want to make records and be in movies and on television. I want a happy marriage with great communication and children I can hold and hug and kiss. I want to make them laugh and dry their tears and sing them sweet lullabies. God willing, I'll have all these things because I took the initiative to give myself a future.

Who knows? I could get hit by a Humvee tomorrow or choke on a piece of tofu. But I have faith that I'll be here with my husband to watch my kids grow up. I'll be here to help others and see my dreams come true. I'll be healthy and I'll be happy—the way I've always wanted to be.

It's up to me to make it happen.

It's always been that way.

I just have to follow my gut feelings.

Asking the Experts

"These are some questions I needed answered. I hope that you find this information helpful, too." — Carnie

Alan Wittgrove, M.D., Bariatric Surgeon

D R. ALAN WITTGROVE IS THE CO-DEVELOPER OF THE LAPAROSCOPIC gastric bypass protocol and the co-founder of the Alvarado Center for Surgical Weight Control in San Diego, California. He is an expert in weight-loss surgery and minimally invasive surgical techniques.

Q: What is morbid obesity?

Obesity is defined objectively by body mass index (BMI). The National Institutes of Health (NIH) definition of morbid obesity is a body mass index of 35–40 with co-morbid conditions, or a BMI over 40 even without other conditions. With a BMI over 40, we know that the patient will eventually experience ill effects whether or not he or she has up to that point. Super-obesity is defined as a BMI of 50 or higher.

Q: What are the co-morbid conditions you referred to that are associated with obesity?

Co-morbidities include such conditions as diabetes, hypertension, and sleep apnea. These, of course, are diseases in and of themselves, but they happen so frequently with morbid obesity that they're really symptoms of the larger problem. In women, co-morbid conditions also include infertility, urinary incontinence, and certain kinds of cancers, specifically ovarian cancer, endometrial cancer, and probably colon cancer.

Obese men are at a higher risk for prostate cancer. For both men and women who are excessively obese, a major complaint is also arthritic symptoms of the weight-bearing joints. These people may not take arthritis medication, but they avoid activity. Because of their joint immobility, they often do not have a full family life or the kind of job they would like.

Q: What about depression?

Obviously, depression is a major complaint. Our society puts a lot of pressure on people of size.

Q: Who is a candidate for bariatric surgery?

Most bariatric surgeons follow the guidelines set down by the NIH in the early 1990s. Those guidelines say that those with BMIs over 40 are candidates for bariatric surgery whether or not they have any other related medical complaints. For those with BMIs between 35 and 40, the criteria are a little more stringent. The NIH says they have to have some other severe medical problem such as hypertension, sleep apnea, or diabetes. The NIH later added arthritic symptoms and immobility that interferes with a patient's normal life or their employment.

I would like to see the NIH take another look at its surgical criteria. Given the dramatic increase in the 30–35 BMI category, and the accompanying increase in diabetes and other problems in that group, I think their inclusion within the guidelines may be warranted.

Q: Are patients required to try less dramatic treatments before opting for bariatric surgery?

Most bariatric surgery programs require some history of failed attempts at diet and exercise programs. But in reality, anyone who is morbidly obese has already been on some kind of diet and/or exercise program. Do I require that a patient must have been on another program? No, because there's no good data that I know of that shows that any of those programs are successful. I don't require it, but in reality, everyone I see has already tried them and failed.

Q: Could you provide a quick overview of weight-loss surgery?

All the types of obesity surgery were developed in the late 1960s, and are of two types: restrictive operations like vertical banded gastroplasty, which make it impossible for the patient to eat as much; and the malabsorptive operations, like the biliopancreatic diversion with duodenal switch, which causes the patient's body to not absorb fats and starches.

Over the next 20 years, the techniques in these surgeries were refined. We learned, for example, that we had to make the new stomach pouch that's created in a gastric bypass very small. The next big evolution in the field came in 1993, when we began to do laparoscopic surgery. Laparoscopic surgery results in fewer complications and problems for the patients.

Q: What are the main types of bariatric surgery?

The most common bariatric surgery in the United States is the gastric bypass. The most common worldwide is vertical banded gastroplasty, which comprises only about 15–20% of the surgeries done in the U.S. because it's still undergoing FDA testing. The third main type is the biliopancreatic diversion with duodenal switch, which is malabsorptive surgery. Most of us worry about the malnutrition that can occur after malabsorptive operations and favor the gastric bypass instead.

Q: Could you describe the gastric bypass?

The gastric bypass is an operation whereby most of the stomach is bypassed, but still functions as a kind of chemical factory of enzymes and acids. We make a very small pouch at the top of the stomach using a stapling device. And then we divide the small intestine and bring a limb of intestine up to that small pouch so that food comes down the esophagus, transiently goes into the small pouch that restricts how much you can eat, and then goes directly into the small intestine where it mixes with bile and pancreatic juices that help the food be absorbed. So you end up with a "Y" configuration with two limbs of small intestine coming down into a common channel where absorption takes place.

Q: What are the differences between open and laparoscopic procedures?

One of the primary reasons the laparoscopic procedure was developed was to decrease the rate of our most common complication, which was incisional hernias. The easiest way to do that is to make smaller incisions off the midline of the body. So the main difference is that instead of a 4- to-12-inch incision in the upper abdomen made in the open gastric bypass, in the laparoscopic surgery we make several 1- or 2-inch incisions off the midline. We then insert long instruments and complete the operation guided by a miniature TV camera without physically handling the tissues.

We believe laparoscopy allows us to be more accurate. The camera can be brought right down to the tissues and magnifies them, allowing us to be very precise. Laparoscopy saves approximately 20% of gastric bypass patients who develop incisional hernias from undergoing another operation to repair them, since our incisional hernia rate with laparoscopy is essentially zero.

Q: What's the difference between the gastric bypass and the vertical banded gastroplasty?

Vertical banded gastroplasty (VBG) restricts what you can eat. It makes a very small pouch out of the bottom part of the esophagus and the upper part of the stomach, then restricts the outlet of the pouch so that everything you eat has to get through an opening about the size of the opening of a toothpaste tube before it can go on to the rest of your intestinal tract. It doesn't rearrange your intestinal tract the way a gastric bypass does. It only restricts what goes in there.

Q: How successful is the vertical banded gastroplasty compared to the gastric bypass?

According to the results reported in medical literature, VBG is not nearly as effective as the gastric bypass. Only about 25% of VBG patients are reported to have lost more than 50% of their excess body weight over a five-year period. Our data show that 85% of our laparoscopic gastric bypass patients have lost over 50% of their excess body weight.

Some surgical centers have reported equal success in terms of weight lost following surgery, but that result seems highly dependent on the experience of the surgeon doing the operation. The vertical banded gastroplasty also can have the effect of teaching patients to eat the wrong foods. High-calorie, sugary liquids—which are not recommended for weight-loss programs—will go right through the restricted opening and into the larger portion of the stomach, for example.

Q: Could you explain the biliopancreatic diversion?

This operation causes a malabsorption of food. There are two ways of losing weight from a dietary standpoint. One is that you don't eat as much, which is the focus of the restrictive operations. The other is that you eat what you want, but you're prevented from absorbing certain foods, and this is the focus of the malabsorptive operations.

The only things we can block absorption of are fats and starches. We can't block sugar. So the biliopancreatic diversion is a malabsorptive operation that causes people not to be able to digest or absorb fat or starches in the same way.

The operation creates two limbs, the alimentary limb where the food comes down, and the biliopancreatic limb where the bile and pancreatic juices come down. They meet in a common channel where the enzymes break down the food and cause absorption. The common channel was originally made very short—about 50 centimeters in length until it got into the colon. Now it's usually about 100 centimeters in length. Even so, there is not a lot of absorption capacity, which leads to malnutrition complications in some patients.

The duodenal switch is like a biliopancreatic diversion except it preserves the pyloric valve in the stomach and a little bit of the first part of the small intestine. Its proponents say it avoids some of the possible malnutrition complications of the biliopancreatic diversion by slowing down the pace of the digestive process, but there's not a lot of data on this issue yet.

Q: What common complications may occur after bariatric surgery?

We operate on some pretty sick patients. That's why they come to us for surgery, after all. A lot of our patients have diabetes, and diabetics don't heal well. So our most common complication is wound infection. But in laparoscopy, the wounds are very small. They may be inconvenient for the patient, but from a surgeon's standpoint, the wounds are a very minor issue. About 10% of our patients may have seromas or some sort of a wound issue.

All our patients have at least a little problem with their pulmonary systems. We operate just underneath the left diaphragm, and all of our patients have a little bit of collapse in the left lung that usually results in no symptoms at all. Even though our patients often do not have great pulmonary function, we have a very low incidence of pneumonia after surgery because our patients are so motivated and follow our preventive instructions.

Q: What are the major risks of gastric bypass surgery?

There are two potentially serious complications. The first is a leak, either at the site where the stomach is attached to the small intestine or where the small bowel is sutured or stapled to the small stomach pouch. This occurs in somewhere from 1–3% of our patients. Half of these patients will need another operation, and half can be controlled by a drain that we place during the first surgery.

The second potential problem is a pulmonary embolism, a blood clot that travels to the lungs. We guard against this by treating people with blood thinners like heparin, getting them up and walking early, and having them wear sequential-compression stockings in bed so they are less likely to form clots in the deep veins of their legs.

Q: What causes the leaks?

A disruption of the staple or suture line causes the leak. If you look at the reasons for that, our diabetic patients probably have a higher incidence of leaks because they don't heal as well. They don't heal down the staple lines and incorporate them, so we have to rely on the sutures or staples to bind things together longer until the body can actually scar them in.

Q: What about intestinal blockages?

There are two kinds of bowel obstructions we worry about.

The first, which occurs in less than 3% of patients, results from kinking of the bowel or a scar forming that would kink the bowel. This usually occurs within a few days of the operation. An obstruction can also form later than that, even years after the operation, as a result of scarring, and there are specific ways of monitoring for this.

The second kind of obstruction is an actual scarring down of the hookups that we make between the small intestine and the small stomach pouch. This occurs in 3–15% of patients depending on the technique used by the surgeon and his experience. This kind of obstruction is treated by an endoscopic surgery and opening up the scarred passage with an inflated balloon, much like what is done with cardiac blood vessels in angioplasty.

Q: What can a patient do to prepare for bariatric surgery?

Probably the best thing a patient could do is to increase his or her pulmonary endurance a little bit. They can help themselves just by going out and walking, not smoking, and coughing and deep breathing to make sure the lungs are clear.

Q: What about trying to lose weight before surgery?

I'm not a big advocate of people trying to lose weight or staying on a diet before they go into weight-loss surgery. I don't think there's much correlation between how well they're going to do after the surgery and dieting before the surgery. I admit that some people differ with me. Some bariatric centers feel very strongly that people should try to go on a weight-loss regimen and stick to it before surgery, and they use that as a predictor of success after surgery. I don't think it's a good predictor.

For super-obese people, however, there are two reasons why we might want them to go on a weight-loss program. The first is that logistically it's hard to operate on people who are really big. Some machinery, like CT scanners, can't accommodate them, and it's hard for nurses to push them around on beds, and so forth.

Second, there's some indication that weight loss right before we operate may shrink the patient's liver down acutely if there's a very large, fatty liver. Since we have to operate underneath the liver, we might have patients go on a weight-loss program if we know from ultrasound that they have a big liver, or if they're diabetic and therefore likely to have an enlarged liver, or if they have abnormal results of liver function tests before surgery. A smaller liver improves the patient's chance of having the surgery done laparoscopically.

Q: What about psychological preparation for surgery?

I think every patient does that in his or her own way. We do a psychological evaluation on all our patients to make sure that they're well informed, don't have any unanswered questions, and have accurate expectations for the surgery. For any surgery, I believe that the patient should be positive going in. It can be difficult for some of our patients whose families or friends are very negative at the time of the surgery. They come in bummed out because of all the negative comments they've had to deal with. Or they may be afraid of negative comments after the surgery, so they don't tell people and have to do this alone, without support. These issues can be difficult to address. But by and large, people do what they need to do from a psychological standpoint and go through the surgery.

Q: Would it be valuable to develop a protocol or program that involves hypnosis, positive affirmations, or methods of this nature to prepare patients for surgery?

A couple of the insurance companies have started looking at programs like that. I think there's good data to support the positive effect these programs can have. I'm all for that kind of stuff. I love it. There is so much that we don't know about surgery and how people heal from surgery. But I do know that people who go into surgery feeling good usually do better than people who are feeling bad about it.

Q: What psychological conditions would eliminate a prospective patient as a surgical candidate?

The NIH guidelines say that patients should be stable psychologically. I think most major bariatric programs, however, have operated on some schizophrenic patients.

Q: Would that include patients who needed to be stabilized by medications?

Certainly. I operated about a year ago on a lady who had a lot of medical problems, who was also schizophrenic and extremely functional. She was experiencing side effects from the medications for her obesity-related diseases, we operated on her, and she's done great. She's still schizophrenic, but she's physically fine.

Q: What is the first post-operative year like for the patient? What factors are most important for a successful result?

Follow-up is the most important factor in success. The operation itself does not cure obesity. The patient needs to have some sort of accountability in following their program.

As for the first year, it breaks down into different segments. The first 4–6 weeks, we want them pretty much only on protein and water. It gets boring, no question about it. And it's frustrating, because patients find they can tolerate a food one day, and the next day they eat exactly the same thing and can't tolerate it. We don't know why. It's simply an indication of how this new little stomach they have is healing. They just need to drop back for a day and try again a couple of days later.

After the first 4–6 weeks, they're usually able to expand what they eat a little bit, and therefore have a little higher energy level. But they're still not giving their bodies much energy, and they're in ketosis. They have to burn up the fat, and that produces ketones. If they don't stay well hydrated and eat protein during this period, they're going to feel even worse.

By the third to fourth month, they're starting to eat more normal kinds of foods, though obviously much less of them. By the sixth month, about two-thirds of the amount they're going to lose has already been lost—and that's about 60% of their excess body weight. Most of the weight loss is in those first six months, and then it slows down so that at 12 months most people have reached the low point in their weight loss.

Q: What is "dumping"?

Dumping is a physiological reaction to a high sugar load. What happens is that people dump a lot of sugar into the small intestine quickly, and the small intestine is not used to this. All of a sudden, your sugar level rises, the body senses that, and it dumps in a lot of insulin, which dramatically lowers blood sugar. This often results in nausea and vomiting, cramping, abdominal pain, flushing of the skin, sweating, and a sense of fear and ill-being. It's frightening for patients because they not only feel sick, but also have a sense of impending doom. It's a negative event in patients' lives, but we doctors like it. We hope that most patients get it and that the dumping experience leads to an aversion to sugar intake. While we can affect fat and starch absorption, we can't keep patients from absorbing sugar—and sugar is addictive. If they can tolerate sugar, they eat it, and they get a rush from it that's pleasant. Unfortunately, this wears off in an hour or two, and then they want some more sugar. Generally, people who avoid sugar do better after gastric bypass.

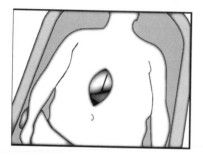

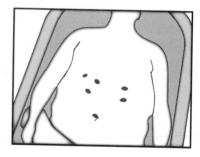

When the gastric bypass procedure is performed "open," an incision extending from just below the bottom of the sternum to just above the navel is made through the abdominal wall along the midline.

When the procedure is performed laparoscopically, six small incisions ranging in size from 1" to 2" in length are made off the midline in the locations above.

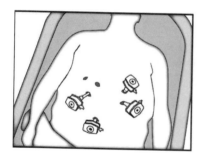

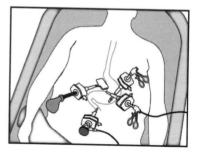

In the laparoscopic procedure, plastic trochars that act as portals for the endoscopic surgical instruments are inserted through the incisions into the abdominal cavity.

Specially designed endoscopic surgical instruments—including the laparoscope (bottom center)—are inserted into the abdominal cavity through the trochars to perform the Roux en-Y gastric bypass procedure.

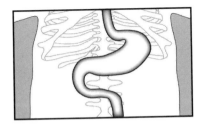

The normal digestive tract consisting of the esophagus leading into the stomach followed by the small intestine.

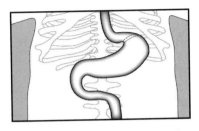

A small pouch approximately 15 cubic centimeters in volume is created at the top of the stomach with a double line of surgical staples.

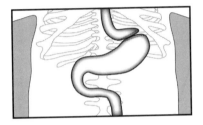

An incision is made between the double staple lines, separating the newly created pouch from the remainder of the original stomach.

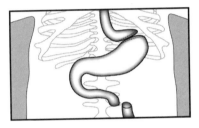

Approximately 18 inches from where the small intestine attaches to the bottom of the original stomach, the small intestine is divided.

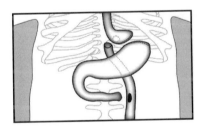

The lower limb of the transected small intestine is moved up and attached to an opening created in the new pouch. The upper limb of the small intestine is then attached to an opening created farther down in the small intestine.

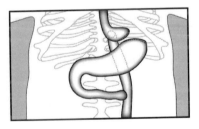

The completed Roux en-Y gastric bypass configuration restores the integrity of the digestive tract. Food comes down the esophagus into the new gastric pouch and then into the newly connected intestinal limb. The remainder of the original stomach continues to produce gastric juices that are essential to nutrient assimilation in the small intestine.

Q: How frequently do patients have plastic surgery after bariatric surgery?

On a cruise a year ago, we asked 120 patients how many of them would like to have plastic surgery after their weight loss, and 100% raised their hands. But only about 10–15% of patients actually have surgery afterward. For some of them, it's medically indicated, no question. For others, it's cosmetic.

Abdominoplasty is by far the most popular procedure. The medical indication for abdominoplasty, and for breast lifts as well, is usually that the places where skin rubs on skin are such a hygiene problem that people develop rashes no matter what lotions, potions, and powders they use. Next in popularity is plastic surgery on the arms and thighs.

Q: How satisfied are patients with the results of plastic surgery?

Abdominoplasty and breast uplifts rank very high in patient satisfaction. Arms may not be as satisfactory because the scar is visible. Scars heal better when you can immobilize the affected area, and that's not possible with the upper arms.

Q: How do morbid obesity and weight loss affect the likelihood of pregnancy?

There's a lot of discussion on this topic right now. There are many women who are infertile as a result of their obesity, and for those individuals, weight loss is certainly the only way that they may ever get pregnant. The question is, is it safe to be pregnant after bariatric surgery? I think it certainly is.

But morbidly obese women are in a higher risk group during pregnancy. They have higher instances of hypertension and diabetes, higher C-section rates, and their babies are at higher risk for all sorts of anomalies. So certainly if they lose weight through bariatric surgery, they're reducing their risk. They're less likely to develop hypertension and diabetes. We have even found that many women who had been pregnant and required C-sections before bariatric surgery did not require C-sections in subsequent pregnancies after the surgery.

Q: What are your guidelines for pregnancy after bariatric surgery?

We discourage them during the first year because we think it's not safe if they're losing a lot of weight. But once they stabilize, I think that they can become pregnant and carry a healthy baby to term. We do ask them to follow up with us as well as their obstetricians because there are some things that the obstetricians don't know that we do.

We have a protocol for women who become pregnant after bariatric surgery that we send to obstetricians, telling them, for example, that if they need to test for diabetes, they should not use an oral glucose tolerance test because it will make the patient very sick. And when a patient is taking her prenatal vitamins, she should take her regular vitamins for her gastric bypass as well. So follow-up and coordination between the bariatric surgeon and the obstetrician is very important.

Sharron Dalton, Ph.D., R.D., Nutritionist

D<small>R. S</small>HARRON D<small>ALTON IS THE</small> A<small>SSOCIATE</small> P<small>ROFESSOR AND</small> Director, Graduate Nutrition Program, Department of Nutrition and Food Studies, at New York University in New York City. She is an expert on food choice behavior, the dynamics of body weight management, international nutrition, and childhood obesity.

Q: What is known about the causes of morbid obesity?

There's nature and there's nurture—your environment and your genes. For instance, we really don't see many fat people in the villages of Nepal or India. There may be a few fat genes among these populations, but because they aren't in an obesity-fostering environment, they aren't fat. So it's always the interaction. I don't think anyone would say it's one or the other, genetics or environment.

That's why I was so interested in Carnie's family history. If there are two obese parents, then of course you know the genetic predisposition is going to be much higher. The standard figures they cite for the genetic responsibility of obesity is anywhere from 20% all the way up to 80%. But that has to be nurtured by the environment, which starts out in the family, and then, of course, is added to by our general social environment.

So what are the causes? We really don't know. There is a lot of work going on right now and lots of attempts to try to pin it down. If it's genetic, it's definitely a group of genes. It certainly wouldn't be just one gene.

Q: Is obesity the result of the breakdown of the body's satiety mechanism?

For someone who starts out as a fairly normal child and then becomes obese in childhood, this is probably where the mechanism gets misled. Leann L. Birch's work at Penn State showed some of that evidence in children. Obese children, just like obese adults—and in particular, morbidly obese adults—do not seem to have a satiety response that the rest of us have. They don't seem to feel so full that they can't eat another bite. They don't stop. They can eat when anyone else would be throwing up.

Q: Is there a way to repair that impairment?

We try all kinds of behavior modification gimmicks, but they're overridden by external cues like simply opening the refrigerator and seeing a Boston cream pie. It's very hard to override those external cues to eat. Then they just keep eating, and nothing happens with the internal responses to stop eating.

For this reason, I think that bariatric surgery is the one answer. I know the research supports this. If people perforate their staple lines after surgery, they go right back to eating. So unless it's mechanically stopped, there seem to be very few ways to retrain the disrupted satiety mechanism.

Q: What is the relationship between morbid obesity, childhood emotional development, and eating behavior?

For starters, I would say as a dietitian that good nutrition celebrates food, rather than the current standard practice among parents and nearly every eater out there that good nutrition is about restricting, controlling, and avoiding. Good nutrition, I think, shouldn't be a dreary daily grind of "shoulds" and "oughts."

In fact, parenting now seems to go well beyond just making the food available. We force-feed young children and then restrict them later without really having taught them how to make choices and set constructive limits. So it becomes a problem of feeding—rather than eating—with a child. There are very few parents today who sit down to eat with their children in an enjoyable way. Children eat their food everywhere—outside, inside, in front of the TV. They have very little structure in their meal plan. That might sound very old-fashioned—the idea of scheduled meals—but most of the current research still supports the idea that children can regulate their eating and their appetite, and they will not impair their appetite mechanisms if there's a division of responsibility.

That means that the parents decide what food will be served and when it's eaten. The child decides whether to eat it, and how much of it to eat. The child decides whether he or she is full or not.

But many parents override that by trying to make their children clean their plate—you know, "Eat this and you can have dessert." All of those things that most of us know—like "Here's the airplane coming into the hangar, down into the mouth"—these reinforcing behaviors are not recommended.

So by the time a child is older, they're caught in a terrible dilemma. They're initially taught that they must eat all their food. On the other hand, they can't then eat all their food if they start to get a little overweight.

With parents like Marilyn Wilson-Rutherford, who was constantly dieting, just being a role model of dieting may have made a big difference to Carnie as she grew up, because dieting for her must have been a conditioned behavior. The psychological and physiological effects of it for many people—but not everyone—become pathological.

Q: How might feeling deprived of parental attention affect obesity?

Emotional eating is thought to be a response to negative emotions such as anxiety, depression, anger, boredom, and loneliness. We know that adults use food to counteract feelings of being unloved, and ultimately to achieve the pleasure that they're lacking.

I picture a child today coming home to an empty house after school because both parents are working, or we have single parents. Many kids have instructions to stay inside, away from outside dangers, so they're in this environment of anxiety, depression, anger, boredom, and loneliness. Often the only things available to these kids are a television, a full refrigerator, and the microwave. We know that many of these children spend lots of time in front of the TV, and that fat kids spend more time watching than thin kids. We also know that full refrigerators are available more often for fat kids than thin kids.

This is a setup to diminish anxiety, to relieve their frustration and deprivation, and even to express hostility—conscious or unconscious—by eating.

Q: How common is morbid or extreme obesity in America?
The 1994 data showed that it's about .5%, which would be roughly 1.5 million people in the category that we're talking about. These numbers have probably increased over the past seven years.

Q: What nutritional deficiencies are present in morbidly obese individuals?
That depends on what people eat. Generally, people who take in a lot of calories don't have many nutritional deficiencies. They actually have a greater chance of not having deficiencies because they eat so much more food that they're very likely to get the 19 to 20 nutrients we have on our list of recommendations.

It's the people who are dieting on very low calories who run the risk of nutrient deficiencies. Morbidly obese people may go on very low-calorie diets, and then they may run the risk of deficiencies. It would be very hard to get all the nutrients you need on a 400-calorie diet unless you mixed them up in a liquid solution and gave it to them.

When we try to work with the extremely obese on decreasing their calories, we work with the standard idea of the five fruits and vegetables a day and reducing the number of breads and cereals. We also have them eat much smaller servings of animal protein and other sources of protein.

We also work mainly on serving size and make sure we get the variety of good foods they need. Once they've had the surgery, there can be problems of absorption, and it's very likely that there will be some deficiencies. It's probably a good idea to take nutrient supplements at that point.

Q: Are there weight-loss regimens that are especially risky?

Yes. Just following a regimen is risky because the biggest problem with weight-loss regimens is that they fail. A regimen means something that usually has to be reinforced and controlled with great vigor for a long period of time, and that just doesn't work for obesity, which is a lifelong thing. That's why 95–97% of these regimens fail, and people gain the weight back.

Of course, maintenance is the biggest problem of all. Failure reinforces failure. I'm not a pro-dieting advocate. I believe in positive, healthy eating, but obviously within reason in terms of calories. I try to promote this type of eating along with increased activity, then let the weight fall into its appropriate place without focusing on weight change, which invariably causes anxiety. The one thing that people want to do is to see the scale move. We try to come up with some sort of stability in weight and eating behavior and then get people moving more—a minimum of 30 minutes a day, up to an hour. That makes the difference every time, but that's also the hardest part to achieve because of the long-term nature of behavior change that's required.

There are only three major ways to promote weight loss—

increased activity, reduced calories, and the cognitive behavior changes. The other two treatment strategies are drugs and surgery. Of the five things we can do, I find that restrictive dieting is the one that fails the most.

Having a full choice of a variety of healthy foods is important, but increasing physical activity is the factor that needs the most work, the most support, and the most encouragement. It's even harder for anyone who has an erratic life to begin with or is prone to depression. That leaves us with the drugs and the surgery.

Q: Do 95–97% of individual diet attempts fail, or 95–97% of the diet plans available?

It's very hard to get a handle on the commercial diet industry in general because programs like Weight Watchers, Jenny Craig, and all the others generally don't report their failures. Most of the data comes from university hospitals—and university medical center-sponsored research. The data from those programs represents people who probably come with a long list of failures anyway. Many successful people are isolated out there and are never reported. So we really don't know what successful people do. All we ever hear about are the failures.

The National Weight Control Registry that comes out of the University of Colorado Medical Center follows people who have been successful at large amounts of weight loss. I believe their requirement is that participants must have lost 30 pounds and kept it off for at least five years. If you think about it, that's not a huge amount of weight loss. But they follow people who have lost somewhere around 8% of total body weight and have kept it off successfully. The one recurring behavior to explain this success is extra physical activity, above what is considered normal—which is 30 minutes a day. In general, most of these people walk the equivalent of four miles a day. They also change some of their eating behaviors. They don't eat fried foods, and they're careful about high-fat foods. So those are the two things that they do, and they just keep at it.

Those are the people who have generally succeeded through standardized programs. But they're not losing vast amounts. Some of them have lost over 100 pounds or more and have kept it off. But keeping that amount off is a real challenge, and the general literature shows somewhere around a 95% failure. People gain it back again. Some of these people coming for surgery have lost 100 pounds and gained it back four times. Imagine the struggle they've gone through.

Q: How does motivational help fit in?

I find that motivational support is the key. I think most of the literature, including the NIH guidelines, ranks it as the number-one factor in achieving weight-loss success. Yet they have very little evidence of how it's done or what it is, because motivational programming is such a hard thing to package. You can't take it as a pill. Motivation is also extremely hard for depressed people.

The best way to describe a motivated person is someone who has good coping skills. So in most of our work, we try to help people develop coping skills. This means learning how to handle the slings and arrows of the world, developing strong and flexible approaches to managing frustration, learning how to nurture oneself without using food, and at the same time setting limits that are healthy. A strong friendship, or family support, is probably the primary coping method used. But that in itself takes skill. Fat people are often isolated and lonely, so they don't have a great support network, and to get help from friends is very, very hard. Interestingly, many of them don't want to have fat friends.

Not surprisingly, finding ways that obese people can go out and move their body and feel comfortable with others in public is the biggest challenge. I use a lot of brainstorming to determine what's the most important thing they can do and what they feel they can accomplish.

Q: What are the nutritional challenges associated with massive weight loss following bariatric surgery?

Foremost, we have to deal with the very small capacity of the stomach after surgery. People can eat no more than half a cup of food at a time at first. This means more continual eating and smaller amounts of food; otherwise, you'll pop your staples.

If it's a smooth post-operative period, there's usually not much diarrhea. But if there *is* diarrhea, that's a huge problem because people lose a lot of electrolytes and a lot of the minerals—particularly potassium. The usual diarrhea treatments are important, then a lot of fluids and replacements of the electrolytes. Long term, a lot of other vitamins and minerals can be lost. So we usually treat with supplements and very concentrated sources of nutrients, such as dense foods.

It's hard to say what percentage of people now experience this problem because most of the evidence pertaining to these problems occurred with some of the older methods of surgery that used to take 18 inches out of the gut. We found that there was a lot more difficulty with absorption and getting enough nutrients in these procedures.

Generally, every patient should be on an across-the-board supplement. Probably some of the vitamin assays would also be a good idea. We want to keep an eye on the mineral loss.

Q: Would that be anything special compared to the supplements people normally take?

No, you know, the daily multiple vitamin tablet is fine. If these are older people, there are specific supplements for different age groups or sexes. Men shouldn't particularly have extra iron, while women may need it if they're still menstruating. But for the most part, it's just the standard daily supplement, which usually brings people up to the recommended dietary allowances.

Q: What nutritional adjustments need to be made to deal with such issues as hair loss or skin elasticity as massive amounts of weight come off?

A lot of people, for all kinds of reasons, think hair loss is related to what you eat, but there isn't any good data that I've ever seen on that. As long as there's adequate protein—and that is definitely an issue—there shouldn't be hair loss. If there is protein urea in the excretion after surgery, this could be very serious and would be cause for immediate concern. It would probably require a good workup to see what's going on, especially if there's kidney involvement. That's why it's always important to make sure all functions are up and going.

Q: Are there safety issues regarding high protein post-bariatric surgery diets?

I would think so. The way the body works is that the first demand is for energy, and it's going to need energy as the priority before it will rebuild and maintain tissue. When there is not enough carbohydrate, protein has to act like a carbohydrate—rather than being used for rebuilding and maintaining tissue. This can cause some problems with nitrogen components going up.

I've seen protein overload with that kind of a regimen. So, the first rule is to monitor the patient to ensure that problems are avoided.

Q: What are the factors in surgical weight loss that are essential to a successful result?

Developing coping mechanisms. These come from family and from the patient herself. I'm sure Carnie is getting quite a lot of psychological support. I don't know if she does, but I would guess she probably gets regular therapy.

I also don't know how strong her support from her friends is, but that is also extremely important. The coping mechanisms are very, very important for surgical weight loss. I was involved in a follow-up phone survey of all of Mount Sinai's 200 post-surgical patients. Patients who had support seemed to manage much better than those who had very little support and led isolated, lonely lives.

This all feeds into successful weight loss. If people have support and the opportunity to make choices and to learn how to set limits for themselves, it's much better than having someone else put the limits on them.

It sounds like Carnie's bought into this for herself, and she's the one who's decided on her limits. She's no longer trying to answer to an outside idea of what she should look like, what she should eat, all of these other rules. There are probably basic guidelines, but she's making the choices within those parameters.

The reason diets fail and the reason people fail at weight loss is because of compliance. They just can't stand the restriction. I've worked with people who have lost 100 pounds under the most compliant conditions. But after a while, they just can't stand it any longer, and then they start gaining the weight back more than ever.

Q: Is individualizing the diet to your own standards and comfort level a major factor in compliance?

Absolutely. I would call it a major factor in successful weight management, rather than compliance.

Q: What are the nutritional considerations related to becoming pregnant after surgically induced weight loss?

Basically, they are the same as for a normal-weight pregnancy. In terms of nutrition, we usually think of a target weight gain for overweight people of only 15–20 pounds, rather than the 25–30 that we would recommend for most pregnancies.

Usually during the first trimester, we would normally expect to see weight gain around a pound or two. But in obese patients, I would hope not to see much weight gain in the first trimester. In the second trimester, maybe five to six pounds is reasonable. Normally we'd expect to see about an 11-pound increase. The third trimester produces greater weight gain, up to whatever limit is considered appropriate for that person.

Gestational diabetes is one of the biggest problems that I've found in obese women having their first pregnancy. I would expect that if someone had bariatric surgery, they may have had a history of elevated blood sugar, and this could be a problem. Most pregnant women have their urine checked quite often for high blood sugar. Of course, if someone is still on insulin, this takes some very special management because ketosis can harm the brain development of the fetus.

The basic advice would be to eat a balanced diet, get plenty of fluids, and don't diet during pregnancy. Even with obese women, we never recommend dieting during pregnancy because there can be a risk to the fetus.

Steven B. Heymsfield, M.D., Endocrinologist

Dr. Steven Heymsfield is Professor of Medicine, Columbia University College of Physicians and Surgeons; and Director, Outpatient Obesity and Human Body Composition Core Units of the Obesity Research Center, St. Luke's-Roosevelt Hospital Center in New York City. He is an expert in human body composition and the treatment and prevention of obesity.

Q: How is morbid obesity diagnosed?
It's pretty straightforward. If you don't already know it from seeing somebody, you get a height and a weight and calculate their BMI. If it's over 40, they're morbidly obese. For a woman, use 100 pounds for the first five feet, and five pounds per inch after that. Carnie is about 5'4" and weighed about 300 pounds. So her ideal weight is around 120 pounds. By any standard you use, she was morbidly obese.

Q: How common is morbid obesity?
It's very hard to get precise statistics on that. There was an old idea that it was about 5% of the population. But because our weight is shifting upwards, perhaps it's more than that now.

Q: What are the causes of morbid obesity?
There are only a few known causes, such as very rare genetic abnormalities. In the large majority of people who are morbidly obese, the underlying cause is not really specifically known.

Q: In what percentage of cases does thyroid malfunction cause morbid obesity?
Thyroid malfunction would never be a cause of morbid obesity. When the thyroid fails, people can gain some weight, but it's usually in the range of 10–20% above their normal weight. It's not double their normal weight.

Q: Why would it stop at 10–20%?

You might consider the thyroid responsible for fine-tuning. It's a fine regulator of metabolism and body weight. If you have an overactive thyroid, you could lose 10% of your weight. If you have an underactive thyroid, you could gain 10–15% of your weight. But beyond that, there are other weight-controlling mechanisms.

Q: What are the other "weight-controlling" mechanisms?

The Leptin hormone feedback loop is one example. Leptin is made by fat cells, and this hormone interacts with various brain regions to suppress food intake. People with a genetic inability to make Leptin lose eating control and become obese because that feedback loop is broken.

People weren't tested for Leptin in the past because it was only discovered in 1994. But it's one of the few specific blood tests that might relate to obesity.

Although there are childhood forms of morbid obesity, they're usually rare and fatal at a fairly young age. So if you get into adulthood, you don't have one of those forms.

Q: Could you elaborate on some of those childhood forms of morbid obesity?

The most common cause of morbid obesity in children is Prader-Willi Syndrome. That is, in the most simple terms, the result of a "broken" chromosome. It's associated with mild mental retardation, severe obesity, and a really voracious appetite. These children often die in their late teens from obesity complications and other genetic abnormalities.

It's fairly rare overall—perhaps one in 100,000 or 200,000 births. But it's common enough so that there are Prader-Willi associations in every large city. The families share a lot of common care problems.

There are some more rare genetic abnormalities that cause

obesity in children as well, like Lawrence Moon Bidell Syndrome. But they are extremely rare.

Q: Are the BMI definitions the same for children as adults?

It changes greatly. Children tend to have lower BMIs than adults, so there is a little bit of a debate over the applicability of BMI definitions for children. The BMI of a normal 5-year-old and a normal 50-year-old are very different.

Q: If your child is gaining weight rapidly, what's the usual course of diagnosis and testing for the cause of their obesity?

You want to exclude all of the conditions like Prader-Willi Syndrome, and rule out a Leptin deficiency. A good family medical history, a physical exam, and blood tests would all be involved. You would do thyroid and hormone testing as well. There are probably other rare hormonal abnormalities, like Cushing Syndrome, but those are unusual, and most physicians easily recognize them.

Q: How accurate is thyroid testing?

If you go back 20 to 30 years, it was an extremely crude test. Today, thyroid testing is very, very sophisticated. It's gotten better and better. So, if you have a thyroid abnormality, the chances are very, very good the blood tests will pick it up.

Q: Is there a role for preventive strategies to reduce the prevalence of morbid obesity?

There is, but I'm not sure we've accomplished it. The risk of becoming morbidly obese is related to some predictable factors, so you could identify children who were at high risk at a pretty young age. For example, if both of your parents are obese, your risk of becoming morbidly obese is pretty good. You have similar genes and a similar environment. Those two factors are really what lead to obesity. It's hard to pull those things apart, but we know that each contributes.

There are other very well-known factors like socioeconomic status. For reasons that are not clearly understood, people of lower socioeconomic status are at a higher risk of developing morbid obesity. One camp says that education plays a role in regulating weight. Knowing about weight and having a low weight is socially desirable in upper socioeconomic circles, so there's some thought that it's a process that people in some ways subtly control.

On the other hand, there's a countercurrent theory that holds that there may be a common genetic factor that leads to both obesity and lower socioeconomic status.

Q: Has any work been done regarding the notion that overeating might be related to a desire for power or status?

Yes. There are a lot of theories like that, but there isn't a great deal of supportive data. Black women tend more often than whites to run their families. Now I'm generalizing very grossly here, but being big and physically strong—which often does come with obesity—is thought in some cultures to carry some value, as opposed to being very thin and frail looking. An anorexic body type would not be desirable in some cultures.

Q: What are the main co-morbidities associated with morbid obesity, and what is their effect on prognosis?

There's a host of them. Just being obese in general carries with it risks of diabetes, heart disease, strokes, joint problems, gallstones, reproductive abnormalities, and certain types of cancers. The risks for purely mechanical problems like sleep apnea also increase greatly. The possibility of pulmonary emboli—blood clots going to your lungs—also begins to increase. Your risk of not surviving a surgical procedure increases greatly at those weights as well. While obesity in itself carries with it all of these co-morbidities, morbid obesity's a special case because just the major mechanical problems of breathing, moving about, and maybe even being operated on can increase markedly.

Q: Is there anything endocrine-related that would be caused by something like sleep apnea?

Not directly. Sleep apnea can, in some ways, be related to high blood pressure.

Q: Would there be a concomitant psychological effect caused by sleep apnea?

Absolutely. There are very significant mood effects. If you can't keep awake during the day, that's a big problem. But also some occult depression and things like that could be related to sleep disturbances.

Q: What kind of hormones would be shooting into the system as a result of this condition?

They're called catecholamines. Epinephrine and norepinephrine could be secreted into the bloodstream, and they constrict blood vessels. That could lead to high blood pressure. But maybe the hypoxia could lead to subtler mood changes.

Q: Is there any relationship between morbid obesity—or some of the co-morbidities related to morbid obesity—and the tendency to use marijuana or other drugs?

I wouldn't say directly, but—I'm going out a little bit on a limb here—I think that sometimes children of parents who are drug or alcohol abusers end up obese. I guess the theory is sometimes that food is yet another form of that addictive behavior. Rather than become alcoholic, they become "food-aholics." I don't know if that's a learned behavior or something you acquire genetically, but quite often physicians see that children of either drug or alcohol abusers will display some of these qualities as well.

Q: Can marijuana use exacerbate the tendency to become morbidly obese?

I think that's definitely a possibility. Morbid obesity and marijuana are a pretty volatile mixture. Marijuana causes a number of biological effects, and certainly one them is an increased appetite.

Q: What are the basic principles in the treatment of obesity and morbid obesity?

For obesity in general, you have to eat less than you expend and thereby lose body energy stores. Somehow you have to either increase your physical activity or reduce your food intake—or both—to lose weight. You can reduce your food intake through either a voluntary effort on a traditional kind of everyday diet program, or through medications. But whatever the program, it involves reducing intake through, and increasing energy expenditure through, physical activity. That's the backbone of weight-control programs.

Sadly, for morbidly obese patients, those measures only rarely work.

Q: Why is that?

We don't really know. Whatever the underlying basis is for doubling your ideal body weight must be fairly powerful. Whatever those genetic and environmental reasons are, they're not easily overcome by voluntary means.

Q: Are there endocrine treatments that would encourage a person to exercise?

At the moment, we don't have anything like that I'm aware of. There's been some hope that you could have hormonal treatments or drug treatments that would have the same effect as exercise, but none that would *encourage* you to exercise.

Q: Are there weight-loss regimens that are excessively risky?

Definitely. Any type of fad diet, such as the grapefruit diet or weird diets that have very abnormal nutrient compositions, have been known to kill people. So any type of diet that promises too much and is very unusual in nutrients could potentially put you at risk.

The second type of thing that could put you at risk is any medication that you would take that is not approved, or has not been studied very thoroughly. This includes alternative medications. They could be risky as well.

Q: What are the endocrine considerations regarding weight-loss surgery?

People should certainly go to physicians who are trained to do that type of surgery and do it on a regular professional basis. It's not something that you just do once or twice every couple of months. The physicians who do this have programs and should do thorough medical and psychological evaluations of candidates before they do the surgery. Good follow-ups after the surgery are also essential. Those are very important considerations that mandate that you go to a real professional.

Q: Is there any risk of endocrine imbalance as a result of surgically induced weight loss?

Definitely. If you lose weight too quickly, you could suffer from things like low blood sugar and hypoglycemia. You could have a fluid imbalance with loss of key electrolytes that in turn would lead to muscle weakness or heart problems.

Q: What about psychological effects?

It's not an unreasonable assumption that overly rapid weight loss could lead to some mood changes, particularly depression. At first, when people who are morbidly obese lose a lot of weight, they feel good. They're elated. But that could change very quickly. We know that people who voluntarily starved in experimental studies developed mood changes. Listlessness and depression are often associated with hair loss and other signs of protein deficiency.

Q: Following the operation, what are the patients' needs in terms of diet, nutrition, and exercise?

Let's start with exercise. If you're morbidly obese, we know that even after the operation you can't start jumping rope three hours a day. I have patients who can't even walk. People have to gradually increase their physical activity. A physical trainer or physical therapist should assist patients just to make sure there are no joint problems or joint damage. It's something you want to do carefully and judiciously so you don't hurt yourself.

On the diet side, it depends on what surgery you have. Each surgical procedure comes with certain dietary requirements, as well as eating smaller meals—sometimes even liquid meals—and chewing your food thoroughly because your gastric size has been restricted substantially.

Nutritionally, you want to make sure you have balanced meals, particularly ones that have adequate protein—if not extra protein—to make sure that the quality of your diet is good and that you don't lose excessive amounts of your muscle as you're dieting. This applies to liquids as well. You don't want to drink high-sugar drinks as your only food source.

Q: Do formerly morbidly obese patients tend to have either muscular imbalances or musculoskeletal problems as a result of rapid weight loss?

There have been some suggested risks: If you lose weight too quickly, maybe you could lose too much muscle or bone. But I haven't seen too much evidence of that.

Q: Is physical therapy often required for post-surgical bariatric patients?

As they lose weight, someone who is morbidly obese will need the help of physical therapists. In the most extreme cases, they learn how to walk again. Once you're above 800 pounds, it's pretty unusual to be able to walk, and many patients who come to see us weigh more than that.

Q: What are the principal characteristics of your patients, and what—if any—are the unique hallmarks of your particular approach?

I see a range of patients, from those who are a little bit overweight to those who are severely and morbidly obese. People in general are treated the same way. First you start with diet and exercise. Usually that's done in collaboration with behaviorists of some type, like a dietitian who's been specially trained, or a psychologist. If that treatment doesn't work after a period of time, then we often add pharmacological therapy.

Q: What do you mean by pharmacological therapy?

There are really only two approved drugs right now. One is a selective serotonin and norepinephrine re-uptake inhibitor, or SNRI. Meridia is the other drug, and it suppresses appetite. It's a reasonably effective drug. But neither one of these drugs will take off the amount of weight required by the morbidly obese patient.

If, for example, you could lose on average about 10% of your weight with diet and medications in one year, that would be a good outcome. But morbidly obese patients need to lose 30–50% percent of their weight, and the only approach now available to get into that range is surgery.

Q: What are the predominant factors that determine a patient's successful outcome from bariatric surgery?

I'm not sure I know that answer, but if they're screened carefully in the beginning, and if they recognize that it's a lifelong commitment and that the surgery is not a magic bullet, then that level of commitment and readiness is very important in predicting whether or not they'll be successful in the long run.

Q: Are these the principal factors with the patients whom you treat?

They're the main things. People have done many studies looking at predictors of long-term success, and one person might find that a certain eating pattern is more consistent with success than others. But in the long run, very few of these predictors have borne much fruit. The main thing is that people are prepared to make a lifelong commitment; that they have realistic expectations of the weight that they can lose; and finally, that they maintain some level of exercise or physical activity.

Q: What role do stress hormones play in this setting?

Stress hormones are not directly related to the cause of obesity. Nor can I think of any relations other than the ones we mentioned, like sleep apnea.

Q: Do some people tend to eat when they feel stress?

Yes, but that's a little different story, and may not be directly related to stress hormones as much as some other behavioral mechanisms that we're not completely familiar with yet. There is that general impression, but it's been hard to nail down in real studies. People who studied students during final exams and in other periods like that haven't really seen as much as you'd expect. We all respond to stress in different ways. Some people eat less during stress.

Q: What effect do bariatric surgery and massive weight loss have on the ability to experience a successful pregnancy?

It substantially improves the possibility. Morbid obesity is associated with increased congenital defects in newborns, and also with infertility. Both of those problems seem to be resolved greatly by weight loss. Often, women become pregnant for the first time after obesity surgery.

Q: What are the most intriguing developments on the horizon regarding the treatment of obesity and morbid obesity?

I think that there's one camp that considers obesity surgery barbaric and right up there with jaw wiring. That camp probably holds the view that there's still a magic bullet to be found, if only we knew the molecular mechanisms regulating food intake for each individual. If we understood them, then we could develop very targeted treatments that would selectively block those mechanisms. That's the kind of futuristic view that says if we really understood the underlying basis for each individual, we wouldn't have to resort to crude treatments such as surgery, which largely reduces food intake through mechanical means.

Q: What are the other theories about the causes of obesity?

One obvious and maybe overwrought idea is that physical activities are much too low and that, as a species, combining so much food and a lack of physical activity means that we're going to become progressively fatter up to some point. As a society, we have to figure out ways to increase our activity, despite having all these luxuries at our disposal.

Q: Are there endocrine factors related to the desire to exercise? What makes a rat want to get on that wheel and just go, rather than lying down and doing nothing?

We can offer some answers to that. One thing we know is that the animals that are Leptin deficient or have blocked Leptin action are also physically inactive in addition to eating too much. When Leptin is replaced, their activity levels increase. So we know from that one example that there are some hormonal mechanisms that underlie physical activity.

Q: What is the status of Leptin replacement therapy?

We already know that when you take Leptin deficient children and give them Leptin, their weight comes down to normal or very near normal. For adults who are adequate in Leptin levels, this replacement therapy has only very minor effects on body weight.

Q: How many people in the obese population would be candidates for Leptin therapy?

I think we're talking about a handful of people in the world, so that's not viable. But the search is on for other mechanisms. There are other pathways within the Leptin axis that have now been discovered that are also abnormal in some people. These haven't translated directly to treatments yet, though.

Q: Is there anything else you'd like to add about morbid obesity?

I think it really brings up a very critical thing for people, and that is that when you're morbidly obese, your whole life is profoundly affected by that problem. It literally surrounds you 24 hours a day, and it makes you very susceptible to all types of fraudulent treatment.

Morbidly obese people spend tens of thousands of dollars in the vain hope of finding a cure. My only recommendation to people would be to seek out the best possible professionals in the area. The American Dietetic Association (ADA) has a Website, and The National Institutes of Health (NIH) has a Website for weight control.

It's very important to seek out the best possible help, but not to try and find the latest supposed cure, nostrum, or herbal preparation that promises something that just can't be delivered.

Myles S. Faith, Ph.D., Psychology Professor

D R. MYLES FAITH IS ASSISTANT PROFESSOR OF CLINICAL Psychology in Psychiatry, Columbia University College of Physicians & Surgeons; and Associate Research Scientist, Obesity Research Center, St. Luke's-Roosevelt Hospital Center in New York City. He is an expert on genetic and environmental influences on pediatric eating and obesity and the treatment and prevention of childhood obesity.

Q: How are a person's attitudes toward food developed?
In part, we come into the world with certain preferences and attitudes toward food, certain likes and dislikes. But in large part, our attitudes come from our early experiences with foods—what our parents exposed us to. We tend to like what our parents liked, and what was presented to us frequently. By the same token, we often dislike foods that our parents didn't like or just didn't serve us.

Q: Aside from preferences, how do we form attitudes about food as something more than nourishment?
Food can certainly become an emotional crutch, and that lesson can be learned from others in your family. It can also come from observing people outside the family, and from the media. Some people learn that one way to handle their problems is through food. It helps to relieve stress and helps them feel better. In effect, the good feeling produced by food can be "over-learned."

Q: Can you explain how food can relieve stress?
There are some hypotheses that food might help to relieve stress through raising serotonin levels, but this is not well understood at this point. Of course, not everyone eats in response to stress, and the underlying physiology is not very clear.

Q: Is there a relationship between smoking marijuana and overeating?

We have a very poor understanding of how overeating relates to the use and abuse of other substances. We know that many of our patients have problems with binge eating and overeating, and often have other problems with other compulsive behaviors. Some, but not all, tell us that they drink excessively, for example, or take drugs. But we don't really understand the relationship between these behaviors.

Q: What is the relationship between morbid obesity and childhood emotional development?

One of the clearest effects we see is that obesity has psychosocial consequences. Feelings of being stigmatized, ridiculed, or rejected by peers are often reported to us by overweight children. For the morbidly obese child, these pressures can be extreme and can lead to emotional problems and problems with peer relationships.

Q: Do some children overeat in order to gain size and power?

I wouldn't read too much into that. When people talk about eating as a way to gain control, we think about eating disorders such as anorexia and bulimia. And in the classic case, a person with these disorders comes from a family marked by power struggles. But with obesity, the family dynamics are not that clear. The families of obese and non-obese individuals exhibit pretty similar psychological makeups. There's no strong evidence that the families of obese individuals have more psychological problems. This is not to say that the family does not play a critical role.

Q: What is the role of the family regarding obesity?

I always say obesity is a family problem, whether you like

it or not. First of all, obesity has a genetic component. Our parents pass on to us a certain predisposition to become heavier. Second, our families provide the environment in which we grow up. They can provide an environment that can make it easy to become obese because everyone is sedentary, or because the house is full of rich snack foods with few healthy choices. And parents can be very accepting and supportive toward their children, or very rejecting. Parents can come down very hard on an overweight child.

Q: Is parental insensitivity a common problem?

Unfortunately, it's very common to see parents who are very, very critical toward their own and other obese children. Obviously, it doesn't help. You would expect ridicule from peers, and even strangers. But a surprising finding is that a lot of it comes from family members. You would think the home environment would be a safe place, but that's not always the case.

Q: Carnie mentioned that as a child her size made her feel powerful in sports. Is this typical?

What we see more commonly is that obesity leads to rejection and teasing by peers. Of course, people can overcome discrimination and look to their strengths. An important lesson is that obese people have strengths and weaknesses just like thin people, and the trick is for everyone to make the best use of their strengths. There obviously was much more to Carnie than her weight.

Q: How does society make life difficult for the obese?

Prejudice against the obese is one of the few prejudices that is publicly acceptable today. It's very common to hear people making comments and jokes about the overweight, and to ridicule them. We live in a society where there is enormous prejudice against the overweight, which is manifested in many ways. It affects their income, the jobs they're offered, even their treatment by sales clerks. It permeates their lives. And overweight and obese individuals consistently have poor body images—that is, they do not like how they look.

Q: What is the relationship between poor body image and self-esteem?

There is some relationship, but it's not a perfect one. Self-esteem is more of a general concept of how you see yourself, and it incorporates all aspects of your life—not only your body image, but also how you see yourself as a worker, as a friend, and so forth. What we see in obese and non-obese individuals is a pretty similar range of self-esteem. But in terms of body image, obese individuals see themselves in a more negative light than the non-obese.

Q: What are the common stereotypes regarding obesity?

The "jolly, fat theory" was big for many years. The idea was that the obese individual was the jolly, fat person on the outside and distressed inside. There is not a lot of evidence to support this. For many years, psychologists tried to find consistent profiles for obese individuals and finally concluded that there are few consistent patterns. It's hard to say that there is a distinct profile of obese individuals. Obese individuals are as diverse and different as non-obese people.

The one exception is the subgroup of binge eaters. These people report to us that they feel very little control when they eat, and eat far more than a normal person would, which causes them great distress. Binge eaters do tend to have a consistent profile. They have more emotional and psychological problems such as depression, anxiety, and poor peer relations.

Q: Can you describe binge eating in more detail?

The hallmark feature of binge eating disorders is eating exorbitant amounts of food in short periods of time. Along with the massive food intake, there's an accompanying feeling of a lack of control, the feeling that they cannot stop eating.

Q: How do you treat the binge eater?

It's a matter of adapting them to a new, healthier style of eating, and forcing them to take control over certain aspects of their life that they feel dominate them. One type of therapy is called cognitive behavior therapy. It targets strategies to change how the patient thinks and behaves. It teaches patients that they can essentially control and master the situation. It provides healthier coping skills, and teaches patients to think through how to handle different situations. The patients practice how not to overconsume, and how to balance out their calories in a healthier way. It's a very practical therapy that confronts the problem head-on, and it's very effective for many patients.

Q: So patients learn to identify their triggers?

Absolutely. The classic approach would be to first keep a diary or log of the situations in which the person binge eats. Were there conflicts with other people? An interpersonal rejection? Did they feel stressed? Lonely? Depressed? For our binge-eating patients, emotions are often a trigger for overeating. Once we've identified the situations and the feelings, we get the person to monitor what they were thinking. Typically, the thoughts are: *I can't stop myself; this is terrible; I'm out of control.* Then we go back with the patient, look at the situation, and teach them healthier responses.

Q: What about pharmacological approaches to binge eating?

There have been some studies on binge eating looking at

different pharmacological agents. For some individuals, they can be helpful. But by and large, cognitive behavioral therapy is considered to be the treatment of choice.

Q: Is there a difference between the obese and the morbidly obese in terms of self-esteem and body image issues?
There are few research studies on the morbidly obese, because they're hard to find and track down for studies. Anecdotally, I would say that they have a very hard time. They are often the recipients of enormous social stigma and abuse.

Q: Do the obese have "addictive personalities"?
Many binge eaters tell us they feel as if they have an addiction, and some say they use alcohol or other drugs in addition. We could say that they believe they have a food addiction. But it's tough to say whether in fact binge eating and obesity are addictions. Most experts would not look at obesity as a food addiction. Addictions have very specific criteria, and most researchers would not think that obesity fits within them.

Q: What are these criteria?
A lot of them have to do with physiological responses and the development of tolerance and the phenomenon of withdrawal. Without going into the details of addiction, most in the obesity community would not consider food an addiction. But if, for example, one of our binge-eating patients feels he or she has a food addiction, we will work with them in those terms. The terminology is not key.

Q: How do you treat the depression that is a problem among binge eaters?
We find that when we improve the eating habits of binge eaters, their moods will often improve, because we're giving them control over their lives. A big reason for depression in

binge eaters is their perception of a loss of control and the inability to stop. So cognitive therapy, by giving them control, reduces a lot of their depression and anxiety.

Another form of treatment that's getting more attention recently is interpersonal therapy, which focuses on how patients relate to the other people in their lives rather than on the eating itself. When your relationships are ruptured, and you're being rejected by others and feel disconnected, interpersonal therapy tries to improve those relationships and help you to connect better with others.

Q: What kind of relationship skills would you teach?

Interpersonal therapy requires looking at your relationships and the ruptures in your relationships. We have patients describe how they have been treated by others, and look at their feelings of rejection, which often relate to weight. Then we try to help them form new, positive relations. This often means forging new relationships and connecting with people in new ways. It is a very positive, forward-thinking, behavioral approach. These relationships are very important to people who are obese and have had bad experiences in the past. They think, *I'm never going to be able to connect with other people. Who would want me?* That creates a self-fulfilling prophecy.

Q: For a parent, when is the appropriate time to seek psychological counseling regarding a child's weight problem?

In terms of psychological counseling for weight problems, I would say it's when one's weight is getting in the way of a healthy lifestyle. That can mean not going to school, not going to work, not having close friends, and not having a good network of people to be with. That might be a time to get psychological counseling. On the medical end, obesity is often accompanied by serious medical complications, even in childhood. If there are obvious medical complications, they should be tended to by medical personnel.

Q: Can an obese child be otherwise relatively well adjusted in terms of their functioning?

Sure. Obesity is a complicated problem because it has medical components, and it has psychological and social components. A child can be overweight and have medical problems associated with it, but not be bothered much by that interpersonally. Maybe the child is not hindered by it, functions well, and doesn't need psychological counseling. On the other hand, we might have a child who's overweight and who has no medical complications. Yet this child is teased or ridiculed, or feels different and is not pursuing friendships or doing as well as they could. Maybe this child might benefit from some kind of counseling to function better socially. Whenever we deal with obesity, we recognize we're dealing with a multifaceted issue. It's medical, it's psychological, it's social—it's everything rolled up.

Q: What psychological preparation is there for bariatric surgery?

Prior to bariatric surgery, the potential patient is extensively interviewed to make sure that he or she has tried other weight-loss alternatives, including behavioral and nonpharmacological approaches. We make sure the person is of clear mind and is prepared for this undertaking. The bottom line is that the surgeon and the surgical team want to make sure the person has tried other options and is psychologically prepared, because when surgery is successful, there are major changes.

Q: What psychological pitfalls typically need to be negotiated by the post-bariatric surgery patient?

Often, when patients lose weight, their mood improves,

their profile improves, and they psychologically do better. They're seeing themselves in a totally new way, so we prepare them for the fact that people will see and react to them differently, and we deal with those sorts of expectations.

Q: How do you do that?

We handle it in different ways. We ask how they expect their life will be different, and how they expect people will treat them differently when they've lost the weight, or as they're losing the weight. We try to get a sense of what their expectations are. We don't want them to be devastated if everything doesn't work perfectly, or if they regain some weight. As in all weight loss, it's getting a sense of what their expectations are, helping them work toward those expectations, but preparing them if everything doesn't happen at once.

Q: Is post-weight loss identity crisis common?

When you go through this sort of surgery and you lose a lot of weight, you're seeing yourself in a new light, and people treat you differently. At some point, that can be overwhelming. Many patients report similar reactions to us. It's not completely unexpected, given the big change.

We try to help prepare patients by dealing with their expectations, letting them know that people often go through periods of stress because they see themselves in a different light. We're supportive and give them different psychological strategies for riding it out, coping with the situation, and helping them stay with their weight goals.

There's no hard-and-fast rule here, but I think the general and common theme is that we want to deal with people's expectations about their life, their weight, and how they hope things will be different after the surgery. We want to give them support mechanisms for when things don't go as they hope or for when they see the differences.

Q: **What effects on interpersonal relationships are typically the result of dramatic weight losses?**

There's not a tremendous database on this, so it's hard to say. Anecdotally, people often tell us that after the surgery—and in general, when they lose weight—they feel better, their relationships often improve, and more often than not, it has positive effects.

Of course there are individual differences, and you will see cases where when one person improves their weight, it can be problematic for the other person in the relationship. This sometimes occurs when you see weight loss outside of surgery. In some relations, a wife might want to lose weight, and the husband might sabotage it. Sometimes they will tell us the reason is that the husband is concerned that when the spouse loses weight, he might not be seen as desirable. Or maybe he feels threatened. A lot of this comes down to the nature of the relationship.

Q: **What about intimacy?**

One of the motivations to lose weight is to be more physically desirable, and that's fine. After patients lose weight, they feel more confident, more comfortable approaching others, and for many individuals, this confidence will help them. But sometimes they lose the weight, but they still have the same challenges in terms of approaching others. So again, there's no hard, fast pattern.

Q: **What about the mind-set of someone who's tried every diet out there and has failed?**

The pattern of losing weight and then regaining it—which is sometimes called yo-yo dieting—is very common. It's the norm to regain weight, and it's a very frustrating process. People lose weight, and they feel great. Then they regain it, and they're upset and frustrated.

One of the problems is that people often have very high expectations. If you look at studies, people who go into weight-loss programs at universities have unrealistic expectations about how much they want to lose, or how much they *can* lose. It's simply more than they probably can achieve. That's unfortunate, because it sets up such a big goal that they're almost setting themselves up for failure.

An important concept now in weight-loss practice is the idea of setting up reasonable goals and expectations. With many good behavioral programs, you can lose a pound to two pounds a week. If you keep the behavior change going and you continue to eat healthier foods and be physically active, people often can sustain this.

But with the re-gain, people will often feel worse. We try to encourage patients to live healthier without putting themselves down, so that even if they regain weight, they can still try to connect with others. They don't need to put themselves down. They can still strive to have friends and be in relationships and live healthy overall.

Q: Is there an increased incidence of suicide among the morbidly obese?

I don't know of any data on that. We did a study looking in the United States population, and being an obese woman was associated with a slightly greater tendency at attempted suicide in the past year. But it's a small relationship. I would say that among the morbidly obese and the heaviest, clinically they report more psychological problems with peer relations, discrimination, and so forth. But I don't have any hard data on suicide.

Q: Are there ethnic factors that affect obesity?

African-American women have a significantly higher obesity prevalence than Caucasian women. This probably results from a combination of inherited genetic factors, as well as lifestyle and environmental factors. I don't have the data on hand about Hispanics, Asians, or Native Americans.

Q: How effective is hypnosis in weight control and preparation for bariatric surgery and in recovery?

Hypnosis for weight loss has been studied quite a bit, and if you look at rigorously controlled scientific studies, adding hypnosis to a strong behavioral treatment doesn't contribute that much. There's really not great evidence that it does much for weight loss.

In terms of preparing for weight loss or surgery, many people tell us that hypnosis has been helpful for relaxing and that it's beneficial to them. So, for some individuals, it might be helpful, but in terms of hypnosis leading to greater weight loss, there's no strong evidence for that.

It comes down to energy exchange, and simply getting hypnosis probably has a small impact on those sustained behavior changes.

Q: If you're an obese or morbidly obese person, what should you look for in a therapist?

I think you want someone who is empathetic, and who's going to be sympathetic to you. Health-care professionals are often just as biased against the obese as non-health professionals, and that's not an environment that's conducive or helpful.

Find a therapist or a counselor who's going to be supportive, who's going to be helpful, who will not be condescending because of your weight. They should also have some good cognitive behavioral training in terms of how to deal with binge eating, how to deal with lifestyle changes, and how to build physical activity into a sustainable regimen.

Q: How would someone go about identifying a therapist with these skills?

There's an organization called the North American Association for the Study of Obesity (NASO). It's on the Web. They could help make the more informed decisions in terms of getting help. There are also behavioral organizations such as the Association for the Advancement of Behavior Therapy, and they're often networked into good health-care providers.

People who have lost weight—people who have made improvements—are often the best sources, and they like to share this information.

Q: What about support groups?

They are often very helpful. Web support groups will be very big in the future. I think any kind of group where there's group support and social support is probably going to be quite helpful.

Q: Are there programs that train doctors to be more aware of their attitudes toward the obese?

That's becoming a big issue. In recent years, there have been more and more research studies showing that obese people feel discriminated against by health-care providers, that they don't feel comfortable, and that they don't want to go to them. Those of us in the health-care community are getting a wake-up call that says we need to treat our obese patients better. It's not just in terms of our manners, but also in having comfortable chairs in our waiting rooms, tables that are size-appropriate, and also structuring our offices so that they're more appropriate.

Q: Do you think that should be true of society in general, or is that essentially encouraging people to remain unhealthy?

It would be nice on a societal level if obese individuals did not have to confront discrimination and prejudices, and it would probably be helpful if things were engineered in a way that was more comfortable for them.

Q: What should society be doing to encourage people to deal with their obesity?

Society would need to reconfigure itself so that healthier foods were more readily available and less expensive, and that physical activities were made more accessible. As it is, we expend less and less energy. Our lives are made more and more convenient all the time, which is very nice. But the tradeoff is that we don't have to go out and hunt and gather food anymore. The foods we have are often very tasty, have high calories, and are readily available. So the way our society is geared right now makes it a challenge for our heaviest people to lose weight.

Q: With 61% percent of the American public now considered obese, should we control the advertising of unhealthy foods in much the same way cigarette advertising is controlled?

I wouldn't advocate any policy changes personally, but we need to take a step back and look at our society. Many people in society condemn the obese individual as having low willpower, low moral strength, and poor interpersonal fiber. That is an unfortunate stereotype that does not help anybody. If ridicule and deprecation really were helpful, people would lose weight, because they often receive that. But it typically doesn't help at all. Our broader environment makes it very challenging for the obese individual. So I think we need to look at the bigger picture of the environment, and if we want to seriously reduce the obesity problem, we need to ask what we would need to do on a broad level.

❀   ❀   ❀

INDEX

A

abdominal surgery, 138. *See also* gastric bypass surgery
abdominoplasty, 250. *See also* plastic surgery
absorption
    after surgery, 255–256
    malabsorptive surgery, 229–230, 239–242
    nutrition and, 259
acting career
    during school years, 50–51, 56–57
    television roles, 112–114
addiction. *See also* marijuana; sobriety; substance abuse
    food, 281
    sugar, 6, 247
advertising industry, 289
African-Americans, 266, 286–287
alimentary limb, 242
Alvarado Center for Surgical Weight Control, 171, 221, 237
American Dietetic Association (ADA), 275
anesthesia, 159–161, 176–177, 180
arthritis, 238
Association for the Advancement of Behavior Therapy, 288
audience, 80
    of *Carnie* show, 93
    for surgery, 164
    of Wilson Phillips, 72, 76

B

Ballard, Glen, 61–62, 67, 68
    "Hold On," 68–69

Shadows and Light, 75
Barbara (aunt), 19
bariatric nurses, 181
bariatric surgery. *See also* gastric bypass surgery
    body mass index and, 237, 238, 263, 265
    complications from, 242–244
    controversial methods of, 273
    dieting prior to, 239
    endocrine imbalance from, 269
    intestinal bypass procedure, 229–230
    making decision about, 128–135
    malabsorptive surgical procedure, 230, 239–240
    preparation for, 244
    psychological preparation for, 245–246, 283
    psychological recovery from, 283–285
    types of, 136–138, 239–242
Bay, Michael, 77–78
Bazillion, Eric, 84
Beach Boys, 3, 5. *See also individual names of members*
    Beach Boys Love You, 25
    tour, 48–49
Beach Boys Family and Friends, 111, 116–118, 204, 217
Beach Boys Love You (Beach Boys), 25
bee incident, 174–175
Bel Air home, 3–4
Bel Air Hotel, 213
Bell's palsy, 116
"Be My Baby" (Ronettes), 47, 214

Bender, Sabel, 51
Beverly Hills Diet, 29
biliopancreatic diversion, 239–242
biliopancreatic limb, 242
Billboard, 70
binge eating
    by Carnie, 27–28, 70–71, 173
    in general population, 277, 279–281
Birch, Leann L., 252–253
bleeding during surgery, 141
blood clots, 173, 180, 181, 243.
    See also pulmonary function
body mass index (BMI), 237, 238, 263,
    265
Bonfiglio, Rob, *149, 151, 156, 157,* 174
    acceptance by, 199
    adjusting to married life, 223–226
    early relationship with, 124–128
    first meeting with, 120–124
    music career of, 125, 203, 225
    during surgery, 180
    views on surgery, 167, 229–230
    wedding, 211–215
bowel function
    after surgery, 183, 220, 243–244
    constipation, 217
    diarrhea, 259
boyfriends. *See* Bonfiglio, Rob; intimacy
breast lift surgery, 250. *See also*
    plastic surgery
Brill, Jenny, 20, *148,* 212
Brother Records Studio, 25
Bruce, Lenny, 87
Buckley, Francis, 62, 68

C
Canata, Ritchie, 124
cancer, 238
career ambition, 57, 63, 234–235
Carnie, 91–97, *145*
Carnival, 57
Carnival Cruise, *155,* 219, 221
Carpenter, Karen, 47
Cassidy, Shaun, 29
catecholamines, 267
Champion, Cherie, 19

Chermol, Cathy, 91–93, 95–96, *145*
children
    body mass index for, 265
    eating behavior and, 253–255
    emotional development of, 277
    hormonal factors for obesity in,
        263–265
    psychological counseling for,
        282–283
    satiety response and, 252–253
cigarette smoking, 14
Clark, G. Wesley, 138, 219
clothing. *See* wardrobe
cognitive behavior therapy, 73, 209.
    See also hypnosis; therapy
    for binge eating, 280–281
    exercise and, 256–257
    token program, 26–27
Columbia University College of
    Physicians and Surgeons, 263, 276
co-morbid conditions, 99–101, 132,
    237–238, 266–267
    benefits *vs.* risks of surgery,
        139–140
    fear of, 115–118
constipation, 220. *See also*
    bowel function
coping skills, 258, 260–261. *See also*
    therapy
cramping after surgery, 160
critics, music, 76
Cushing Syndrome, 265

D
Dalton, Sharron (interview), 252–262
Dee Dee (aunt), 5, 19, *40, 157*
    dieting by, 29
    supportive of surgery, 173, 176
depression, 238
    binge eating and, 281–282
    emotional eating and, 254–255, 276
        (*See also* eating habits)
    weight loss motivation and,
        258–259
Dexatrim, 30
diabetes, 237–238

gestational, 251, 262
obesity and, 142–159
suture leaks and, 243
in Wilson family, 2, 142
diarrhea, 259. *See also* bowel function
dieting. *See also* weight loss
for bariatric surgery patients, 239,
244–245
as conditioned behavior, 254
crash, 65–66
cycle of, 27–28, 133, 285–286
maintaining weight after, 256–257
principle of, 268
risky weight-loss regimens,
256–257, 269, 274–275
Wittgrove on, 138
digestive tract, diagram of, 249
discrimination. *See* prejudice
diuretics, 30
divorce (of Brian and Marilyn Wilson),
27. *See also* Wilson, Brian; Wilson-
Rutherford, Marilyn
"Don't Worry, Baby" (Brian Wilson),
170
"Dream Is Alive, The" video, *45*
drug abuse, 267–268. *See also*
marijuana; sobriety
drugs, weight loss, 256–257, 271–272,
280–281
"dumping," 184, 191–192, 196–197,
247
duodenal switch, 136, 239–242

E

eating habits. *See also* dieting; nutrition
attitude toward food and, 276
behavioral mechanisms of, 253,
272–273
emotional, 266, 276
food selection post-surgery,
186–189, 194–196, 205, 241
satiety and, 197–198, 252–253
of Wilson family, 2–4, 6–7
Elliot-Kugell, Owen, 59–61, 89, *148*,
211–212
Elliott, Cass, 59

embolism, 181, 243. *See also*
pulmonary function
Encino home, 27
endocrine factors of obesity, 263–275
environmental factors of obesity, 1–2,
252–253
epinephrine, 267
esophagus, diagram of, 249
ethnic factors of obesity, 266, 286–287
exercise
behavioral change and, 256–257
hormones and, 268–269
lack of, 273–274
motivation and, 258–259
post-surgery, 191, 218, 270
treadmill incident, 25
Ex-Lax, 29–30

F

Faith, Myles S. Faith (interview),
276–289
family plans, 233–234
fans. *See* audience
"Fantasy Is Reality?" (Brian Wilson),
105
fashion industry, plus-size, 198
fat camp. *See* Weight Watchers camp
Fat Chick from Wilson Phillips, The,
112
financial problems, 91, 112
"Flesh and Blood" (Wilson Phillips), *45,*
104
follow-up program, for surgery,
190–191, 247–248, 270
food journal, 64
Forum (Los Angeles), 48–49
fraudulent treatments for obesity,
274–275

G

gastric bypass surgery, 136–138. *See
also* bariatric surgery; nutrition;
plastic surgery
average weight loss from, 221
body mass index and, 237, 238,
263, 265

bowel complications from, 183,
217, 220, 243–244
controversy of, 167–168, 207,
220–221
day of, 174–177
defined, 240
diagrams of, 248–249
eating immediately after, 183–184
emotional reaction to, 205–211,
226
follow-up program, 190–191,
246–248, 270
hotel stay after, 185–189
Internet broadcast, 179–180
laparoscopic protocol development,
237
laparoscopic *vs.* open, 136–160,
240–241
length of procedure, 159
pain management for, 159–161,
176–177, 180–182
pictures taken immediately after,
154
pictures taken immediately before,
153
popularity of, 239–240
pregnancy after, 233–234
reconstructive plastic surgery after,
222–223, 250
risks of, 138, 229
seromas, 188–189, 242–243
skin elasticity and, 218
success of Carnie's procedure,
188, 190
success rate for general population,
233, 241, 272
vertical banded gastroplasty *vs.*,
241
genetic factors of obesity, 1–2, 277–278
environmental factors *vs.*, 252–253
hormonal abnormalities, 263–265
overcoming, 64–65
substance abuse and, 267
in Wilson family, 2, 28–29, 142
gestational diabetes, 251, 262. *See also*
diabetes; pregnancy

Ginger (cousin), 20
glucose tolerance test, 251
Good Morning America, 207
Great Changes (North Hollywood), 110

H
hair loss, 194, 260
health concerns. *See* co-morbid
conditions
hereditary factors. *See* genetic factors
of obesity
hernia, incisional, 137, 240
Heymsfield, Steven B. (interview),
263–275
Hey Santa! (Wilson Sisters), 88–90
Hoffman, Steve, *43*
"Hold On" (Wilson Phillips), 68–69
Holland, 5
homes
in Bel Air, 3–4
in Encino, 27
in Holland, 5
in New York City, 92
in Philadelphia, 199, 206, 217
honeymoon, 217–218
Honeys, The, 5
hormone problems, 263–275
hotel stay, after surgery, 185–189
Howard Stern Show, The, 87, 89–90,
207
hunger. *See* eating
husband. *See* Bonfiglio, Rob
hydration after surgery, 217, 220
hypertension, 237–238
hypnosis, 245–246
post-surgery, 186, 209–210
to prepare for surgery, 170, 172
for weight control, 287

I
identity. *See* self-image
incisional hernia, 137, 240
infection, 188–189, 242–243
infertility, 238, 250–251
instruments, surgical, 136–137,
240–241, 244–245

insulin, 247. *See also* diabetes;
    "dumping"
insurance companies, 245
interpersonal therapy, 282
intestinal bypass procedure, 229–230
intestines, 137–138, 240
    blockage of, 243–244
    bypass procedure, 229–230
    "dumping," 184, 191–192,
        196–197, 247
intimacy, 198–201. *See also*
    Bonfiglio, Rob
    after bariatric surgery, 198–201,
      285
    early feelings about, 51–53, 55–56
    relationship patterns and, 119
Irv (grandfather), 7–9, *41*
Italy trip, 217–218

J
Jackson, Janet, 77
Jardine, Adam, 124
Jardine, Al, 61, 111, 116–119, *147*,
    204, 217
Jenny Craig program, 30, 112
Jester, Leslie, *153*, 171, 208, 211,
    222, 230
Johnston, Aimee, 171
joint problems, 238
journal, food, 64

K
Kay, Shawn, 20
ketosis, 262
kidney disease, 142, 230
Knott, Jeffrey, 52
Koppelman, Charles, 67
Kugell, Jack, 89

L
Lake, Rikki, 95
Landy, Eugene, 25–27, 103–104
Lassner, Andy, 93
Lawrence Moon Bidell Syndrome, 265
laxatives, 29–30
leaks, from surgery, 243

Leptin deficiency, 264, 265, 274
life expectancy, 229–230
Lindora Clinic, 28, 30
liver, 245
"Love Will Never Do Without You"
    (Jackson), 77
lungs, 172–173, 243, 244. *See also*
    blood clots

M
Mae (grandmother), 2, 7–9, *41*, 142
malabsorptive surgical procedure, 230,
    239–240
malnutrition
    dieting and, 255–256
    from malabsorptive operations,
      239–240
Mama Earth character, 113
Mamas and the Papas, 59
marijuana
    addiction to, 53–54, 62
    first experience with, 14
    morbid obesity and, 267–268, 277
    sobriety during Beach Boys Family
      and Friends tour, 111
    use after surgery, 208–209
    use during Wilson Phillips period,
      70–71, 80–81
Marx, Richard, 71
McCartney, Linda, 29
McCartney, Paul, 29
meals, scheduled, 2–4, 254
men, nutrition for, 259–260
Mercury Records, 103, 108
Meridia, 271
metabolism, 66
Metzfield, Karen, 164–165, 176
Miller, Tiffany, 20, 116–118, *148*, 212
Million Pound March, 99–100
mineral loss, 259
"Miracle" (Brian and Carnie Wilson),
    107
"Monday Without You" (Carnie and
    Wendy Wilson), 108–110
Montel Williams Show, 231
morbid obesity

causes of, 252–253
defined, 237
diagnosing, 263
fraudulent treatment for, 274–275
hormonal causes of, 263–265
obesity *vs.*, 281
pregnancy and, 250–251
preparation for surgery and, 244
prevalence of, 255, 263, 289
risks from, 230
morphine, 180, 181, 183
music. *See also individual artist*
  names; individual titles of works
  critics, 76
  harmonization, 50, 60, 69, 108
  importance to Wilson family,
    47–50, 203
  piano playing, 49
  videos, *45*, 69, 71, 77–81
Mustard's (Napa Valley), 193

N
naming, of Carnie, 9–10
Napa Valley trip, 192–193
narcotics for pain, 160
National Institutes of Health (NIH), 275
  body mass index defined by, 237,
    238, 263, 265
  guidelines for surgery, 246
National Weight Control Registry, 257
New York City home, 92
New York University, 252
norepinephrine, 267
North American Association for the
  Study of Obesity (NASO), 288
Northwest Afternoon, 227–228
nurses, bariatric, 181
NutriSystem, 30
  nutrition. *See also* malnutrition
  Dalton, Sharron (interview),
    252–262
  Lisa Roth on, 64
  surgery follow-up program,
    190–191, 247–248, 259, 270
  vitamins, 191, 251, 255–256, 259

O
Oakwood school, 10, 50, 56
obesity. *See also* co-morbid conditions;
  morbid obesity
  diabetes and, 142–159
  morbid obesity *vs.*, 281
  prevalence of, 289
  risks of, 139–140
  size acceptance movement, 99–100,
    114–115, 134
  societal attitude toward, 98–100,
    210, 224, 278–282, 288–289
Obesity Research Center, 263, 276
O'Donnell, Rosie, 97
Oprah, 166, 207
overeating. *See* binge eating; eating

P
pain
  anesthesia for, 159–161, 176–177
  reaction to medicines for, 183
  from surgery, 180–182
Palmer, Robert, *46*
Panzer, Jeff, *45*, 71, 79
Paratore, Jim, 97
parenting, food and, 253–255, 265–266,
  277–278
patient-controlled analgesia machine
  (PCA unit), 159
Pennsylvania State University, 253–254
People, 208
Perry, Richard, 61
Pet Sounds (Brian Wilson), 227
pharmacological therapy, 256–257,
  271–272, 280–281
Philadelphia
  home, 199, 206, 217
  visit, 129–130
Phillips, Chynna, *43–46. See also*
  Wilson Phillips
  "Beautiful at Last," 84
  childhood of, 1, 81–82
  "Flesh and Blood," *45*, 104
  "Hold On," 68–69
  Shadows and Light, 75, 104
  sobriety of, 62

solo career of, 81
suggested Wilson Phillips, 59
support by, 12
Wilson Phillips, 74, 75
"You're in Love," 71
"You Won't See Me Cry," 77
Phillips, John, 59
Phillips, Michelle, 59, 61, 63, 81
physical therapy, 271
plastic surgery, 222–223, 250
pneumonia, 243
potassium deficiency, 259
power
overeating in children and, 277
size and, 22–23, 70
Prader-Willi Syndrome, 264–265
pregnancy
gestational diabetes, 251, 262
nutrition for, 261–262
plans for, 233–234
prejudice toward obese, 98–100, 210, 224, 278–279, 288–289
protein
hair loss and, 194
intake after surgery, 270
overload, 260
surgery follow-up program, 190–191, 247–248, 270
publicity. *See also* SBK Records; *individual titles of works*
for gastric bypass operation, 163–164, 207–208
Internet broadcast about surgery, 179–180
radio station interviews, 70
before surgery, 173–175
unwanted, 184
for Wilson Phillips, 63
pulmonary function, 172–173. *See also* blood clots
embolism, 181, 243
preparation for surgery and, 244

R
racial factors of obesity, 266, 286–287
radio station interviews, 70, 87, 89–90

reconstructive plastic surgery, 222–223, 250
recording industry, 84, 108. *See also individual record company names*
Regis and Kathie Lee, 96
religion, 13
"Rhapsody in Blue" (Gershwin), 49
Ritts, Herb, 77
Ronettes, 47
Roseanne, 114–115, 207
Rosie, 97
Roth, Lisa, *44,* 177
accompanied Wilson Phillips tour, 70–71
initial training with, 63–67
views on surgery, 167–168
views on therapy, 73
Roux en-Y procedure
description of, 137–138, 240
diagram of, 248
Rutherford, Daniel, 18, *148,* 176

S
Sackier, Jonathan, 131–132, 136, 164, 173
satiety, from eating, 197–198, 252–253
Savick, Peter, 79
SBK Records, 67, 70–71, 76
cancelled contract for Wilson Sisters, 90
solo contracts for Wilson Phillips, 87
Scared to Be Thin (Carnie Wilson), 112
scarring, 244
schizophrenia, 246
Schoen, Marc, 228–229
influence of, 73
initial therapy sessions with, 62–63
post-surgery therapy, 209–210
preparation for surgery, 168–170
(*See also* hypnosis)
Seabury, Warren, 63
"Secret Show, The," 96
self-esteem, 279
self-image, 23–24, 71, 133
audience and, 98

fears about weight loss, 169,
205–211, 226
of post-surgery body, 177–178,
199–201
power and, 22–23, 70
self-esteem in general population
and, 279
sequential-compression stockings, 180,
243
seromas, 188–189, 242–243
serotonin, 276
serotonin and norephinephrine
re-uptake inhibitor (SNRI), 271
sex. *See* intimacy
Shadows and Light (Wilson Phillips),
75, 104, *146*
Shapiro, Mickey, 87, *158*
Carnie, 91
Mercury Records contract, 103
proposed broadcasting surgery, 163
Spotlight Health website started
by, 131
Sharp, Ken, 121, *149*
Siegel, Julie, 20, *148, 212*
Silk Stalkings, 113
'60s, The, 113–114
size acceptance movement, 99–100,
114–115, 134
skin elasticity, 218, 222–223, 250, 260
sleep apnea, 116, 237–238, 267
small intestine, 137–138. *See also*
intestines
"dumping," 184, 191–192,
196–197, 247
scarring of, 244
Snickers incident, 13
sobriety
to prepare for surgery, 172
during production of *Shadows and
Light,* 75
socioeconomic factors of obesity, 266
Spector, Phil, 47
Spector, Ronnie, 47
spleen, 141
sports, 22–23, 278
Spotlight Health, 88, *154,* 131

accommodations during surgery
stay, 173, 185
future work for, 225
interviews on, 166–167
on-line support group, 133–135,
195, 227–228
progress recorded by, 198
surgery broadcast, 163–164,
179–180
St. Luke's-Roosevelt Hospital Center,
263, 276
Star, Paul, 79
stereotypes about obesity, 279. *See also*
prejudice toward obese
Stern, Howard, 87, 89–90, 207
Stiles, Julia, 113–114
stomach
capacity of, 259
diagrams of, 248–249
pouch size of, 141–142, 239
scarring of, 244
surgical placemet of, 137
stress hormones, 272
stylists, for music videos, 78
substance abuse, 267–268. *See also*
marijuana; sobriety
sugar. *See also* diabetes; nutrition
addiction, 6, 247
"dumping," 184, 191–192,
196–197, 247
suicide, 286. *See also* depression
surgeon, choosing a, 141, 269,
274–275. *See also individual
names*
sutures, 243

T
technology. *See* instruments, surgical
Telepictures, 91, 97. *See also Carnie*
television appearances, 207. *See also*
acting career; *Carnie; individual
television show names*
therapy. *See also* hypnosis
choosing a practitioner, 287
cognitive behavior approach, 73,
209, 256–257, 280–281

Faith, Myles S. Faith (interview),
  276–289
  importance of support groups,
    221–222, 288
  interpersonal, 282
  with Landy, 25–27, 103–104
  post-surgery, 209–210, 226
  preparation for surgery, 168–172,
    245–246, 287
  recommended by Chynna
    Phillips, 62
thyroid, 263–265
Tordol, 160
treadmill incident, 25
20/20, 166, 207
Tylenol with codeine, 183

U
University of Colorado Medical
  Center, 257
urinary incontinence, 238

V
vertical banded gastroplasty (VBG),
  136, 239–241
VetRock concert, 120, *147, 150*
videos, music, *45*
  "Hold On," 69
  Shadows and Light, 77–81
  "You're in Love," 71
vitamins, 191, 251, 255–256, 259. *See
  also* nutrition
vomiting, 196. *See also* binge eating

W
Wanderlust, 125
wardrobe
  financial problems and, 112
  for "Hold On" video, 69
  importance of, 110
  post-surgery, 198
  for *Shadows and Light,* 78–79
  wedding dress, 212–213
"Warmth of the Sun" (Brian Wilson),
  214
Warner Brothers Television, 91.

  See also Carnie
Wasserman, Rob, 105
wedding, *157*
  anxiety about, 211
  engagement, 203–205
weight loss. *See also* bariatric surgery;
    gastric bypass surgery
  average, from gastric bypass, 221
  feelings about, 205–211, 226,
    270, 284
  goal achievement, 218–219, 226
  goal setting for, 286
  maintenance of, 256–257
  motivational support and, 258–259
  pregnancy and, 250–251
  prior to surgery, 244–245
  success rate for general population,
    260–261, 272
  for wedding, 213
weight-loss surgery. *See* bariatric
  surgery
Weight Loss Surgery (WLS) cruise, *155,*
  219, 221
Weight Watchers camp, 12–15, 22
Williams, Montel, 231
Wilson, Audree, 2, 9, *41,* 48, 142
Wilson, Brian, 3–4, *32–34, 37, 156, 157*
  "Don't Worry, Baby," 170
  eating habits of, 27
  "Fantasy Is Reality?", 105
  father-daughter relationship, 49–50,
    57, 104–107, 226–227
  "Miracle," 107
  musical favorites of, 47
  Pet Sounds, 227
  supportive of surgery, 170
  therapy with Landy, 25–27,
    103–104
  touring with Beach Boys, 48–49
  "Warmth of the Sun," 214
  at wedding, 213–214
  weight problems of, 2, 25
  The Wilsons, 103, 106, *152*
Wilson, Carl (cousin), *42*
Wilson, Carl (uncle), 11–12, 175
Wilson, Daria, 104

Wilson, Delanie, 104
Wilson, Jonah, 5, *42*
  childhood of, 10–11
  treadmill incident, 25
  weight loss by, 24, 29
  on Wilson Phillips tour, 71
Wilson, Justyn, *42*
Wilson, Melinda, 104, 107, *157*, 212
Wilson, Michael, *42*
Wilson, Murry, 2
Wilson, Wendy, *33–36, 38, 40, 42–46,*
  143–144, 147–148, 157. See also
  Wilson Phillips
  Beach Boys Family and Friends
    tour, 117
  childhood of, 1, 3, 5, 48
  "Flesh and Blood," 104
  Hey Santa!, 88–90
  "Hold On," 68–69
  maid of honor, 211–212, 214–215
  reaction to surgery, 166–167, 173,
    182, 207
  relationship with, 12, 20–22, 68
  Shadows and Light, 75, 104, *146*
  thirtieth birthday celebration,
    192–193
  treadmill incident, 25
  at VetRock, 120
  The Wilsons, 103, 106, *152*
  Wilson Sisters, 87–90
  "You're in Love" video, 71
  "You Won't See Me Cry," 77
Wilson Phillips, 59–85
  "Beautiful at Last," 84
  breakup of, 81–85
  "Flesh and Blood," *45,* 104
  future projects for, 84
  "Hold On," 68–69
  management of, 77
  marijuana use and, 54
  preparation for touring, 67
  Shadows and Light, 75, 104, *146*
  solo contracts for, 87
  touring with, 70
  Wilson Phillips album, 74, 75
  "You're in Love," 71

"You Won't See Me Cry," 77
Wilson-Rutherford, Marilyn, *33–34, 40,*
  143–144, 148, 152, 157
  dieting by, 2, 28–29, 254
  mother-daughter relationship with,
    2–4, 17–20
  Spotlight Health interview, 166
  during surgery, 171–173
  views on drugs, 54–55
  views on sex, 53
  at wedding, 211, 215
Wilsons, The (Brian, Carnie, Wendy
  Wilson), 103, 106, *152*
Wilson Sisters
  Hey Santa!, 88–90
  management, 87
Winfrey, Oprah, 166, 207
Wittgrove, Alan, *153, 155, 158,* 188
  Alvarado Center for Surgical Weight
    Control, 171, 221, 237
  attended wedding, 213
  developed laparoscopic procedure,
    138
  first meeting with, 138–161
  interview with, 237–251
  on preparation for surgery, 173
  Weight Loss Surgery cruise, *155,*
    219, 221
women
  African-American, 266, 286–287
  co-morbid conditions in, 237–238
  nutrition after surgery for, 259–260

Y
"Y" configuration. *See* Roux en-Y
  procedure
"You're in Love" (Wilson Phillips), 71
"You Won't See Me Cry" (Wilson
  Phillips), 77

Z
Zax, Steven, 222
Zucker, Katrina, 211, 219–220
Zucker, Marty, 219

ABOUT THE AUTHOR

BORN THE DAUGHTER OF MARILYN WILSON AND BEACH BOY LEGEND Brian Wilson, **Carnie Wilson** has overcome a lifelong struggle with obesity to achieve personal satisfaction, professional success, and new dimensions of physical and emotional health.

As a young child growing up in the fast lane, Carnie turned to food for comfort. As she grew into adulthood and achieved success with the multiplatinum pop group Wilson Phillips and her own talk show, *Carnie,* her dysfunctional relationship with food led to life-threatening morbid obesity. In the summer of 1999, she made the dramatic decision to undergo state-of-the-art weight-loss surgery live over the Internet. During the next two years, her life was transformed as she lost more than 150 pounds, married the man of her dreams, and fashioned a new future of exciting career opportunities. Carnie and her husband, Rob, are living in Los Angeles with their three dogs—and are looking forward to expanding their family soon.

Now dedicated to helping others, Carnie is a spokesperson for Spotlight Health (**www.spotlighthealth.com**), a group of dedicated celebrities, medical experts, and media and marketing specialists whose goal is to dramatically enhance consumer and physician awareness of vital health issues.

❀ ❀ ❀

We hope you enjoyed this Hay House book.
If you would like to receive a free catalog featuring additional Hay House books and products, or if you would like information about the Hay Foundation, please contact:

Hay House, Inc.
P.O. Box 5100
Carlsbad, CA 92018-5100

(760) 431-7695 or **(800) 654-5126**
(760) 431-6948 (fax) or **(800) 650-5115 (fax)**

Please visit the Hay House Website at: **www.hayhouse.com**

❀ ❀ ❀